Artists in the Texas Hill Country

Artists in the
Texas Hill Country

Don Minnick
Jan Fitzhugh
Jim McJunkin

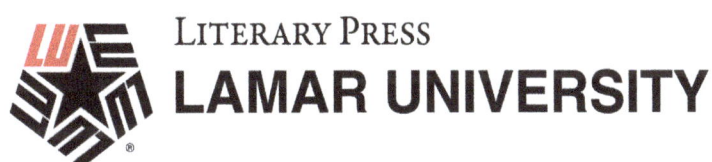
LITERARY PRESS
LAMAR UNIVERSITY

ISBN: 978-1-942956-89-1
Library of Congress Control Number: 2021937414

Manufactured in the United States

Lamar University Literary Press
Beaumont, Texas

We dedicate this book to

Bert Ray, Majory Macdiarmid, Erin Hoyt, Betty Rhodes, and Solon Williams

During the course of preparing this book, our art community lost five lovely members.
Life is short, but art is forever.
Our friends captured permanence for us in their own way.

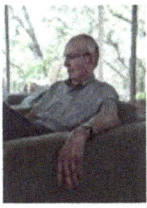
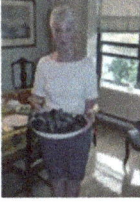
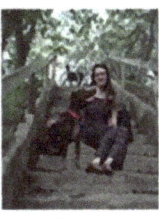
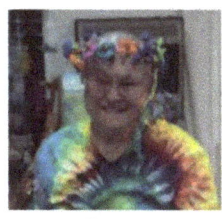
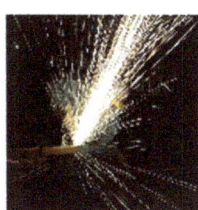

Bert   Majory   Erin   Betty   Solon

"When you think about it there are an astounding number of incredible artists in this little town. We need to revel in the glory of this environment, living in a place so dedicated to creativity. After all, art is to make us enjoy the world." —Bert Ray

"I started to paint when I turned 60. I was so pleased when I first started. I was seeing things so differently: shades of colors, seeing shapes in a new way. That has become such a part of me now." —Majory Macdiarmid

"Immune deficiency is an aspect of my life, and something I deal with 24/7. When I picture myself, there's no wheelchair, no tubes, no devices—just me. My goal is to simply embrace the beauty of having an illness and the freedom to experience life." —Erin Hoyt

"I met my husband Barry while I was dancing on a bar. I was going through Bandera, Texas on my way home from school. I didn't have a penny in my pocket, and I had car trouble along the way. I saw a nice hotel that I wanted to stay in, so I checked into a room and started trying to figure out how I was going to pay for it! I went downstairs to the bar and told the bartender my dilemma. He said if I danced on the bar, I could earn enough money to pay for the room. Pretty soon, in walked a tall guitar player named Barry and we got busy entertaining the crowd. The rest is history." —Betty Rhodes

"You're the only person who ever afflicted me with the title of *artist*. I just think of myself as retired. Twenty years ago, when the kids were in college, I thought, 'I'll start another hobby'. I'd taken some welding classes because I'd worked in a chemical plant. I thought that would be fun to do. I decided to make a bed with a metal headboard and footboard. You think I'd be smart enough to figure out that a half-inch rod doesn't go through a half inch hole. So, after five-hundred-something holes I learned that I had to ream them all out. That makes more noise than grinding does, but it doesn't make as many sparks." —Solon Williams

CONTENTS

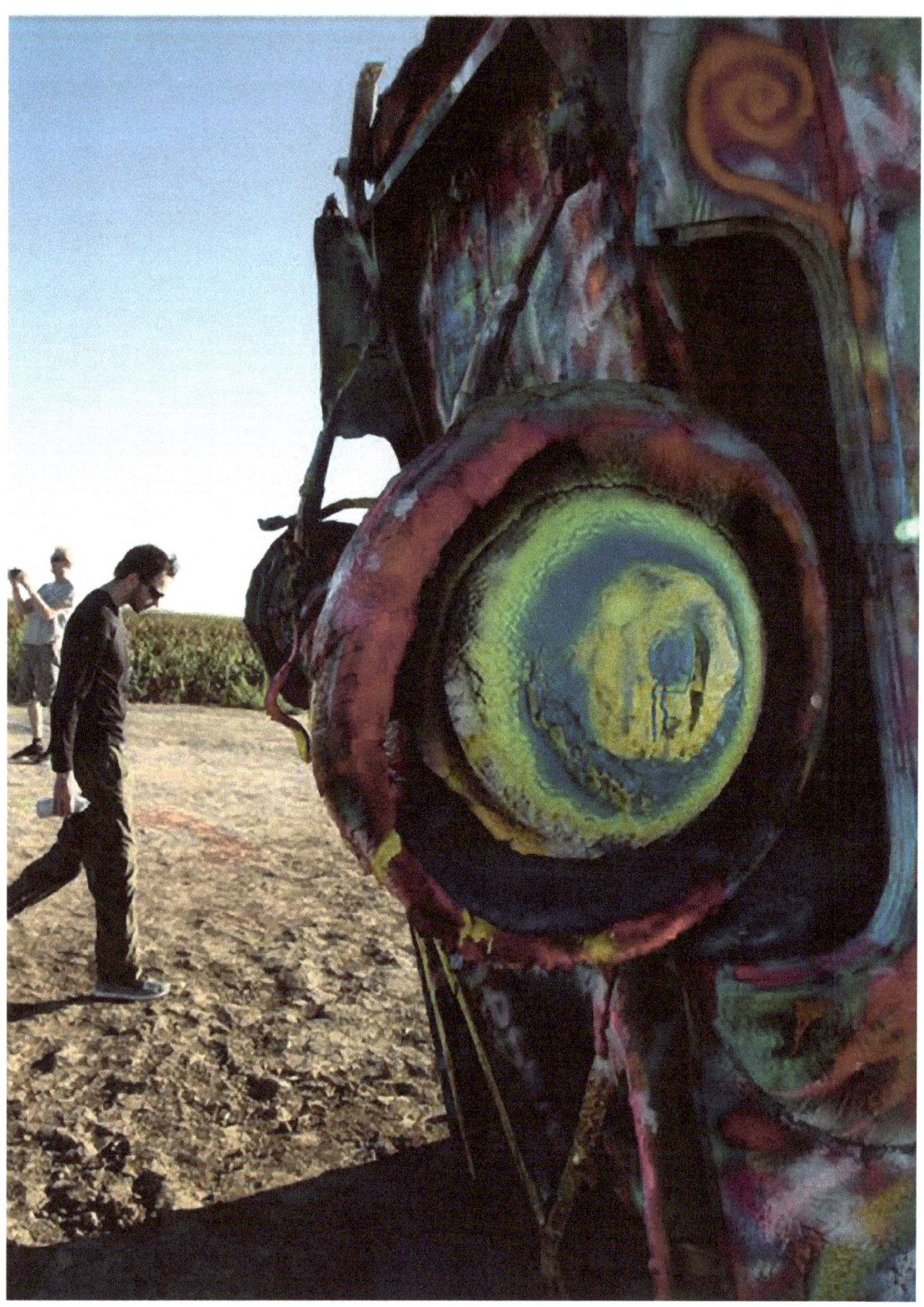

Some Artist at Cadillac Ranch

Why Artists?

Artists are different from the rest of us. Like us, a good percentage of their lives are spent in spectacularly mundane activities: buying groceries, chauffeuring children, doing dishes and trying to locate the car keys. Unlike the rest of us, they are able, on occasion, to dip into the transcendent, to create. Miraculously, in living their lives, they can string these two dramatically different states of mind into a consistent whole. Or so it would seem. So rather than learning about artists, we should learn through them something more important.

We discovered from talking with the artists in this book that with our asking very few questions, or no questions at all, the artists speak the most extraordinary insights about life, about art, and about how we are all connected.

We have chosen artists over any other group that may have stories just as beautiful to tell because we are interested in art. We have a fascination for the act of creation and for the amazing individuals who are in various stages of the mastery of this phenomenon.

The artists in this book exhibit creativity, imagination, exquisite skill and an arc of a story in their work. Best of all we know them. They are our friends.

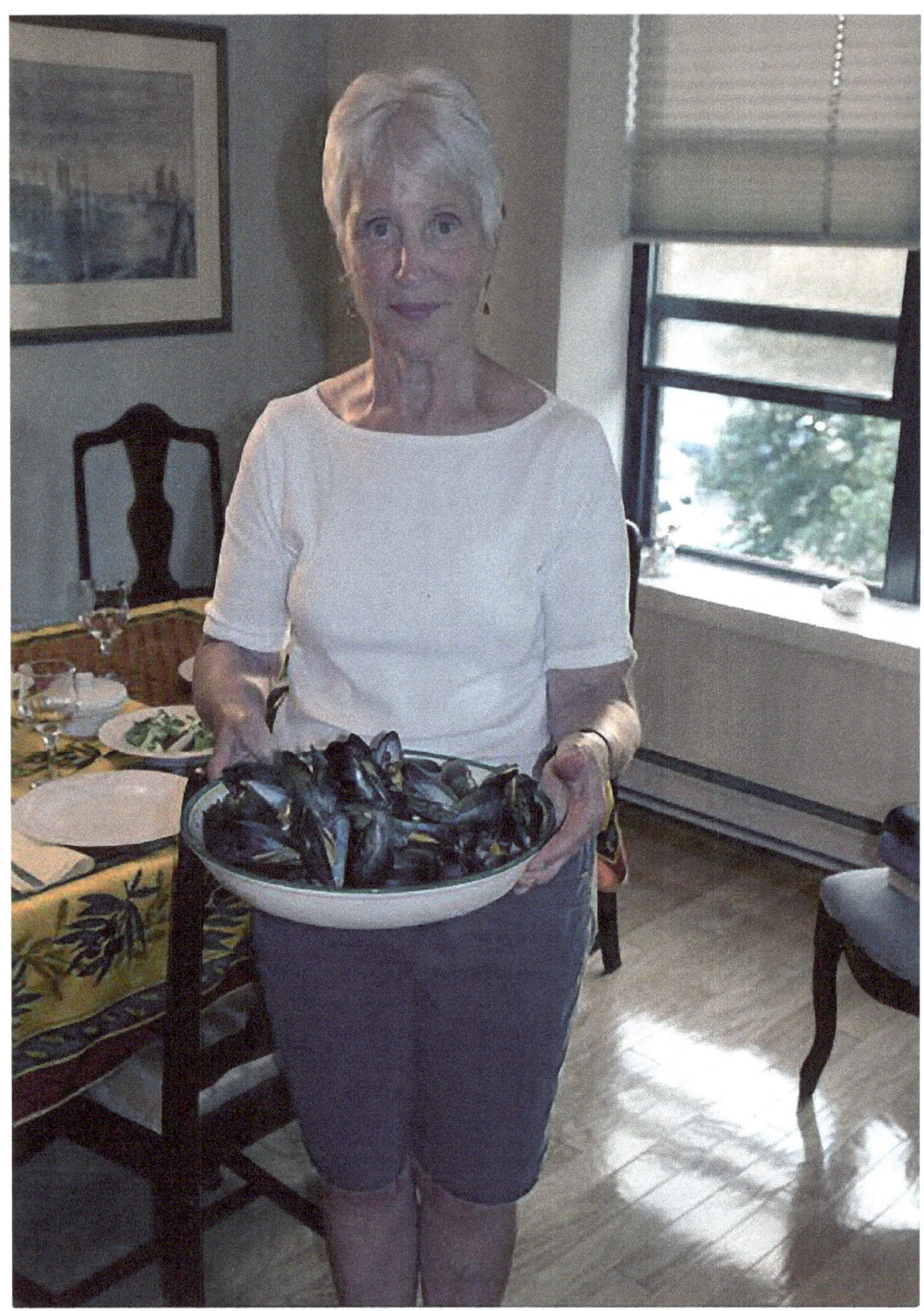

Marjory Macdiarmid

Artists Are Storytellers

There is no single pathway to creativity. There are no rules or guidelines, and no definitive environment that produces an urge to create. It is an individual thing, born from a desire to communicate on a personal level. Creativity comes from kindergartens and prison camps and everywhere in between.

There is something about art that transcends commerce, and something about being an artist that is more than a desire to create. There are also conflicting amounts of rebellion and need for acceptance, and a dichotomy of solitary behavior and exhibitionism.

As this book progressed, it became apparent we would not have to stray too far from our home base of Wimberley, Texas to find enough talent to fill these pages. Initially, we were not fully aware of how many regional, national and international artists live in the hills and valleys around Wimberley. That is an anomaly, because unlike some large metropolitan areas where artists tend to congregate for the sake of commerce, the commercial potential in this area is limited. None of the artists in this book mentioned commerce as a reason for settling in the area, though they often mentioned the region and landscape as a source of inspiration. It's not so much that there is something in the water that makes artists, (somebody else's explanation) rather, it is something in the area that attracts them. Some of the people in this book have sold their work all over the world. One or two have no desire to sell at all. They all have a desire to create.

Not all artists may think of themselves as story-tellers, but this book lets us know that they are. The arc of a story prowls around each work of art and often in the complete body of each artist's work. With little or no prompting, the artists in this book tell rich and funny, tragic and poignant stories about their lives. They offer observations about life in general, and about their work. Even those artists who consider themselves to be introverts or reclusive can relate an engaging, enthralling or otherwise charming story. It is as if making art compels them to connect in profound and meaningful conversation with others. So left-brain or right—wherever it is that creativity lies—these artists not only produce stunning visual imagery that connects us all on a deep level, they can also spin a mesmerizing story, even if those stories are sometimes brief. A connection is what they forge with all of us. And connection is perhaps the most human of all our intentions.

We owe these artists a debt of gratitude. They ensure that the beauty of our culture is enshrined in the stories that give their art context and guarantees its preservation. This, in fact is how society is preserved. This is how culture is passed. These artists are both our archeologists and our futurists.

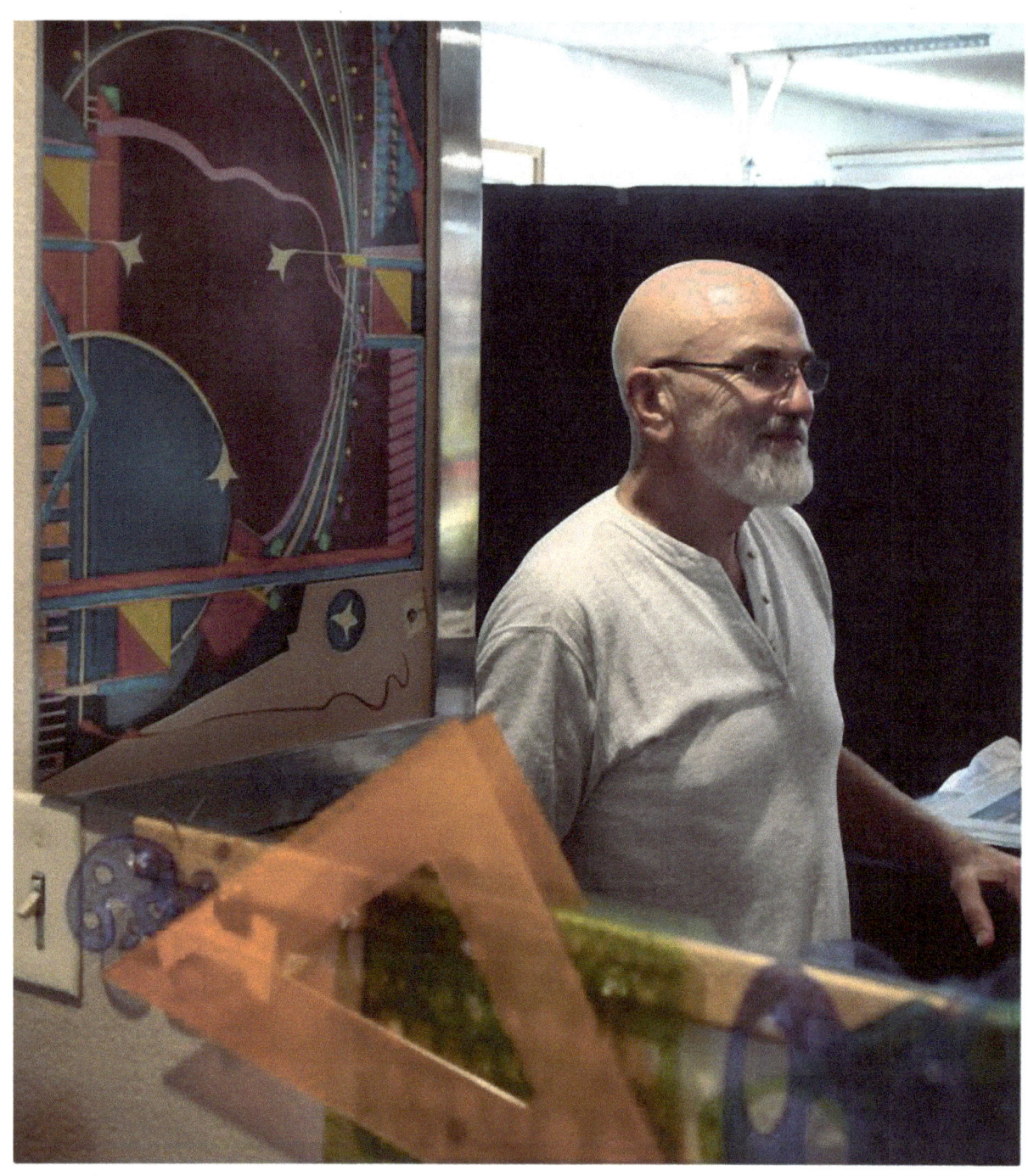

Taylor Dueker

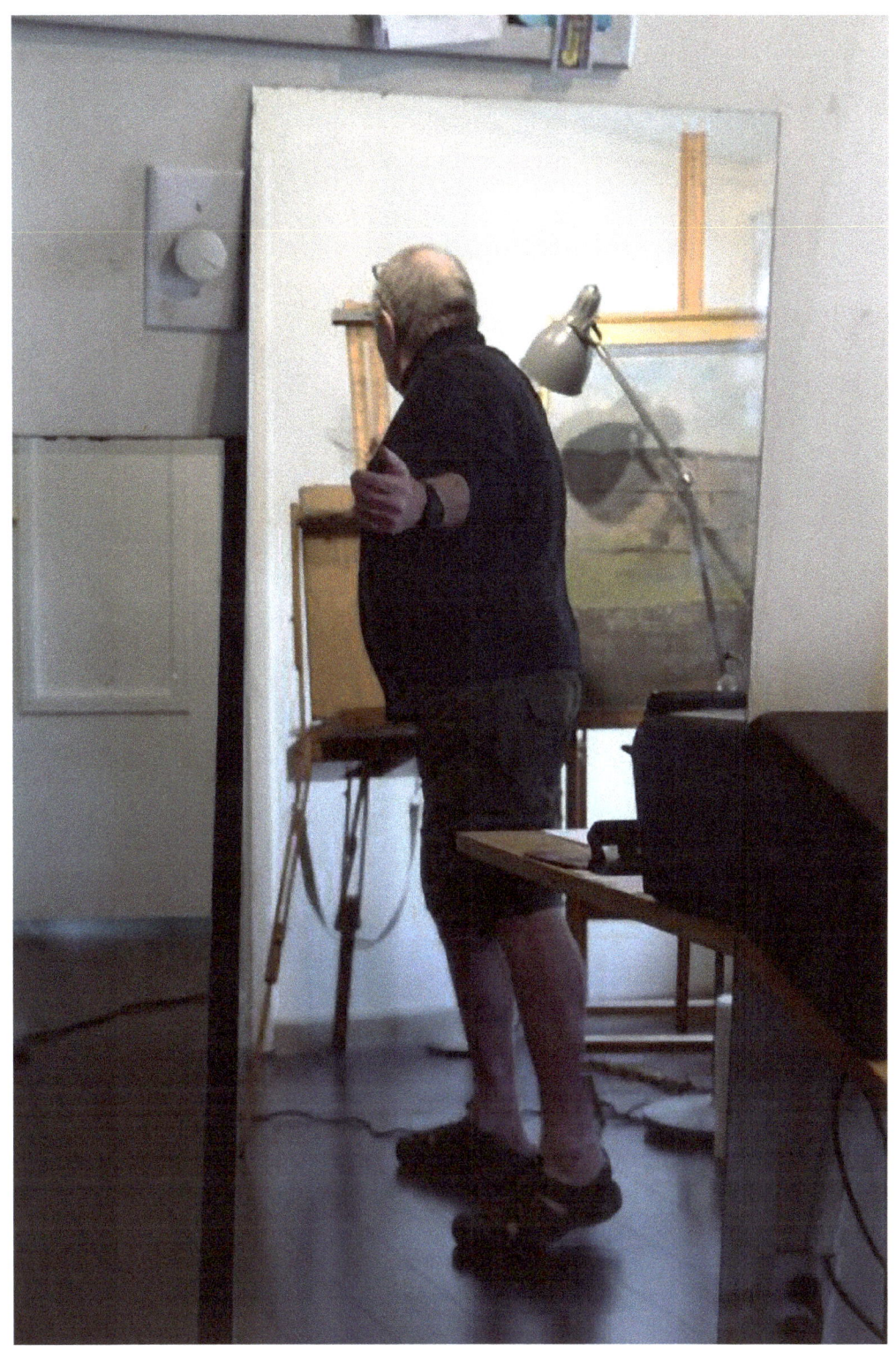

Jim McDonald

13

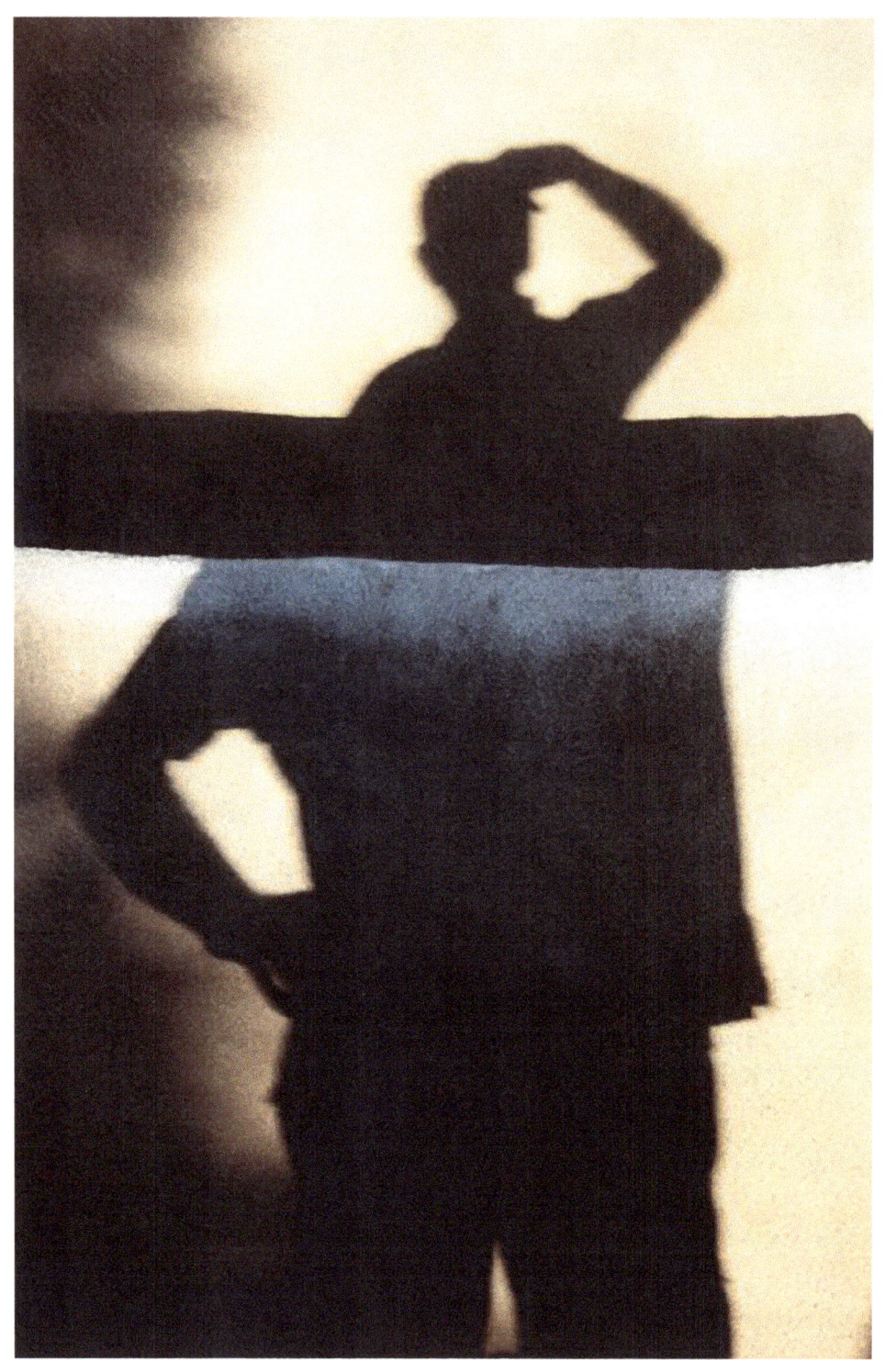

Shadow Portrait / Jim McJunkin

14

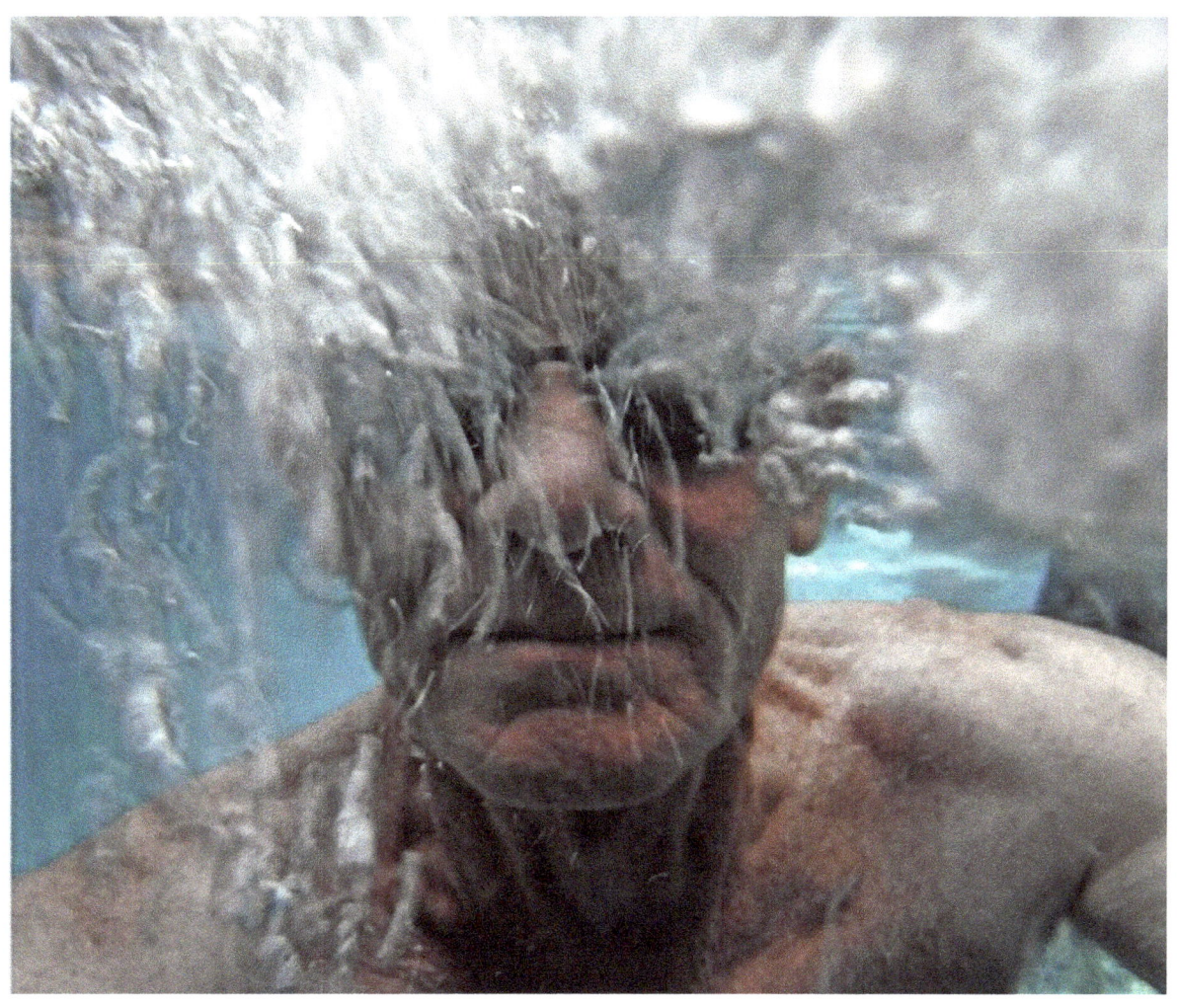

Self Portrait / Jim McJunkin

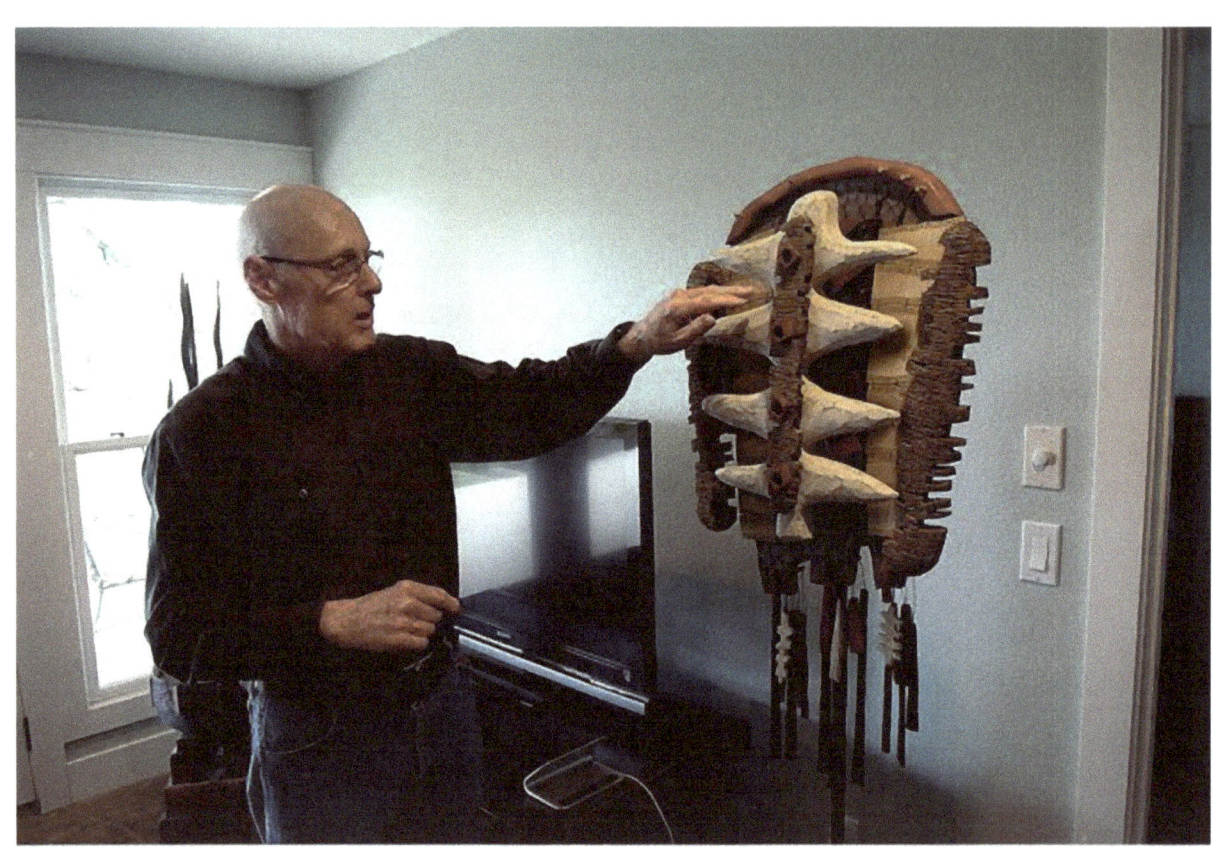

Steve Shellenberger

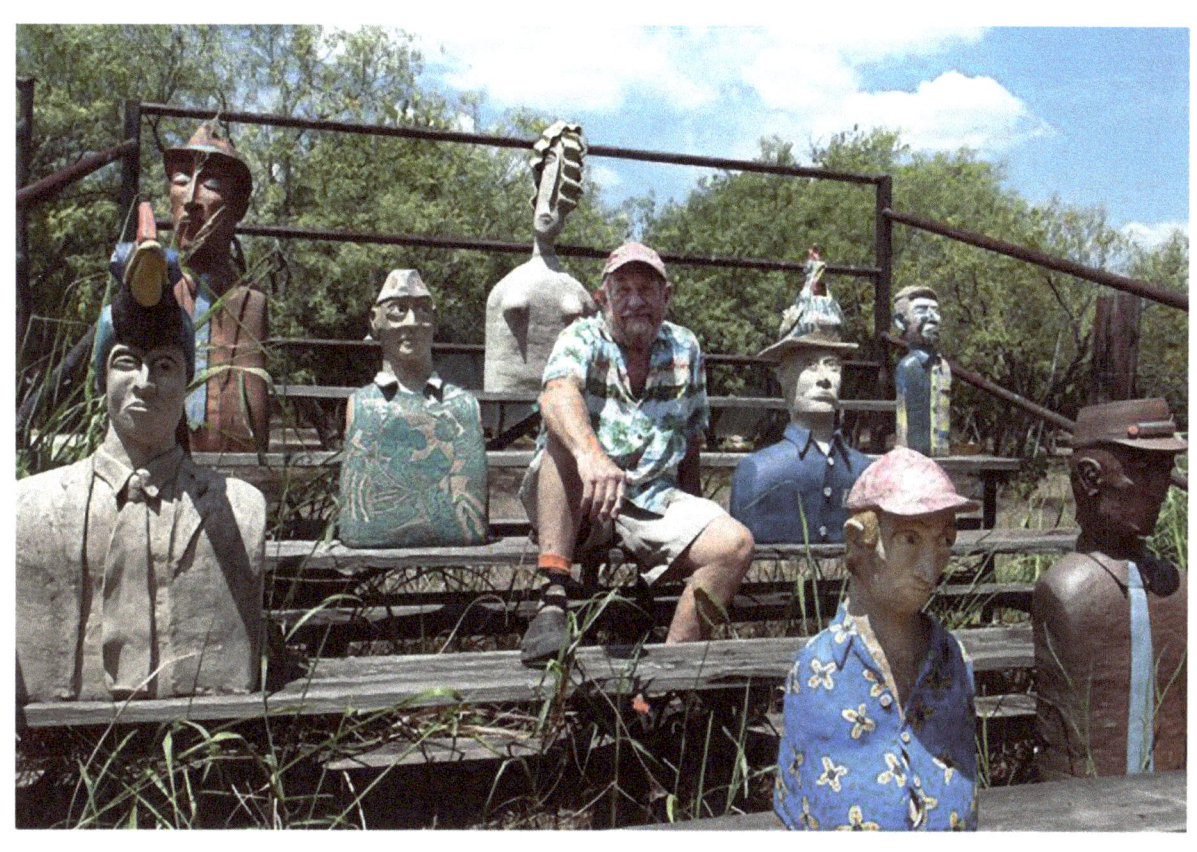

Billy Ray Mangham at Eye of the Dog Art Center

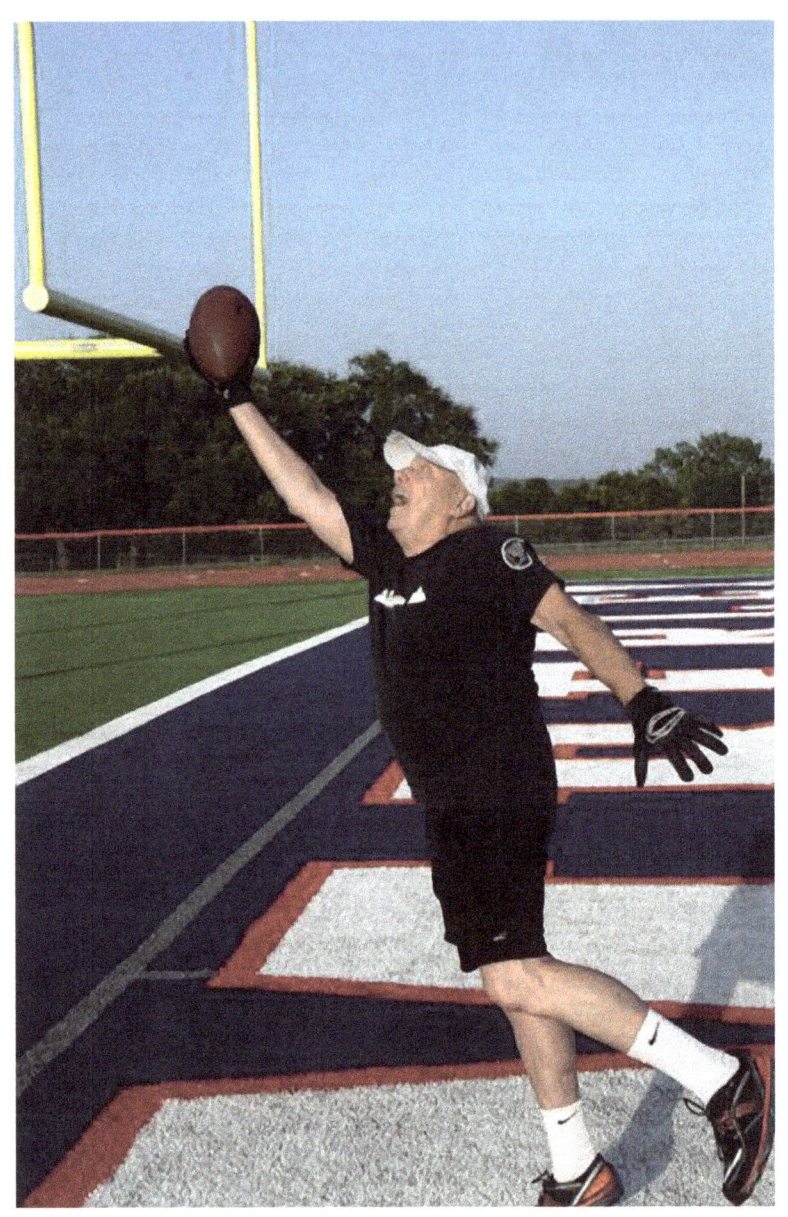

George Krause at football practice

The Artists: In Their Own Words

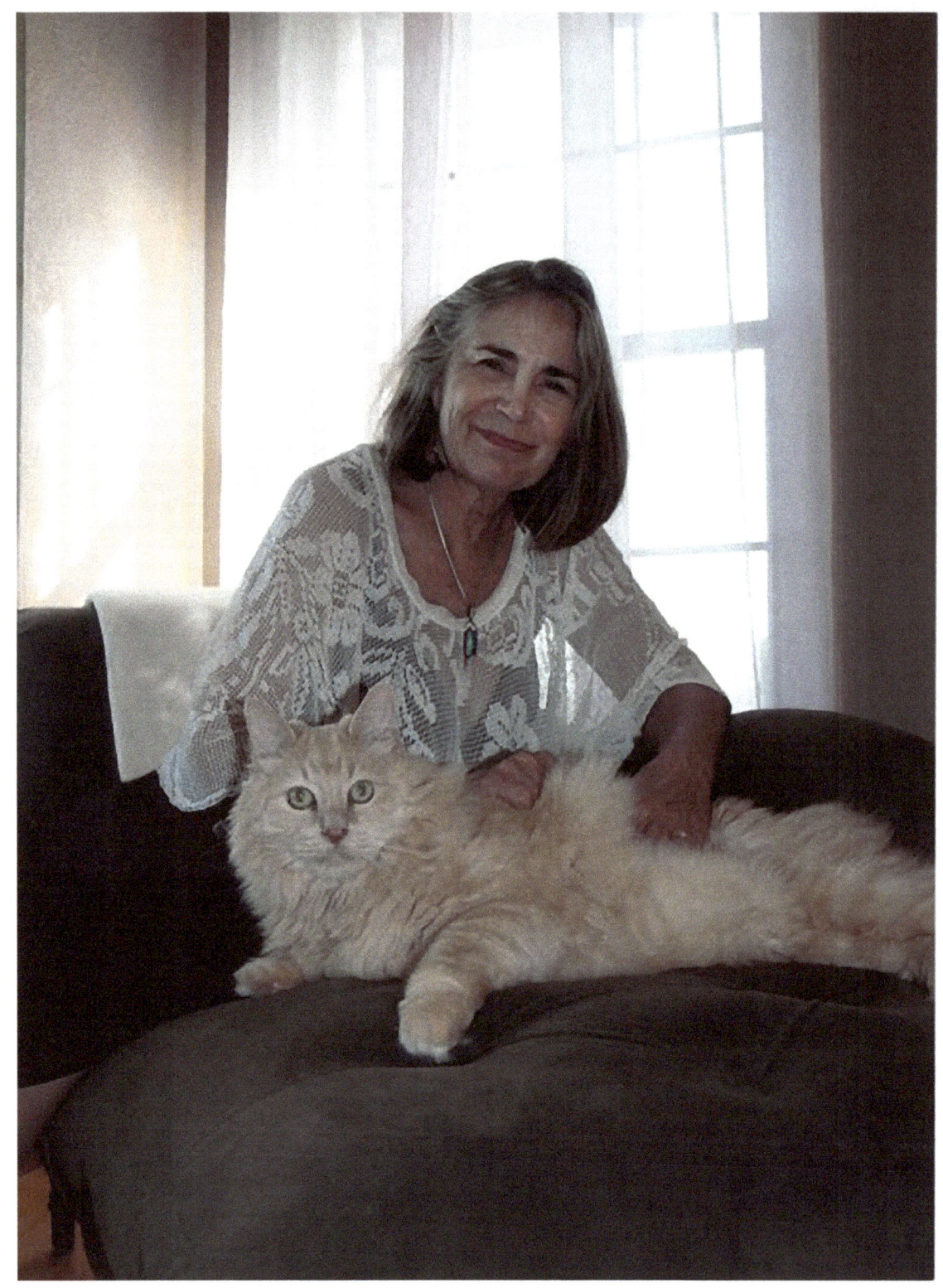

P. Cleve Ragan

P. Cleve Ragan

I found the challenges of being an artist pretty early. When I was about three years old I made some drawings and showed them to my mother. I was all excited. But I didn't get the reaction that I wanted. She was not happy because I'd made the drawings in the family Bible. Little figures drawn all through the Bible. I was so proud, really, I was so proud. But I can understand why she freaked out. After all it was the family Bible. Actually, that moment has probably held me back a lot. When you show somebody one of your creations and they have a hissy fit, it tends to make you hesitate. You expect one reaction and you get exactly the opposite reaction. I've done a lot of therapy about that. Looked at it later. I think that's what stops me so often, to have had one of my first creations cause such a bad reaction. I remember drawing with the crayons so carefully, and the cool black inside of the Bible. I don't remember what I drew, but my mother really had a fit. That moment is really pretty firmly etched. My mother did encourage me in other ways. She was an artist too, and took me to some of her classes. I drew my first portrait was when I was about four years old, and she recognized the person I had drawn.

About ten years ago, my Dad got really sick—he was dying actually—and he told me some more things about the family. When I was in about the third grade, my mother took a lit cigarette and put it on my bed and closed the door to set my room on fire. They said they were going to the laundromat and I asked, "Can I stay home?" Luckily she said no, you can't stay home. I can't even imagine what her intention was. Later we found that Bible in the chest that was in my room. I don't know if there was any connection.

Right outside my room was my bird who died of smoke inhalation. I figured out only last year why I have this thing for birds in my artwork: it is because of that bird, I think.

These are things that I've worked on for years. I go to a breath-work therapist. I'm trying to get past so many things, but also to be able to use my art as a release. I seem to have this blockage. My mother was proud that I was an artist, but she never wanted me to be better than she as an artist. She'd only encourage me so much. In fact, I gave her a painting once, and she ended up kicking a hole in it. I think it is important to marry all these memories with my art. So I don't object to people knowing about them. I want to do a painting of a burning bed. I'm going to get a doll bed and set it on fire. I have this old birdcage and I might put that in there too.

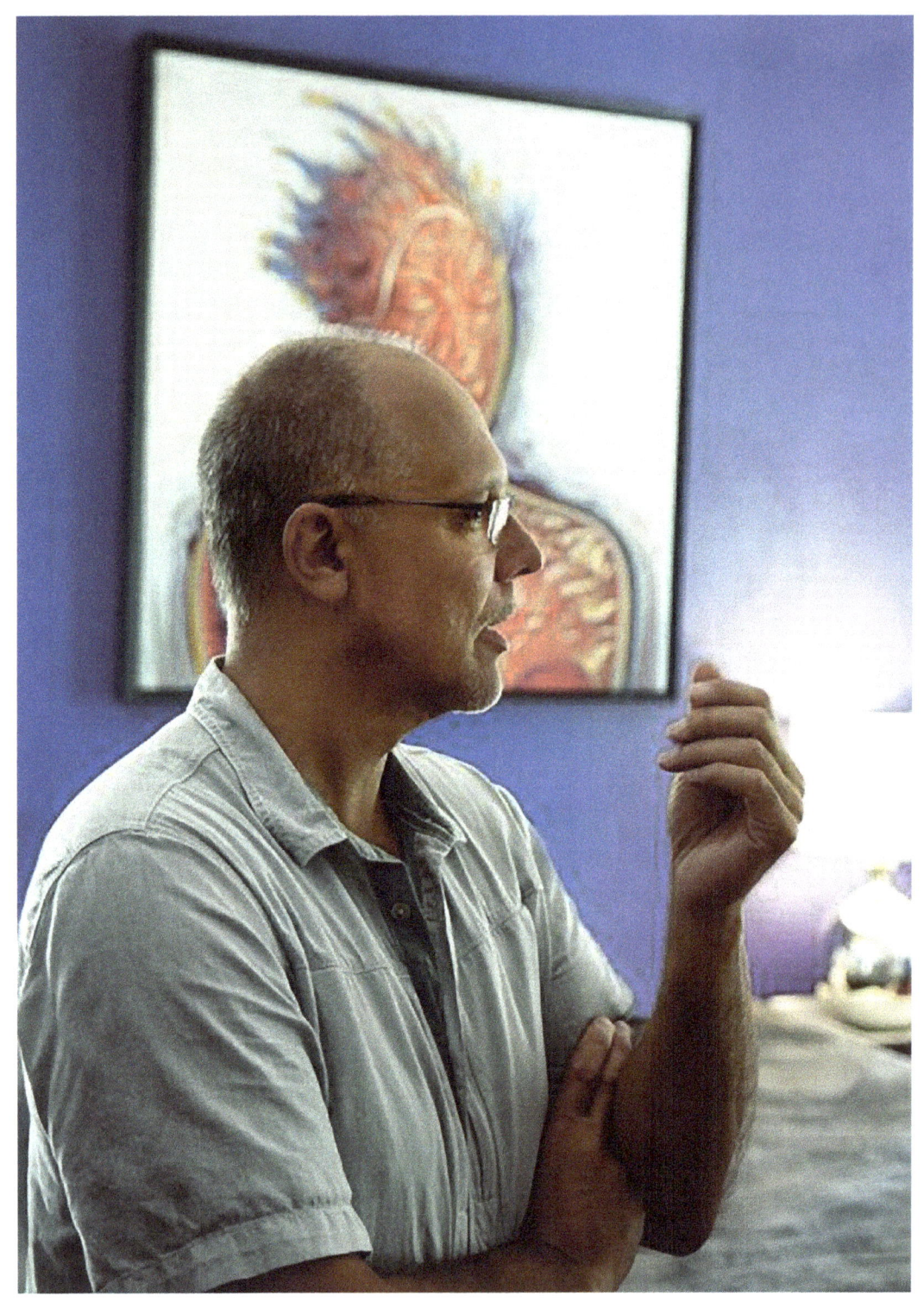

Gil Bruvel

Gil Bruvel

I wanted to create a sensation that could be physical, like the wind pushing through the grass or the trees, creating all these natural patterns, creating sensations. The sands are who we are in a certain way, because we are naturally attracted to pleasure. This work is called "The Flow Series." The combination of the sensations, the elements, the erosion, the wind in this case, is all a little bit of our identity. We never see ourselves as we really are. We have these fantasy images, the constructs. That's the fun part of it. The patterns could be the neural networks, so it's not one single perception of ourselves. The first idea I came up with for "The Flow Series" was in an international competition in Perth, Australia. They wanted a St. George and the Dragon in front of St. George Cathedral. At the time I was more figurative and casting in bronze, and I said to myself, I need to make a departure, artistically and for myself—you know where I would be taking a more contemporary approach. So, I thought, why don't I create the motion of the dragon and the horse with this ribbon? From concept to completion takes a long time because you have the idea, and then you have to put it together, and then you have the casting part, which is super labor intensive and more related to teamwork. So to translate the concept, even though it's made out of a mold (I use the lost wax process), you still have to infuse it with what you want it to do. So there is a little bit of supervision to make sure the work is right, the casting is right. It's all process, so it takes months. Once it's at the foundry I go there a few times a week to see how things are coming along.

This piece is a little bit biographical. I was going through my divorce, so I did these two people. I saw it as two characters parting, but a lot of people see it as two people kissing, fusing. I think it was such a co-dependent relationship that it was like pulling apart, but also they are fusing together. This one is more emotional because it's two people coming apart and realizing they are not what they were, or what they thought they were: the usual illusion we create for ourselves.

Here is one that is more abstract, flowing in one single way—energy. There is something about the stainless steel, in the way that it's layered, that it really does capture the emotion. This one is the same concept. It's called "Never Ending." It's a bit about the Mobius ribbon. The outside of her forms the inside of him and vice versa. Again, just the tail end of my self-inflicted suffering. This one is more intellectual because I am adapting a concept. That's good for art, no? You don't want to deal with too much of it, but you can feed off it for a long time. I started with an image. I don't pretend that I know what I'm doing. Sometimes I just start in the morning thinking that I have something to do. Sometimes it's just a very faint impulse and I go with it, sketch for a bit first.

I use a lot of techniques. I've been doing Vipassana meditation for about 40 years now. It's Buddhist meditation based on concentration, observing the breathing and then observing sensation. That has been a process I have been using a lot. So the idea is to reach your state of equanimity, sitting for a very long time and observing the sensation without conceptualizing and just trying to see things as they are. We identify with the laws of attraction/repulsion—oh this is pleasant, this is horrible, this is painful. I'm going to lose my legs because I can't stand this pain. When we pass that, it is realizing the good and bad we conceptualize in our head is really relative. So in this moment of true observation, there are layers. You know meditation is only practice, it's not intellectual at all. It's based on these kinds of serene moments or peaceful moments where these layers of the mind bring out this clarity of certain things. I've been using that process a lot for creative juice, I guess. Typically, I'll wake at 4:30 in the morning and sit until 9:30, then take a break. It's one meal a day, sensory deprivation. You're not talking, you're not doing anything but just meditation. You close your eyes, you sit down try to have a straight back and just do it over and over. It can be horrendously horrible or absolutely ecstatic. So over the decades you don't even pay attention, you just know that's part of the process. This type of meditation is not so popular because it's intense and time consuming. Now we know that creates some kind of brain wave that is not some voodoo, it's an observable thing, a mystical experience.

As a kid, I was drawing all the time. I had lessons when I was nine - sculpting lessons from my Dad who was a cabinet maker. He was training my older brother and I to help and a lot of what he did was carving. My first lesson I had about sculpting was to take a piece of wood and draw an elephant and then cut out the profile and start to shape it up.

In France, when I was 19-years old, I worked in a restoration workshop where we were restoring old masters from the past—very detailed work.

I feel I am much better now as an artist, but creating involves the laws of repulsion and attraction—the law of failure. You fail all the time, but you don't see it this way, so you keep on doing it. People call that talent, but you don't see it that way because you don't see failure like failure. I think that's a cultural value. In order for me to do a piece even today, I have to do a bunch of sketches, really focus on it and it still completely tanks sometimes. And then it's like, OK how do I go about this thing? Maybe I'm not going to be able to do this project. Because that's where your brain will go. It will tell you in all kinds of little voices, Oh you're terrible; it's not working. My way of evaluating my work is to hear from friends, other artists, collectors - people whose opinion I respect. Because it's so easy to think to yourself, oh this is great! When I feel something is right, I just need to double check it. Meditation helps with that, to have a little bit more non-biased view of things. Kids are the best. They will tell you exactly what it is. The way they see things, and the way they tell you - right there is an inspiration. So why not listen? You know your ego is not your amigo. In London there was a super-famous violinist, world famous, and they took him into the subway dressed like a tramp and he played. Nobody paid attention, except the kids. All the kids stopped and were enthralled.

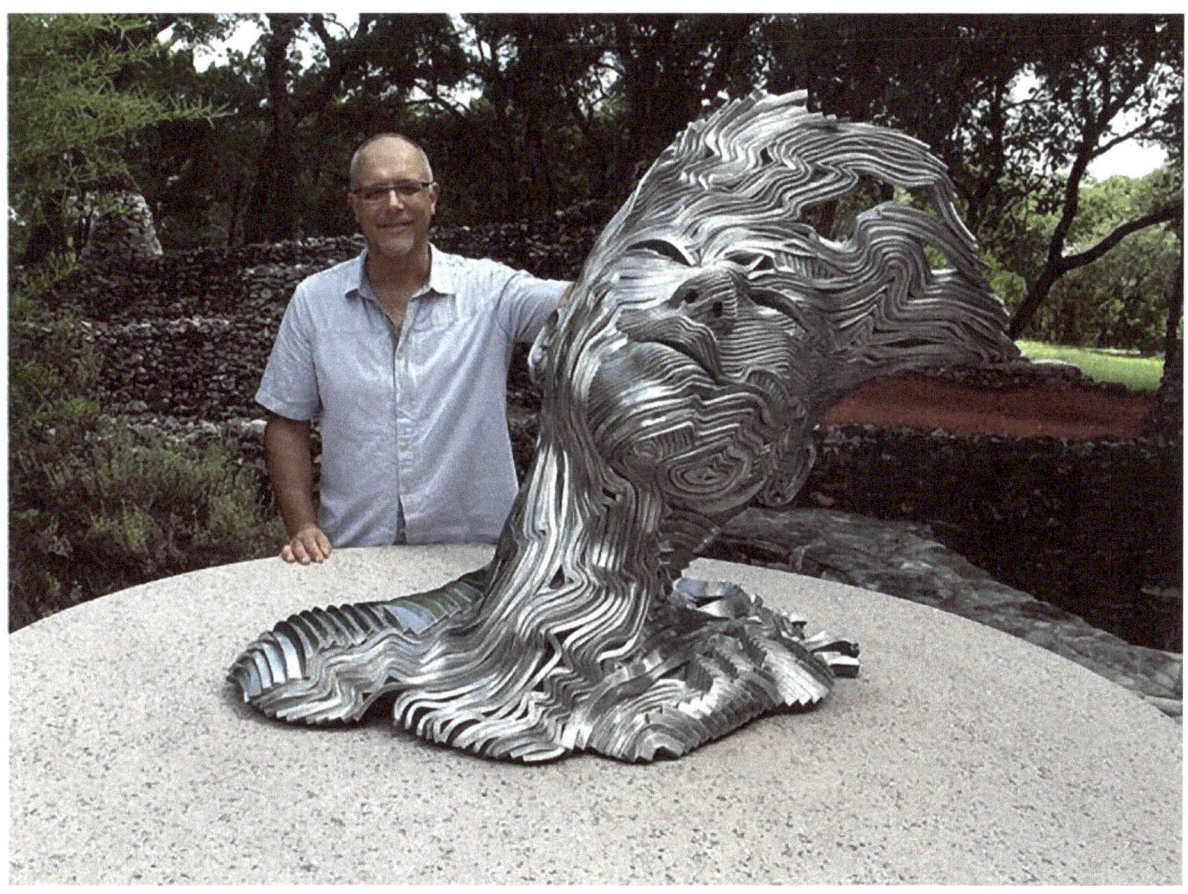

Gil Bruvel with "Flow Series" sculpture

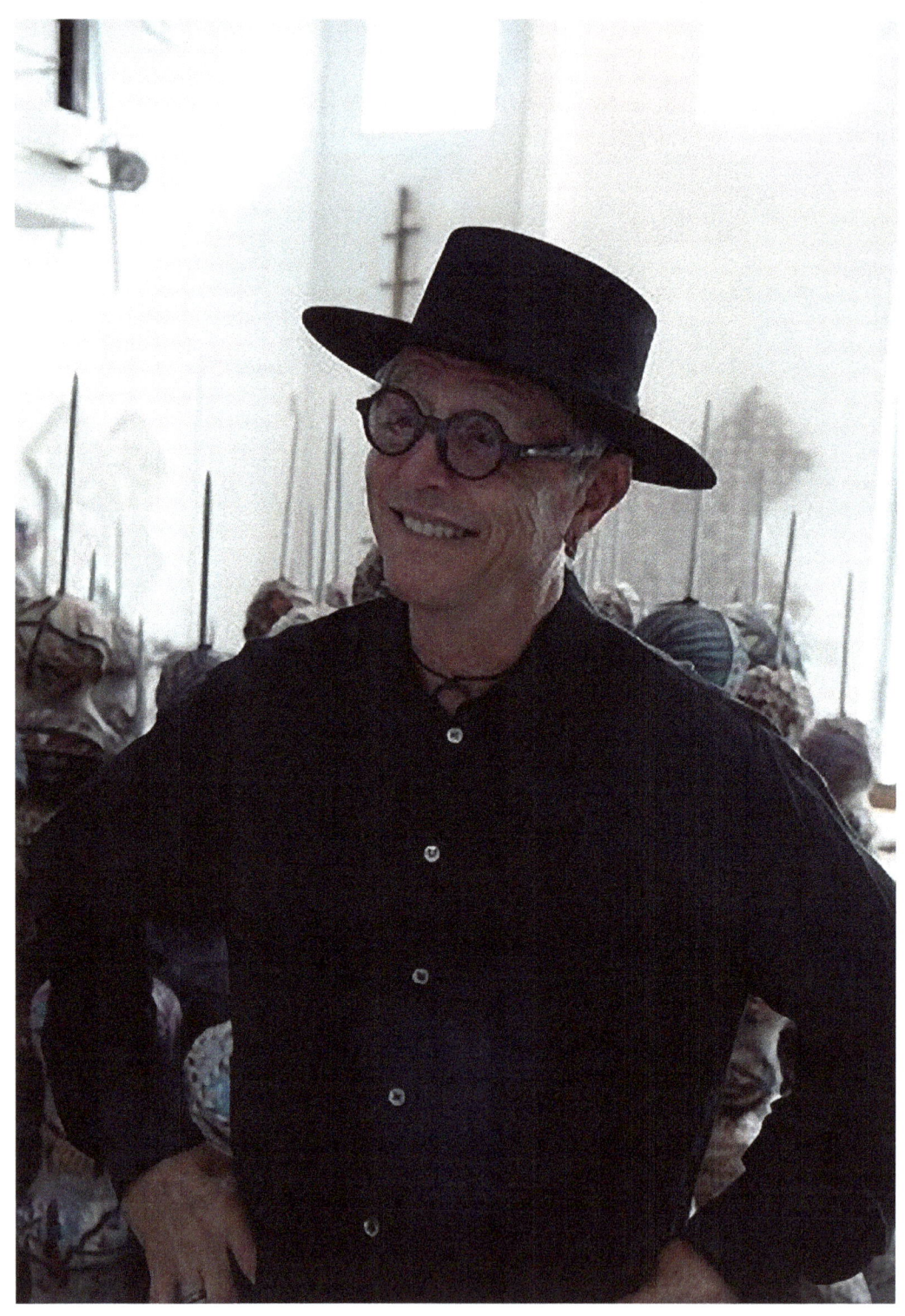

McKay Otto

McKay Otto

I've been making ladders for many years. It's that whole thing of stacking , the way we stack our lives. It's interesting. With each step, and between the steps is a portal. There's an empty space and I think that's what I've been most interested in—that empty space, that silence. It's like meditation beads. You can go up the ladder and come down; go up and come down; go up and come down. Or maybe it's like Rosary beads. The first ladder I ever did was a protest piece against a corporation that was cutting down the virgin redwood forests in California to service junk bond debt. So that first ladder was a protest piece. These ladders are made with virgin redwood. When I was in high school my dad said, I have a summer job for you. You're going to tear down this redwood water tower, which was in one of Texas's oldest oilfields, on my great-great grandfather's ranch. So I spent the whole summer reclaiming this redwood lumber and that's what I've been making my ladders out of for thirty years.

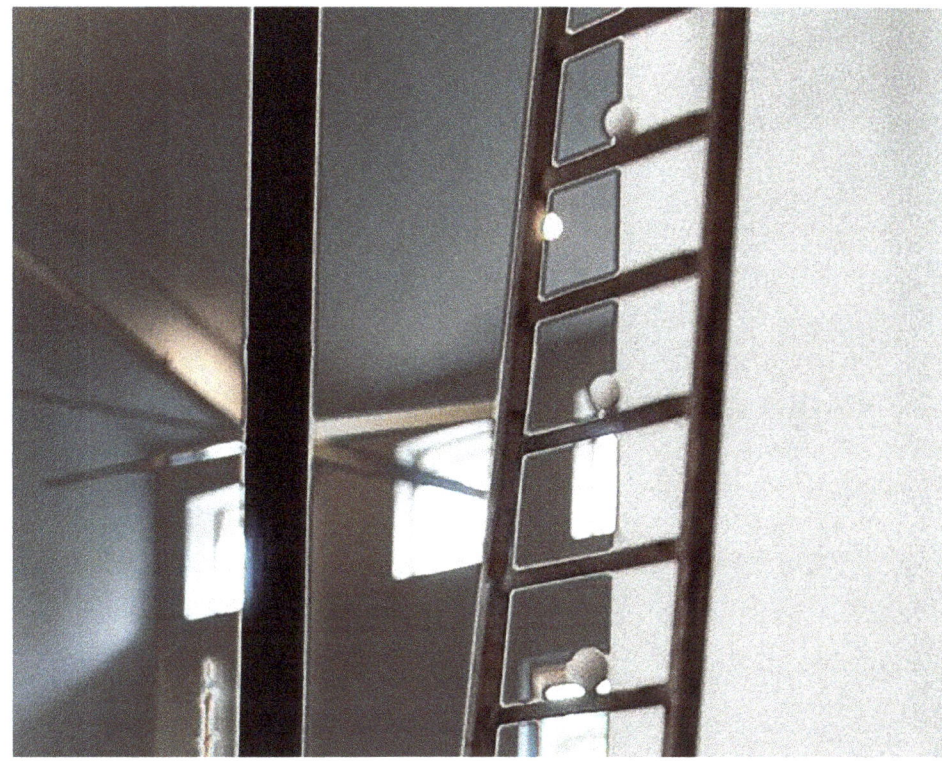

Shapes Inside
Spaces

I'm now involved in making these standing figures from rags. My mother sewed. We were not the richest people around, so she sewed her own clothes, and my sisters' clothes, and shirts for me. These are all saris from India and the rope is made from women's dresses—rags from India. I started thinking about how we've been sending rags all over the world and now they're sending them back to us. Then I started to buy rags, and if you look at the tags, they're from all over the world, clothes from all over the world. They're universal. The material has been worn by a lot of people and I really think objects take on energy. So you really have the energy of multiple people involved here. It speaks again to meditation. It's meditation beads, Rosary beads. The rods coming up through them I think look like needles - women's sewing needles. All of these rags that would have been discarded and all this clothing that would have been worn by all these people, I've been able to repurpose.

These are my signature paintings. These take you right into the work and beyond. I was mentored by one of the world's greatest artists and she did grids. I've been doing grids—horizontal and vertical lines—for over fifty years, and I've done them on a 2-dimensional plane. Every painting in the history of art is all on a 2-dimensional plane. But we live in a 3D world. She challenged me. I've done all this work on a 2D plane and I didn't know how to go beyond the 2D, and she said, I think you are the artist who is going to take art and free it from two dimensionality. The grid is the only thing that talks to and through the intellectual mind. It's the only way you can get to consciousness— through a grid. Everything in the universe is on a grid, and the minute you tie a person or a landscape to a 2D plane you've tied it down. But we're many dimensions of spirituality. We have just forgotten it. We carry it every day with us; it's our soul. And great art is supposed to touch the emotion, not just feeling. It's not great art if it just touches feeling. Anybody can touch feelings, but great art, like the Mona Lisa, touches the soul. It has to go beyond the material. A ladder is nothing but a grid. And you can meditate on a grid, think about it. There's something there for everybody if they just silence their mind. All this chatter that's going on in the world. Everything that's great, someone had to get silent to do. I have to leave my ego at the door every day when I go into the studio. Because if my ego comes in, I'm not creating the work. So I meditate and get out of my body so I'm not doing the work, the work is flowing through me. The universe is doing the work. I work in total silence. Let me get out a Tibetan bowl. My assistant plays a Tibetan bowl. That's where I have to go, that's where the energy in my studio has to go. This tone is a *B* and that's the crown chakra. So it opens up unlimited possibilities. I've got some of the best Tibetan bowls. A friend of mine bought one from me the other day and it was the best *F* I've ever had. It's going to be hard to replace. So that's the sound of the universe. You can get there and that's where you get when you meditate on this work. I think that's why I've been put on the planet right now. We all have a purpose and we don't know what it is. These paintings go everywhere, all over the world. I really think the day will come when millions of people will see these. I use sacred geometry. It's all sacred geometry—all the counting, the numbers are all sacred. The yin and yang create the balance. You'd never see the clouds if there wasn't the shadow. It's all about illumination. Bottom line, you're looking at illumination.

I am producing these phosphorescent paintings. Many layers of phosphorescence are involved in this. It came out of a dream. My mentor came to me at 3AM one night and said,

Where's that paint; that paint that glows? You'd bring those stupid little paintings to me in Taos and I'd tell you to take them home and destroy them. Where's that paint? I got up and I found just a little bit of it and started painting at 3AM. Two weeks later I finished, and I realized I'd created a light box painting. She'd tell me if it looks like paint, if it looks like glow paint, it's not a good painting. If a painter paints and it still looks like paint, they haven't gone past first base. A lot of what you see in galleries still hasn't gone past first base; it still looks like oil paint, or acrylic paint. Now I've incorporated phosphorescence in every painting and every work since. I told Agnes, I had this dream and you came to me and you asked me where's that phosphorescent paint? And she said, I had that same dream.

I was the last artist she critiqued in her lifetime. I took two paintings two weeks before she passed away. She told me not to destroy them, that they were really good paintings, and she said, "You'll be able to retire if you sell either one of these, but remember, if you're a great artist, you'll never want to retire."

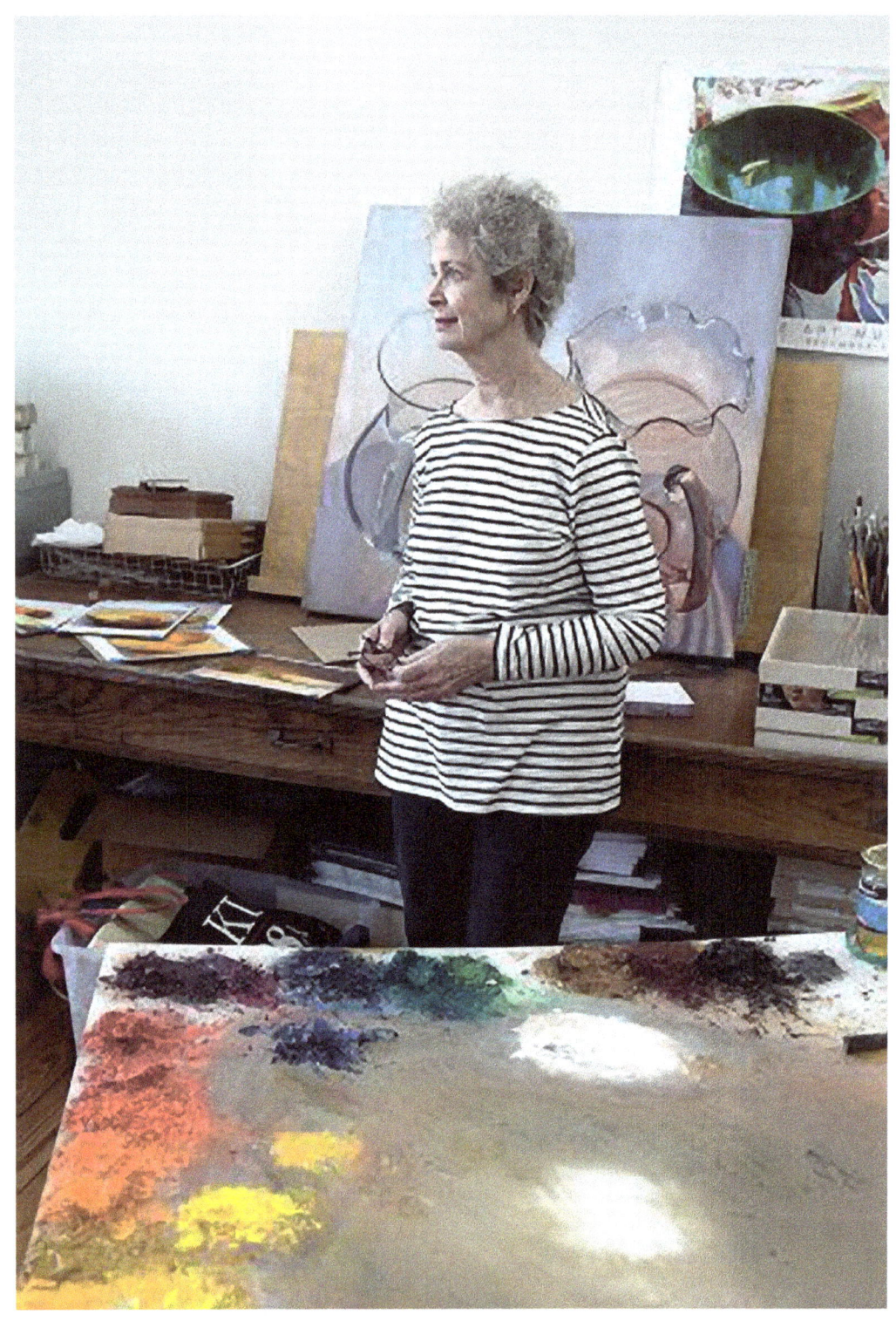

Ellen Berman

Ellen Berman

I really like being private in my studio, and I don't want people in here until I'm ready for them to be in here. I want to be private in general. So I've been lucky enough to have studio situations where I can work on my own. This is the third studio we've built. I've learned as we go along. I've been doing art for a very long time and I always have known that I didn't want to be in a communal environment. I have so many friends in Houston who, both for financial reasons and because they preferred it, worked in big warehouse type situations. That's just not for me. That doesn't work for me. When we moved to Wimberley I could make my studio much bigger and we could turn it any direction we wanted it to be. It faces north. It has these great windows to let in the north light. When I finish a work, I put it across from this north wall. I like to be able to look at it for a period of time, so I needed all this wall space. My studio here is 20'x40' because I went into someone else's building and that was its size and it just felt right. This space is not raw, it's finished. To me it's beautiful. It can be messed up. This is a cheap floor. So that's how I think about it: it's a work space. But I'm aware that for an artist's studio, it's really luxurious and it's beautiful. I'm aware of that every day.

I do work every day. I've been showing regularly since 1985, really a long time it feels like to me. And except for some strange happening, like moving, or somebody in the family dying, or somebody getting sick, I've been painting every day for all those years. It's just going to work, it's going to my job. At this point in my life I don't paint all day. I can't paint all day. I paint standing up, which is another reason why I can't paint all day. I used to paint in the morning, and now I paint in the afternoon. I don't know why that is.

When you are in elementary school there are always one or two kids who are the class artists and I was one of those. And then I gave it up in junior high and high school. I just gave it up. I was doing other things. When I started back up, I was in my mid-30's at the time. I had things I wanted to say, and through painting I found the language with which to say them. So the world opened up for me.

I work from photographs to capture the right light. People do self-portraits by looking into a mirror, but not me. This very early series were self-portraits. It was about grieving. My art creates a narrative. Before I became a painter I was an English teacher. I have read novels my whole life and I love narrative. So my approach to the world is through storytelling and narrative. That's how I make sense of the world. When I first began painting all those years ago, I painted the figure - some self-portraits, but mostly paintings of my daughter who was severely handicapped. I had much that I wanted to say to the world about her, and about our relationship, and I had no words to express this. But I found that through painting I could tell this story. And that story was received, which was remarkable to me. But then she died. And I

31

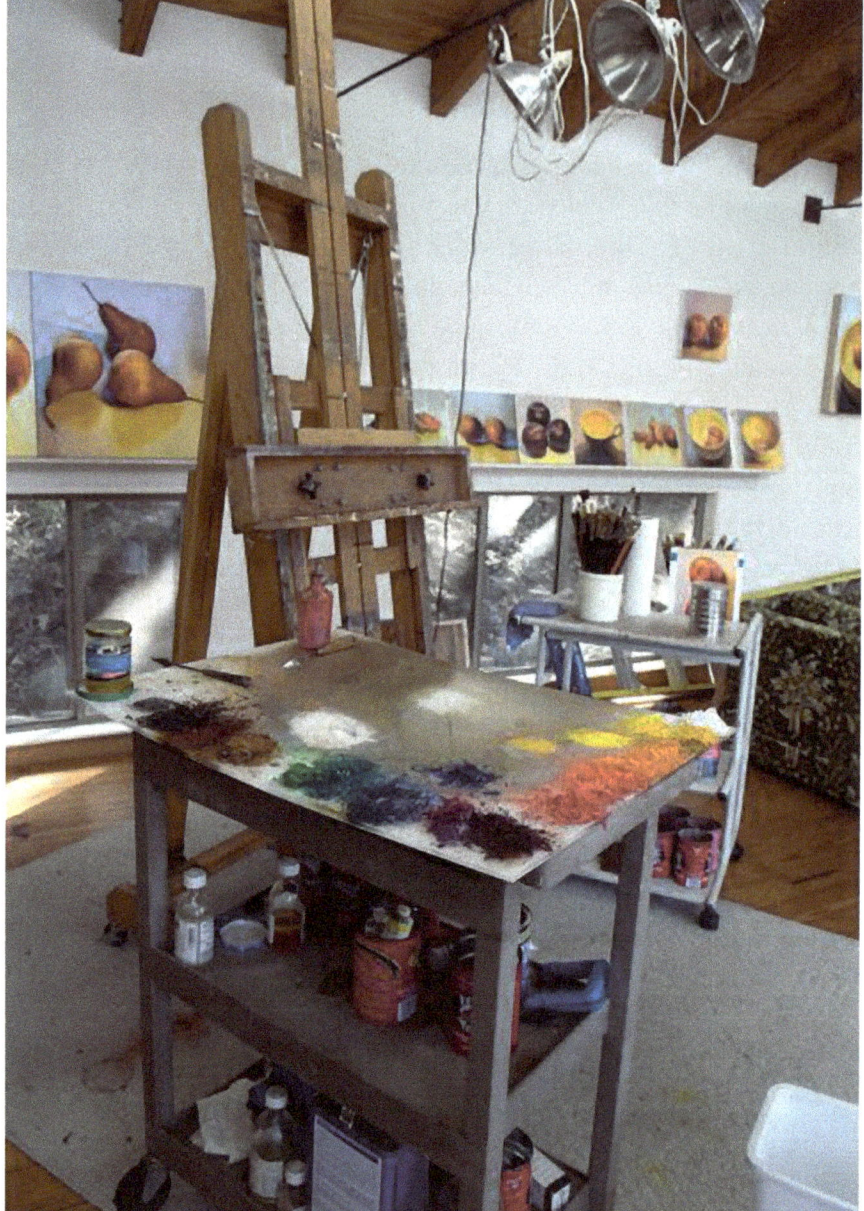

Ellen Berman's
studio

was casting about for what I wanted to paint. I came back to still life. I discovered that I could regard these objects as portraits as well as still life. They became portraits of these domestic things. That's how I approach it. To me, as I painted them, there were these relationships occurring between and among these objects. Even if there was only an empty cup or an empty bowl there was still something occurring, some narrative. And during the course of my making the painting, that idea would help me maintain my interest in making the painting. I hate to say that gave me a reason for making a painting, but it did! And I do believe that there are stories in those paintings.

I've always been interested in painting objects that come from my personal daily life - objects that I know well and am really familiar with; objects that I have some reason for creating a narrative about. If I have an object and then I have two objects, I have a relationship that's set up and that's the beginning of a narrative if they're apart, if they're closer, what is the light?, how sinister is the light? I move the light and the story changes. The story doesn't have to go very long or very deep. I'm easily entertained. When you step back from the paintings, they do look very realistic, and they hold together and they look like objects that you recognize and that you know. But when you look at them very closely, they completely fall apart as objects that you know, and they look abstract and are not realistic at all. That's what I'm after.

D. R. Jones

My artist bio says I'm working through a mythic reality that never existed. Growing up in the 1950s and 1960s with all those westerns: *The Lone Ranger and Tonto*; John Wayne; *Gunsmoke*. They depicted a mythologized American west. But that's what I grew up with. As far as being a painter, I'm relatively new. I was 50 before I started painting. I've been a cabinet maker and carpenter, always involved in creating things. And then I was a computer programmer.

When I was growing up, about age eight or ten, we lived in Lubbock and went to Santa Fe, New Mexico a couple of times every year. And that's when I really got interested in art and the kind of art I ended up pursuing. When I started painting, I thought back to those artists and that art I admired in Santa Fe. That's when I first got the concept of fine art. John Nieto is my hero. He does pretty simple compositions, but bright bold colors, very lively, very active. So I wanted to recreate what I felt seeing those works of art as a kid. I kept coming back to western themes and Texas themes. In the westerns on TV and in the movies, I always rooted for the Indians. So there is a Native American influence and that's what I kind of picked up. I try and create works of art that let me travel back to that mythic American west, and I hope those who see my art go along with me on that journey.

At age 50, I finally just decided I was going to do it. It was pretty rough at first, but then I finally started to hit my stride in fits and starts. When I started painting, it was like every painting was supposed to be a masterpiece. And it took several years to find out that's not the case. I had to work through that mindset. Now I can keep going if it's not a homerun every time.

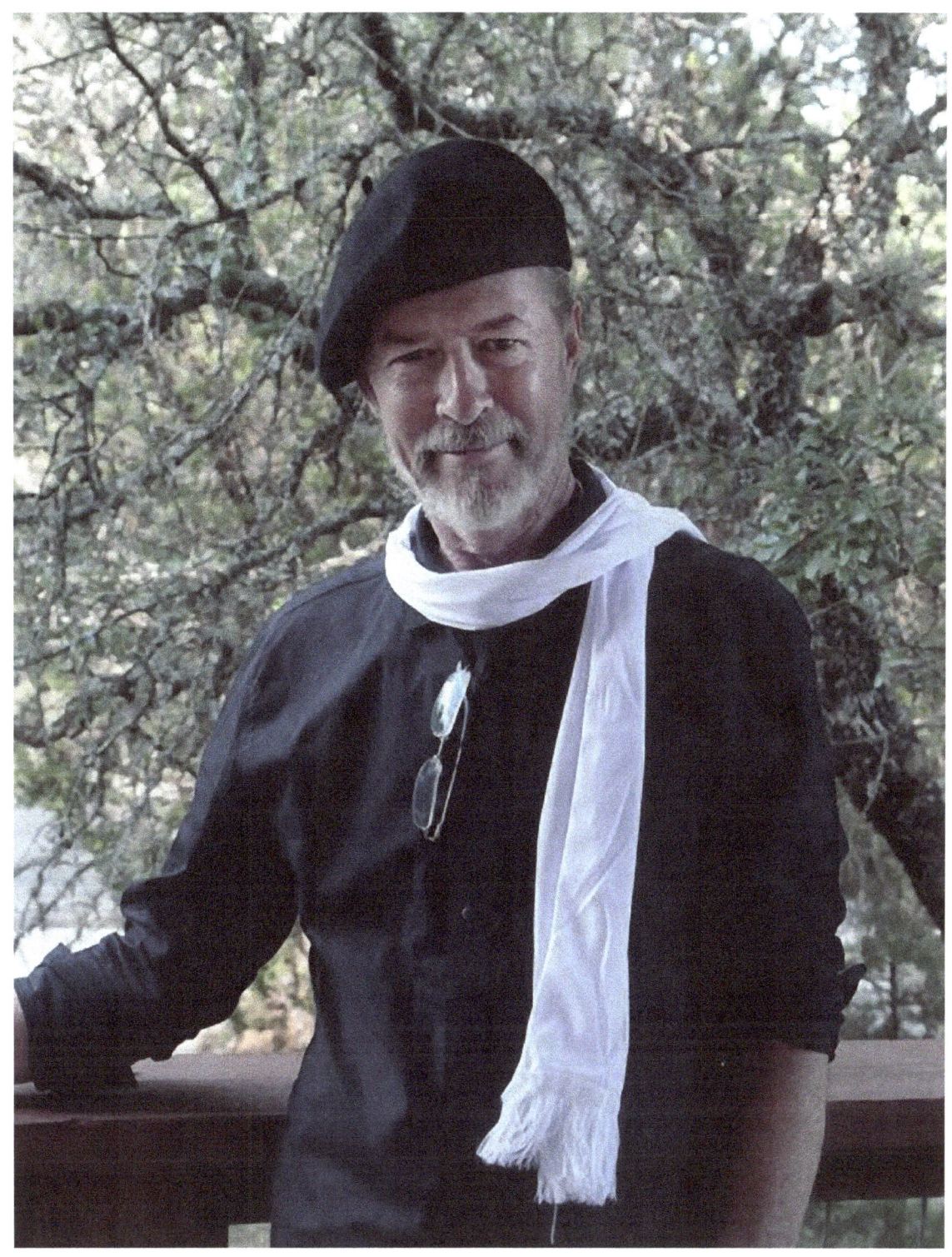

D. R. Jones

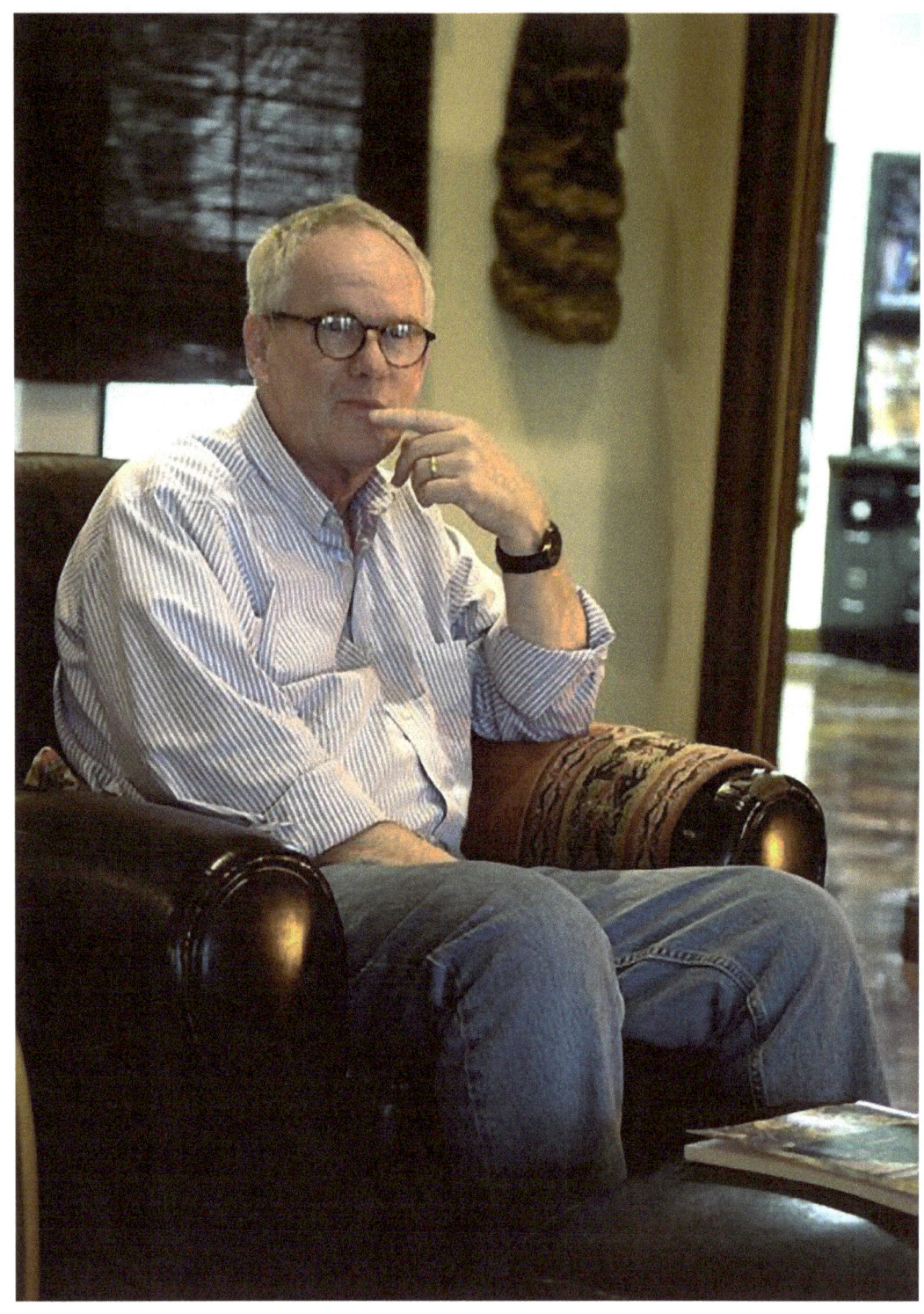

Dennis Darling

Dennis Darling

Basically I've covered the entire arc of photography from 1700's to now. The actual developing techniques are from the 1700s. I use cameras from the 1960s and then I process it and I scan it on this Nikon Cool Scanner, and then I digitalize the negative and then I print it on this printer, a Canon 2015.

When I was teaching photojournalism in Prague last year, we traced part of my father's roots. He was a B-17 bombardier in WWII and he got shot down over Belgium. He was on the lam for about nine months from the Nazis. The French Resistance hid him, and just before he was about to be rescued the Nazi's found him and he was taken to Stalag 13, you know from, *Hogan's Heroes*. But he never told any of the children about that. We only found out later. While I was in Paris I got in contact with a connection to a holocaust survivor: a survivor of Terezine. Somebody said he had died and I thought, aw shit, but then I thought I'd just give him a call and see. And he answered, and he said, "Oh yeah, why don't you come right over." I was so excited. I went to photograph him, but when I got there I realized I didn't bring a damn camera. I only had my iPhone 6. So one of the last photos I took in the holocaust series was made with an iPhone.

I've done photo projects with Hell's Angels and the Klan, and now the Holocaust. You know, just family stuff (laughs). I was brought up in Catholic School: a lot of people in uniforms and a lot of violence, a lot of bloody statues, that really scarred me. I guess I never got over it.

Now, I don't really work, I just teach at the University of Texas. I got started in photography because I was in design school at Georgia State University in Atlanta. A guy I was in school with was from England and he wanted to go back home and he needed plane fare, so he sold me his Minolta SRT 101. So then I took a class to learn how to use it. I took a couple of classes in Georgia, and I took a couple of classes more in graduate school. I have a Masters of Fine Arts degree from the University of Chicago School of Design. I was more interested in design and graphics at the time. But when I came out of graduate school I realized, I'm not going to make money drawing or painting. I'm going to have to do something that's salable on a regular basis. I became an editorial photographer.

I did the Nazis when I was in graduate school. I had to pick something to work on for a year, so I split it. I did the Nazis for six months and the motorcycle gangs for six months. And then I moved to Atlanta to take a non-photographer job: an art director job, and I lasted for about a year before I just got bored silly. That's when I started following the Klan. When I got to Atlanta there was this guy, James Venable. He lived in the shadow of Stone Mountain where the Confederate generals are carved. He had been instrumental in founding the Georgia Klan in the 1920s and 1930s, so I went out and talked to him and he gave me some leads. A friend of mine (our girlfriends were close) vaguely mentioned that he knew this guy named David Duke. He was in Louisiana. I wrote to David Duke, and he said, "Come over and see me if you can, and let's talk." I met with him and he invited me to the next rally. So that's when I started. Louisiana was the big time. I showed up and people were looking at me with the evil eye. So I got out of my car and said, "Is David here yet?" And then everybody relaxed and everything was OK. I learned that in college. I took some anthropology courses and read a book called Visual Anthropology by John Collier. He was working in the 1930s. He basically said if you're going to do this kind of stuff, go in at the top, and then everybody below will fall in line. I photographed the Klan for about five years and then I got critically hurt when a guy plowed his car into the Klan rally at Plains, Georgia back in the mid-1970s. I have all these scars: every finger broken, some broken vertebrae. That happened in 1976. I photographed them until the late 1970s early 1980s. With the last name of *Darling*, you don't take pictures of flowers. You've got to do stuff that's hair-raising, soul-raising.

I tell my students, "I can teach you and you'll know how to take pictures, but to take good pictures, I can't teach you what that takes." It's curiosity. Not just curiosity when you're standing in front of your subject, but curiosity about what it's going to look like from the other side, or from above, or below, or off to the side. There's nothing technical about what I teach. I teach seeing and looking. Somebody said that a camera is an instrument that basically teaches you how to see. That's when it stops being just taking pictures.

I teach the Rosetta Stone of photography the first thing. Proximity, disturbing the frame, getting people out of the center, the rule of thirds, vantage point, sense of place and then, really I don't have much else to say. You have to have the vision. I teach graduate students but you can't really teach graduate students. They know everything. I'm not young enough to know everything, but they do. I was Director of the Photography program at the University of Texas for several years and I'm sort of working my way down now. I always select the first class, the basic class: 144 students. Our enrollment is so shrunken because of the Internet and the iPhone. Journalism is a trade school. I don't care how you glorify it, you're in a trade school and people are there to get a job. Now with the iPhone everybody is a journalist. I used to get people calling me all the time and I had a bulletin board that I would post job openings, internships: newspapers, magazines. Now I haven't had anybody call me in six or seven years. Or, now I get calls that say, *I'm having a wedding—this would be good for somebody's resume or portfolio*. This is a term I hate. But now they say, *You're not really a photographer, you're a creative'*. Anybody that's in the arts, he's a new creative on the scene. Photography is the medium of the nearly talented. If you can draw a picture, there is something there. If you can take a crayon, or a stick and draw something in the dirt then there is something there. It's true. If you give a chimpanzee a camera, after a while he'll get a good shot. He might get an interesting vantage point. But, if you give him a pencil, probably not. Occasionally, you'll see an elephant doing something interesting with a paint brush stuck in his trunk.

In the Holocaust Series I don't think I've ever taken more than 24 frames of any one person. I tend to go in and talk to them for an hour or two. I enjoy it. It's a sick enjoyment, because it makes me so nervous. I'm traveling with lots of film and going through X-ray machines and traveling thousands of miles, to get a portrait and not knowing if I've got it. You have no control of the day they said you could come, or the weather, or the light in their house, or what their personality is. It's kind of a weird calculus you have to get in there. So I find that if I go in and spend time with them, and talk to them, and spend time with their scrapbooks, and that kind of stuff, I can always be sizing up the place and seeing where the best light is; how much I can push them out the door or someplace else. So it's fun to come back and see if there is a picture I like. I just go in with four rolls of film, a camera, and a smile.

I photographed the oldest WWII survivor: Richard Overton in Austin. And the first day, I accidently grabbed a bag with exposed film rather than film I could use. But I ended up just sitting on the porch with him for several hours, all afternoon, just chit-chatting. I mean what else has he got to do? He just sits there in his chair, watching the traffic go by. He always has a crowd there. People stop by - like a reception line. People come up the stairs and talk to him for a minute and then they move on and the next one in line comes up.

Now I write this blog, and I send out photos and some narrative to go with it every week. But I'm a really slow writer. I failed high-school English, but that kept me out of Viet Nam. They couldn't draft somebody in high school. So when all of my friends graduated in 1964, they all were swept up and off to southeast Asia. And I was just hanging out at the house and taking English again. And now I'm the senior faculty member of the School of Journalism at the University of Texas. Life's weird. Dorothy Parker said, I hate writing, but I love having written. Photography is the same thing. When I was in Jerusalem last year photographing holocaust survivors, I'm schlepping all this equipment around, and it's hot and I'm thinking, I'm 70 years old. What am I doing? But then when you get back with these images . . .

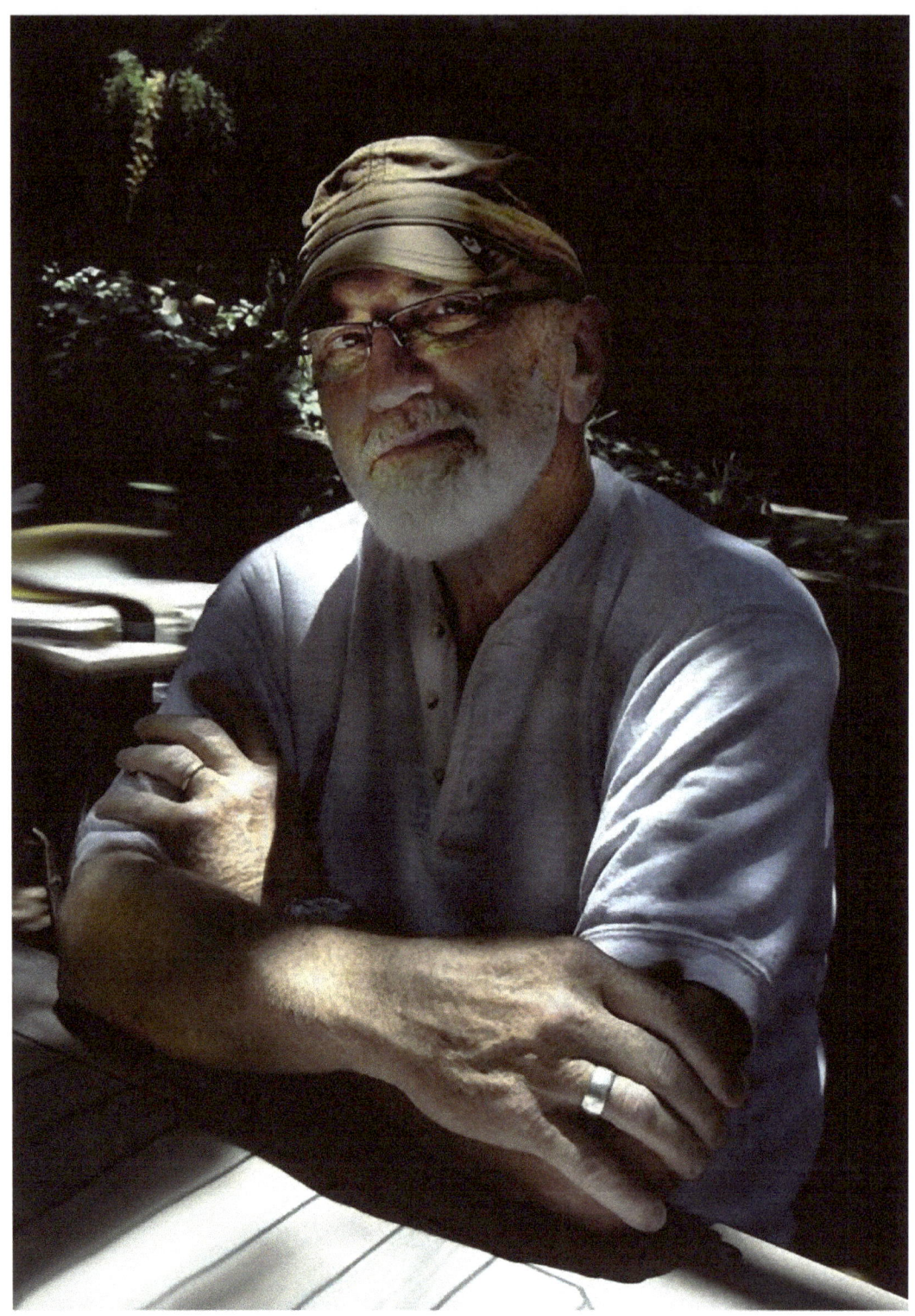

Taylor Dueker

Taylor Dueker

From an early age and throughout my life I have been drawing, painting, and creating. I was always interested in making art. In fact, I chose to major in architecture at Massachusetts Institute of Technology because of my dual interests in math and art, and I liked the discipline and order involved in math combined with art. I think you see that in my work.

One Saturday morning my wife was away, and I thought, If I don't just do it, I'll never get started. I went down to the art supply store and bought a bunch of paints, brushes, and canvases and just started—without any instruction or anything. I usually sketch something first, then I enlarge the sketch and put it on a canvas and start to paint. I usually like a rectangular format, either vertical or horizontal, that allows directionality and flow.

A piece called "Untapped" is what I consider to be my breakout piece, because most all of my other work is sort of rectangular and disciplined. This has figures and colors overlapping. Lots of people started to say I should do something sculptural, 3D. So I found a piece at Goodwill. It was wooden, a wall hanging: like something from Big Lots. It was very sculptural, ugly as sin. I stripped it, sanded it and now I'm doing a painting on that. It's very regular, a square, so you don't have the directionality to work with like a checkerboard.

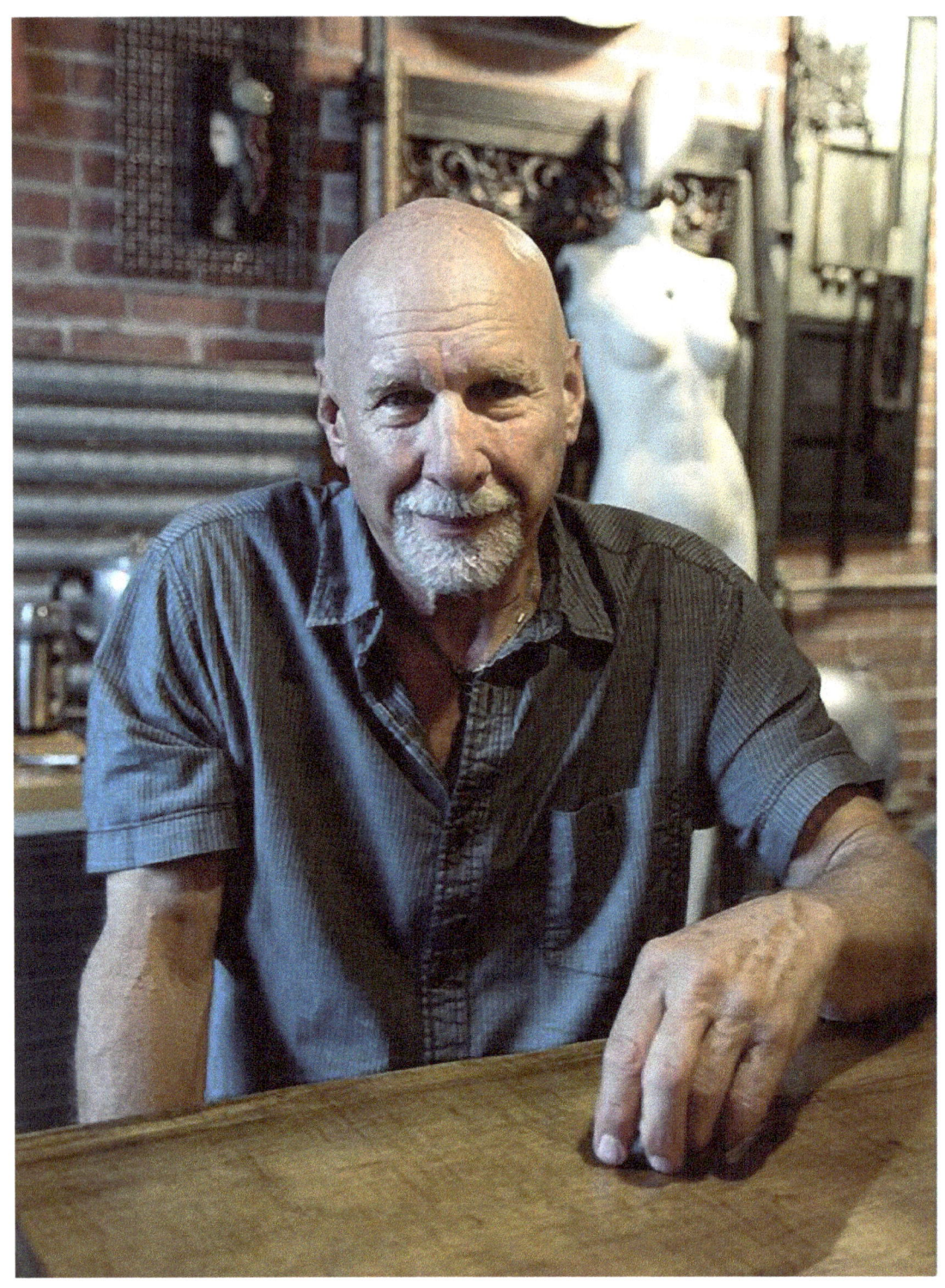

Ronnie Weeks

Ronnie Weeks

My history in art is really short. I just turned 70 years old, and other than doing some pencil drawings and a little bit of water color—all that would fit on that little table there—that's all I've ever done until I started doing this assemblage work. I have no formal art schooling. I took a drawing class back when I was in junior high, and that is the full extent of my art training. I always loved old things, old architectural salvage: metal, wood. I didn't care what part of the world it came from, and I started collecting - sometimes just pieces of things - part of something that came off of an old antique wardrobe, an old door off of a barn. I actually started off making these huge birdhouses back fifteen years ago when I was living in Taos, New Mexico. They were neat old birdhouses - really wild looking. And nobody was doing that at those big flea markets I went to. I took about ten there at one show and they were gone in the first two hours. Some of them went to California, some to New York. I was like, Wow, maybe I don't need to just sell that old dresser, maybe I need to tear it up and make something out of it! And that's really the way it started. I started putting things together that looked pretty cool and hanging it on the wall. Taos is a wonderful place to be creative and to be around other artists. My very first showing was at The Bean: a little coffeeshop on the north side of Taos. All kinds of eclectic people came in there out of the mountains. I just sold like crazy out of there. So it really kind of got me generated and I started making bigger pieces.

It's always been a challenge to me to take a pile of junk that's sitting over there that most people would want to bury in a landfill or torch. The challenge for me is to some way or another, take those things that no longer have the value or the purpose that they originally started with, and send them in a whole other direction with a new value, a new purpose, and give them a new life. I really enjoy that part. That and the fun of just being a junker, just out there scavenging junk materials from all over the country. And then people I know are bringing me stuff from all over the world, really. It gives me access to some really cool junk. Because there's good junk and there's bad junk.

In the early days, when I was in Taos, there were a lot of people who were purists. They'd say if you're gonna do found object art, you need to have found it laying on the side of the road instead of paying somebody $3 for it. So I tried that a little bit and I saw the kind of work they were putting out and what limited work I could come up with, and I wasn't satisfied. I decided that wasn't the way to go because none of it I saw was of any interest. It was basic junk that somebody had put together and stuck up on the wall. It was pretty rough. I wanted to have something more interesting, more appealing, more of a story, something behind it other than some plastic bottle caps. Not that you can't do some interesting things with that, but I just wanted to go in another direction. So now a canvas for me is an old shutter off of an old building in France; or a foundry mold that came in from Detroit. I start on that canvas and just go crazy. I really don't know exactly how the process works in my head, except that when I get an idea going it can be something as little as one small piece and explode into something else. But sometimes, it's very, very easy for me to see the thing quickly and lay it out, sometimes in as little as thirty minutes. Or it might take me a few hours another time. And I always tweak them when I'm putting them together, because you always run across problems, but that's part of it. Then, it might take me weeks to actually put it together and finish it. It's extremely difficult, and I'm not always sure I can actually do it.

I got taught an important lesson in Taos. I'd been doing real good at that little gallery in the coffee shop, so I decided to hit up one of the "real" art galleries about showing my work there. I brought a couple of pieces into this gallery owner, and I could tell initially he really was very interested. I could tell they were appealing to him. He liked the sense of design. But he looked them over real good, including the back of the piece. And then he said well I don't think I can show you here right now; I don't think you're quite ready. And I said, really? Because I've been selling real good over at that little coffee shop gallery. And he pointed out a couple of things that I could see weren't professional—they weren't finished, and that's including the back of the piece, he said, it really needs to look like what it is, a nice piece of artwork, and you took the effort to finish it out right, make it complete. It knocked me back a line or two. I thought, dang, I thought I was on the right road. But that was all I needed to do was just tweak and clean it up. That's the kind of constructive criticism you get that increases the quality of your work.

The medium that I work in as an assemblage artist is one where you really have to have a lot of inventory to pick from. So I've had to have a warehouse-size space to be creative in. And for financial purposes, I needed to live there also. I'm living here, and I have my art gallery in here, and a tremendous amount of inventory that you have to dig for to even find. When you have this much inventory to choose from it's great, but you can't have it all buried down so you have to go dig every time you need something. You have to have it laid out so you can choose from all the options. It's kind of a trial-and-error process. I can get a little idea going and put it on the table. Then I'll take a box around and start collecting up stuff that I think might really put something together here. I just go hunting around the studio and start digging into things and that's kind of how it happens. If I was a painter, I could do with a fourth of this space - some canvasses, some paints. But when you're doing assemblage work, if you want to come up with something unique and creative, you need a lot of materials.

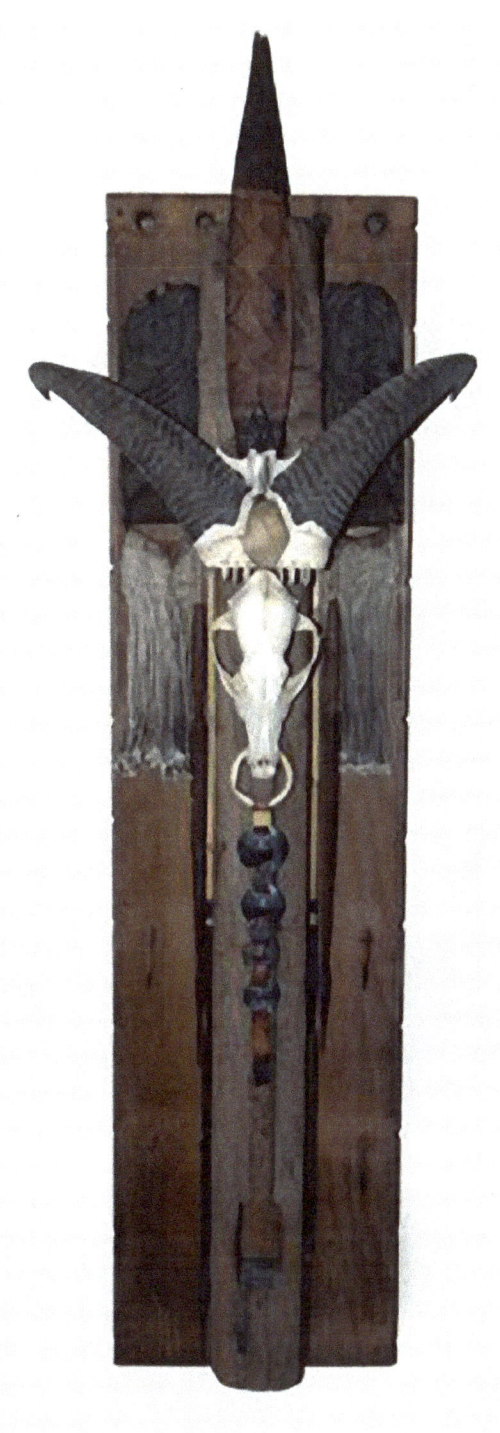

"Assemblage" by Ronnie Weeks

45

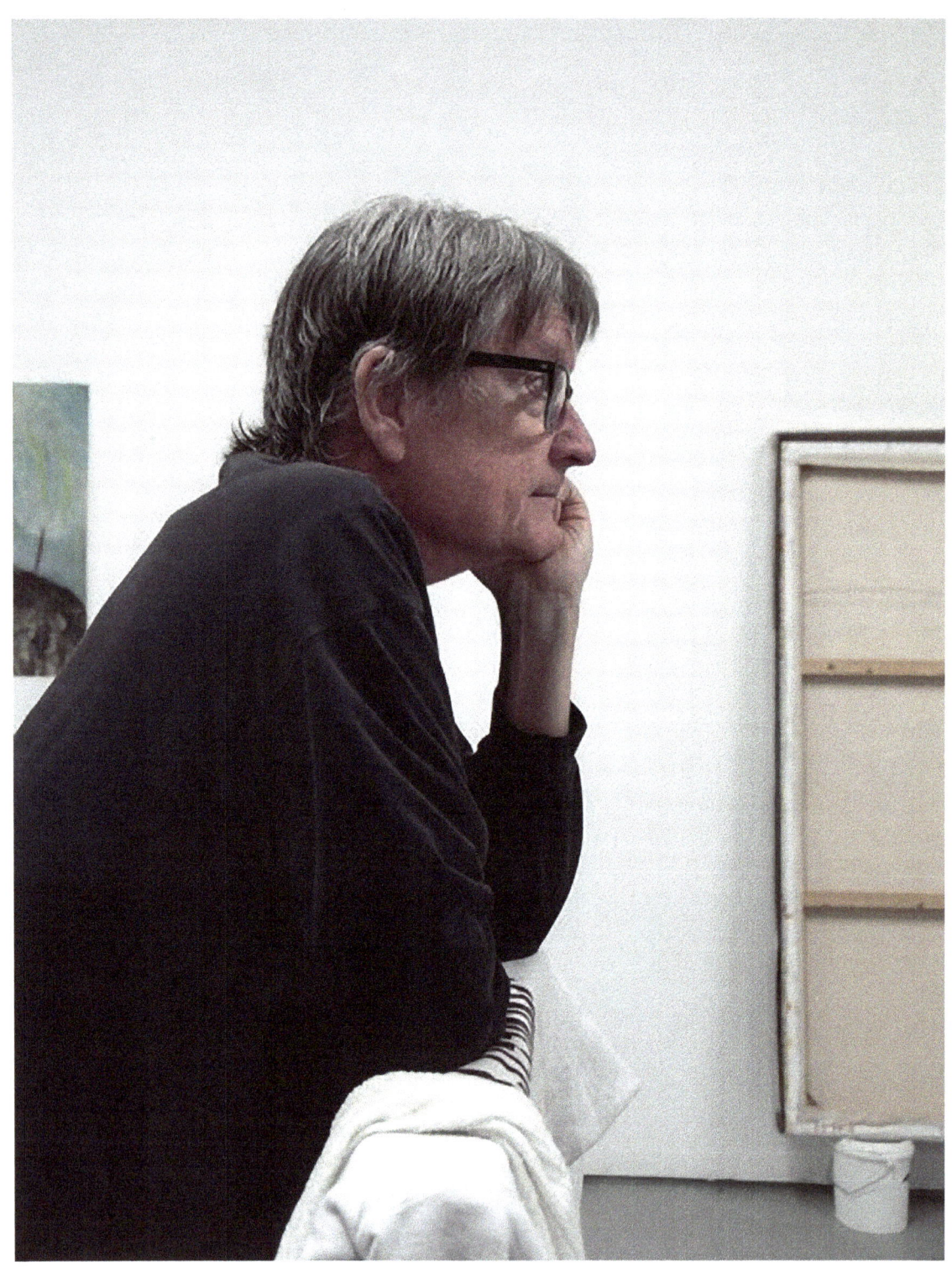

Denny McCoy

Denny McCoy

I've been working with vertical bars of color for nineteen years. In 2013 we went to Japan and that trip had a big effect on me. I had recently had surgery and was really not well. I went with my wife and one of her college roommates. We traveled around and they would go out in the mornings and I would go out in the afternoon. We saw so many wonderful places. We were there for about two weeks. That culture really impressed me. I've always liked Shakuhachi flute music. The whole Japanese way of being in the world just really impressed me.

The paintings I did from 2014 started to change and they've just gotten darker and darker and more and more subtle. I'm not sure what has happened, but this is completely different for me. It's very meditative and very quiet. I'm just an old guy that likes to sit and look. I will sit and look at a painting for just as long as I will be actively working on it because it's hard to get to that point of really being able to see it. That's really tough to do. Somehow, this work is just correct. I don't know what's happened but somehow things have just become more complete.

It's not easy. I don't think art should be easy. I think it should put you back on your heels a little and make you think and wonder. I've been reading a book by Alva Noe about art and philosophy. What they share is that both present a means of questioning or a process of thinking. These paintings are really subtle. It takes about twenty minutes for your eyes to adjust and really see what's there. It takes me that long. I really try and see things I've never seen before. I try to be in places I've never been before. I've been painting since I was in fourth grade, so I have all these skills that I continually try and repress... try to not use them because not using them is the same as using them, and at some point I just try to be in a place I've never been before and to see things in ways that I haven't seen them. And these have just become more and more subtle.

Twenty years ago my painting included some little something that would compel the viewer to look at it. The paintings were much more immediate. My work was more about the act of seeing and understanding and finding some source of visual something that would compel you to look a little longer. With this work you have to stay longer with it. My other work was much more immediate. For me there is a sense of understanding and completeness that is in this new work. I sometimes read things that are hard to read. I've been to Ireland four or five times. I've started reading *Finnegan's Wake* again, and it's just impossible. I've been able to find some recordings of it, because it's meant to be read aloud, meant to be heard. One point of view is that you have to start at the back and work forward because it's cyclical. Reading it, I feel like I'm becoming more and more untethered, and that's OK. I'm in here all day by myself. It's hard to get to that place that you need to get to really do any of this stuff. I try to just look and respond to what's there.

My wife and I were married at the Rothko Chapel in Houston, so Mark Rothko is obviously an important influence. These paintings respond really well to different lighting because two-dimension is an illusion. Normally in my life I have not had my work in the place where I spend the rest of my time because it's a little like cooking a nice big meal and not feeling like eating it. But for this work I have a giant one in my living room.

My earlier work was really luminous—they really kind of glowed. It's almost impossible for the camera or computer to capture it. The vibration between the color bars is something I intended.

Early on I worked in a SavOn in Santa Monica, California. At that point I was making art from anything and everything. They would clear out the nail polish, and for a nickel I could get a jar full, and so some of those paintings were made with fingernail polish. I didn't have any money and just used what I had. You know it doesn't really matter. The most factual thing in the world for me is that things are moving, changing all the time. Those diagonal bars of color really did that. They were very active. They had to do with illusion and they had to do with movement. And for me the most real thing in the world was movement. I was in my thirties then and had all that activity.

I moved to Texas in the 1990s and found that there is a kind of Texas art where the artist says, *Here's some art, and I'm not taking it seriously, and you shouldn't take it seriously either.* I was that guy for a while when I lived in California, but by the time I moved here, I had moved on. It's been my experience that gallery owners like my work, but they're just not able to place it. They'll say, *You know I can't sell black paintings.* During the years when I was raising my son, I worked at many different jobs. I worked in drugstores and I was a meat cutter. I taught art for a while and ran an art gallery. I did other things to try to sell my work and live off my art.

I have come to accept the days when I'm in here and it's such a piece of shit and nothing's going right. And it doesn't matter that it's not going right because that's all getting it to the place where it needs to be. Except when you're there and it's not going right—it's a piece of shit, and some days it's just very hard. There have been times when I've caught myself—either I've been putting tape on or mixing paint, and I was just cussing a blue streak. That's when I just clean up and put everything up and turn off the lights and close the door because this is too hard to do and I'm not enjoying doing it. If all you're doing is swearing at it and this is supposed to be getting you to that higher level, you're certainly not at that level now. Or sometimes you just work through it. There is a degree of discipline. There are certain things that I read when I am depressed or really down. Beatrix Potter is a great stabilizer for me. Someone found the original scores from the old Hal Roach, Little Rascals comedies and a Dutch orchestra recorded it just as it was supposed to be played. I have a two-CD set. When is gets really stupid in here, I just put that on and I just have to laugh.

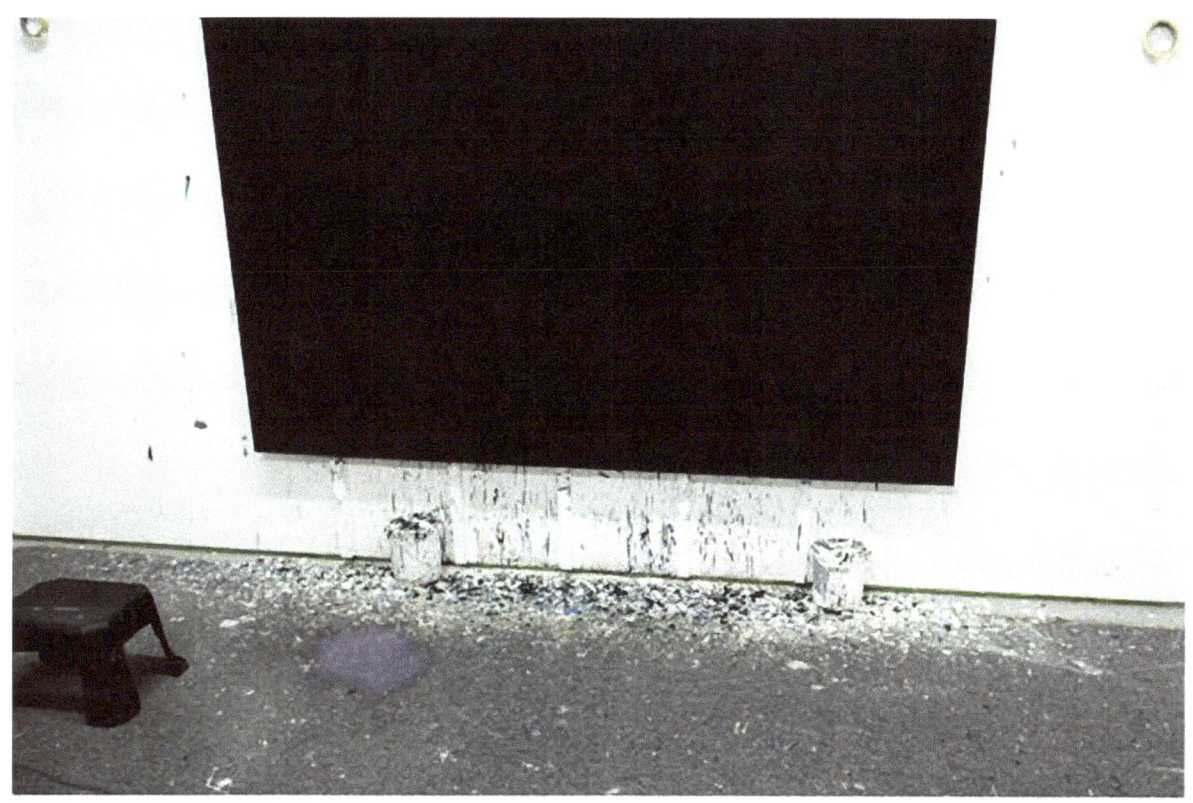

Unfinished painting in Denny McCoy's studio

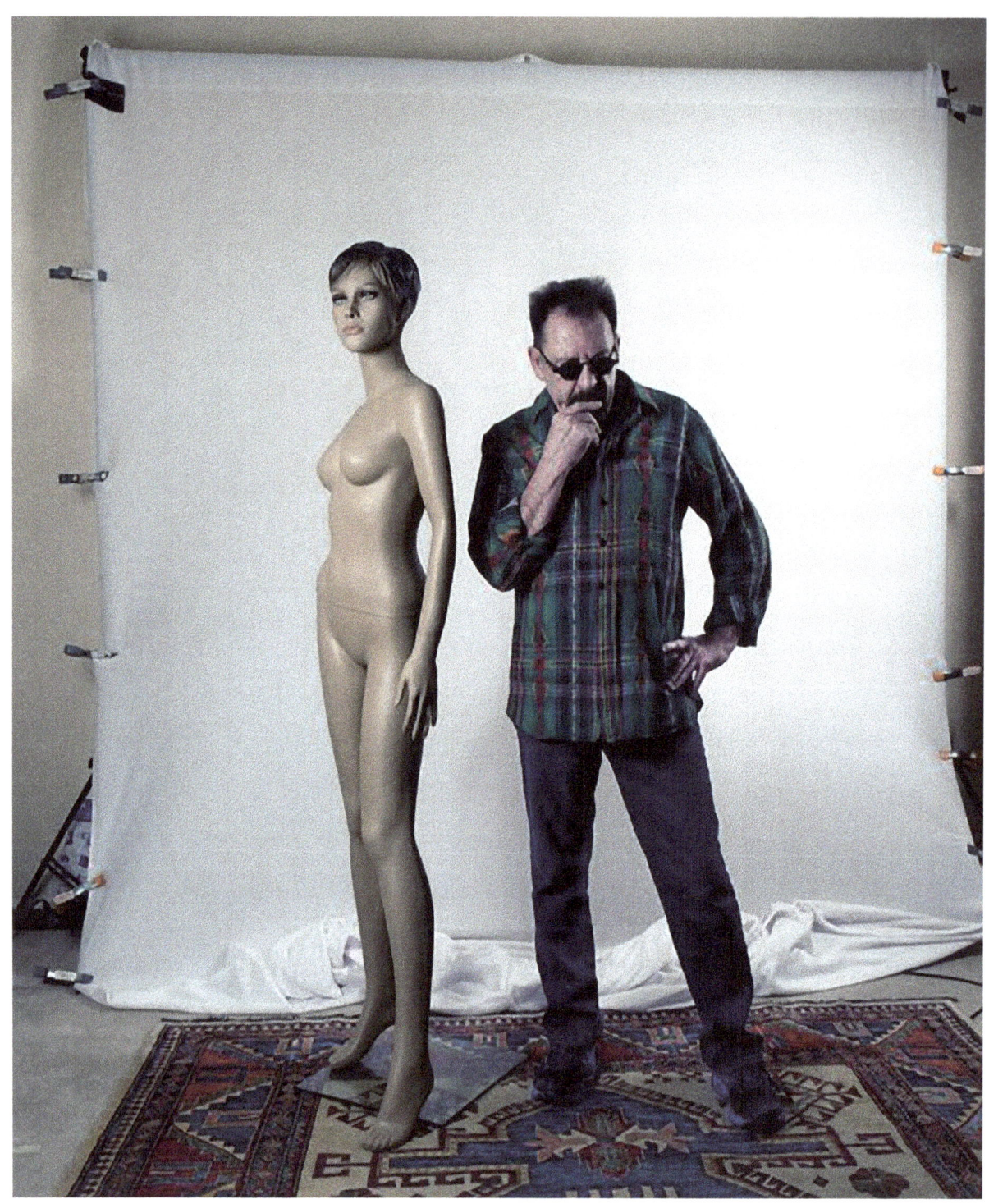

Roger McBee

Roger McBee

When I was in grade school I drew a lot and I was pretty good at it. The teacher would say, OK class, let's pull out our math books and Roger you can draw.

I learned to read very early and was an avid reader. I got very imaginative from reading so much. I lived in a small town, so my view of the world was through the books I read. I'd visualize the characters and places. I could see them so clearly.

I was an English major in college and also studied radio, TV and film. I ended up as a technical writer and manager of technical writers. I finally got worn out from writing the really structured stuff and convinced the company I worked for to let me become a writer and producer in the company's video studio. I spent the next ten years as video script writer, producer and director. As a director I would block out shots for the videographer. I used one of the old-time lenses they used for blocking shots for movies. So I finally got to where I didn't need it anymore. I could look at a shot and mentally block it out. That helps with photographic composition. Then, one day I bought a digital camera and discovered I liked the moment in time of still photography. On a whim I took a course in studio lighting and I was hooked. I swore I'd never shoot people, but that's been one of my most enjoyable activities. Especially some of my work with models where we do role playing. It really brings out different personalities. I especially like shooting artists. They have more creative personalities and can give you a more interesting look.

I've always been the creative sort. Even when I'm taking out the garbage, I have a photograph in my mind that I'm working on mentally. I'll take the photograph and then I'll start thinking about what I can do with that particular image: enhance it, change it, bend it to my photographic will. Those wheels are always turning no matter what I'm doing.

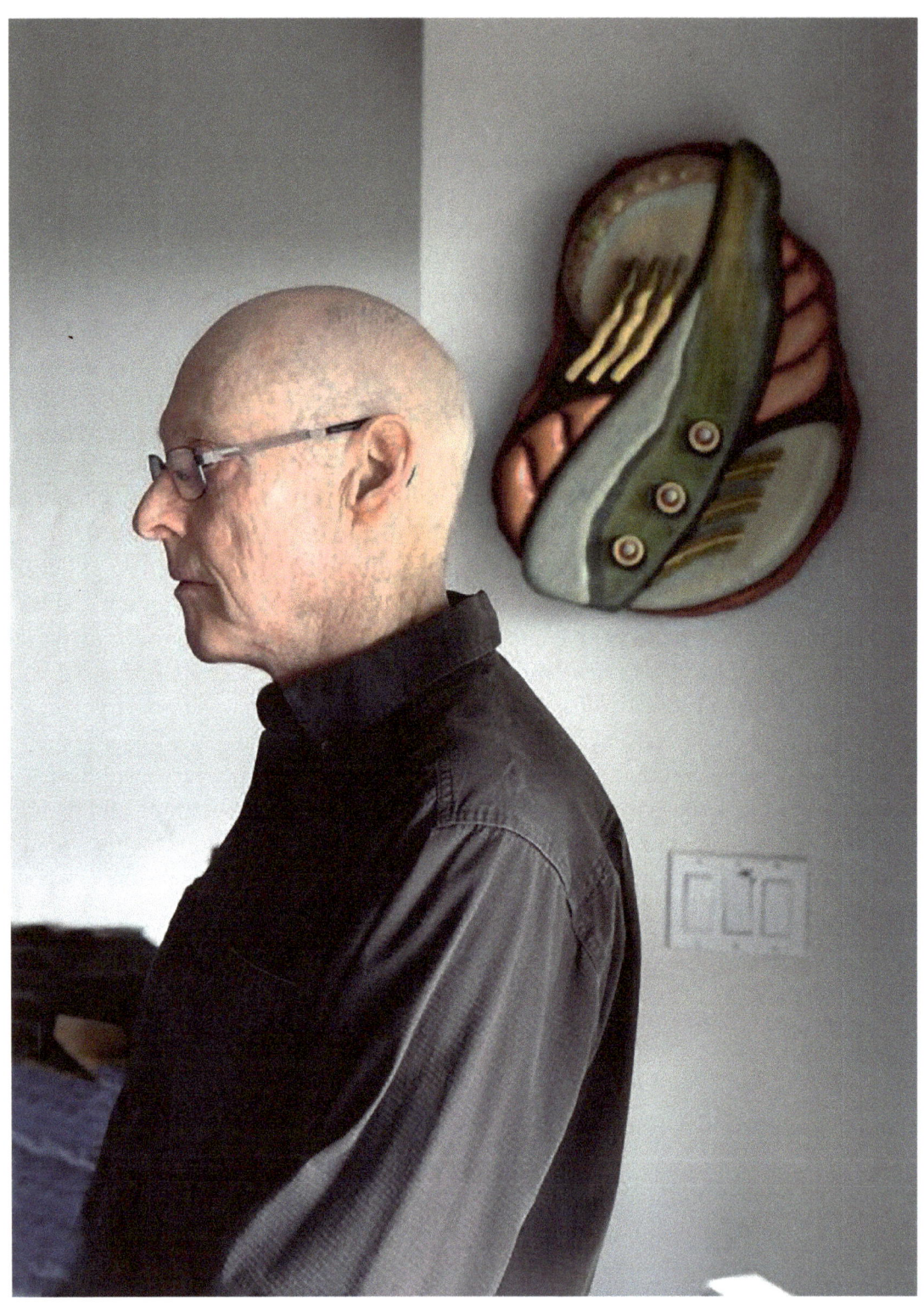

Steve Shellenberger

Steve Shellenberger

I start with a small sketch. Then I enlarge it, put it on wood and cut it out. Then I've got tons of stuff from grinders to sanders to hand rasps that I use to shape it. You can never have enough clamps. I've got a book full of designs. So if something catches my eye I'll enlarge it. I have a projector that I use, but it has to be at night, it's not strong enough to project in the daylight. I've got way more designs than I'll ever have time to accomplish.

The process is really labor intensive. There's lots of sanding and shaping. Then by the time I put color on it because I paint each individual piece, it's time consuming. But it's a joy. I used to have a hard time getting to sleep. Now I go to sleep and I'll wake up, sometimes in the middle of a dream things will come to me. Other times, I'm just sitting there in front of the TV, or I'm by myself. One sketch leads to another and then I'll put it away and come back later. I look through art magazines like a lot of people do. I saw the work of Vicki Grant. She was an architect, but she started working in ceramics and I really liked her textures and patterns. It just spoke to me. I thought, well I could do that in wood. So that just opened up what I'm doing now. I don't know that I have enough to go to a gallery, so a lot of what you see is never going to see daylight. I've enjoyed doing it, and I've learned something from it. I don't know that I want to put it in competition, or even let others know that I did it. I want the quality to be there. I try to make the presentation of these good, even on the back. Make sure it's finished. I sold what I thought was a really nice piece to some guys who lived down below me here. And they had it hanging in a really prominent place in their home. After they had it about three days, the guy called me up and said, you know we were walking by that piece and you could see into it that it wasn't finished. So I said, well I'll take care of that, and I got it back and painted the inside where you could see it. That taught me a lesson.

A little history: I've always enjoyed art. I took arts and crafts in junior high and art in high school. I was a cartoonist for the junior high and high school papers. My college degree is in education: art and English were my teaching fields. I taught sixth-eighth grade art and seventh grade shop class for seven years. And then I went to work as a union carpenter and apprentice for two and a half years. Then I went to work for Dow in Shreveport. I got to do a lot of creative things for them. I started out as operator, moved to the carpenter shop, was an insulation inspector for a while, a gasket guru (asbestos gaskets when they were trying to get rid of them and get new stuff). I taught there too. I worked in training as a quality person for a while. I ended up in Health, Safety & Environment. So I was really pleased to be able to do a lot of different stuff. That is when I started doing the linocuts: pen and ink drawings. I like architecture, shadows on houses, very detailed pointillism—anal-retentive type of stuff (laughs). I loved doing those and those I did show. I was in several national shows and several schools purchased the prints. They sold well. I was President of an art guild, and President of an art museum in our little community.

As far as being in a gallery now, I just don't know if I want to get started in that rat race. Right now I'm enjoying what I'm doing. I'm not sure I want to get too successful (laughs). Maybe if I was younger. I have fun making the pieces. If people like them and they want to pay the prices I'm asking, OK. Some of my pieces look like particular things to people: sometimes really personal body parts. I've got a piece that was rejected at the local art league show because of what somebody thought it looked like.

I mostly use yellow pine. It's easy to carve. I've got some expensive wood, but for what I'm doing, especially with color, it's so dark the color wouldn't show up. If I lived in another part of the country, I might be using something else. For me, this seems to work.

For studio space I've got the best of both worlds. I do woodworking upstairs and painting down in a space below. I couldn't paint up there, and I couldn't do woodworking down here. I construct up there and then bring it down here to paint. My wife is so nice to allow me the time and the space to do this, because art is really selfish. So I play golf with her once a week for atonement.

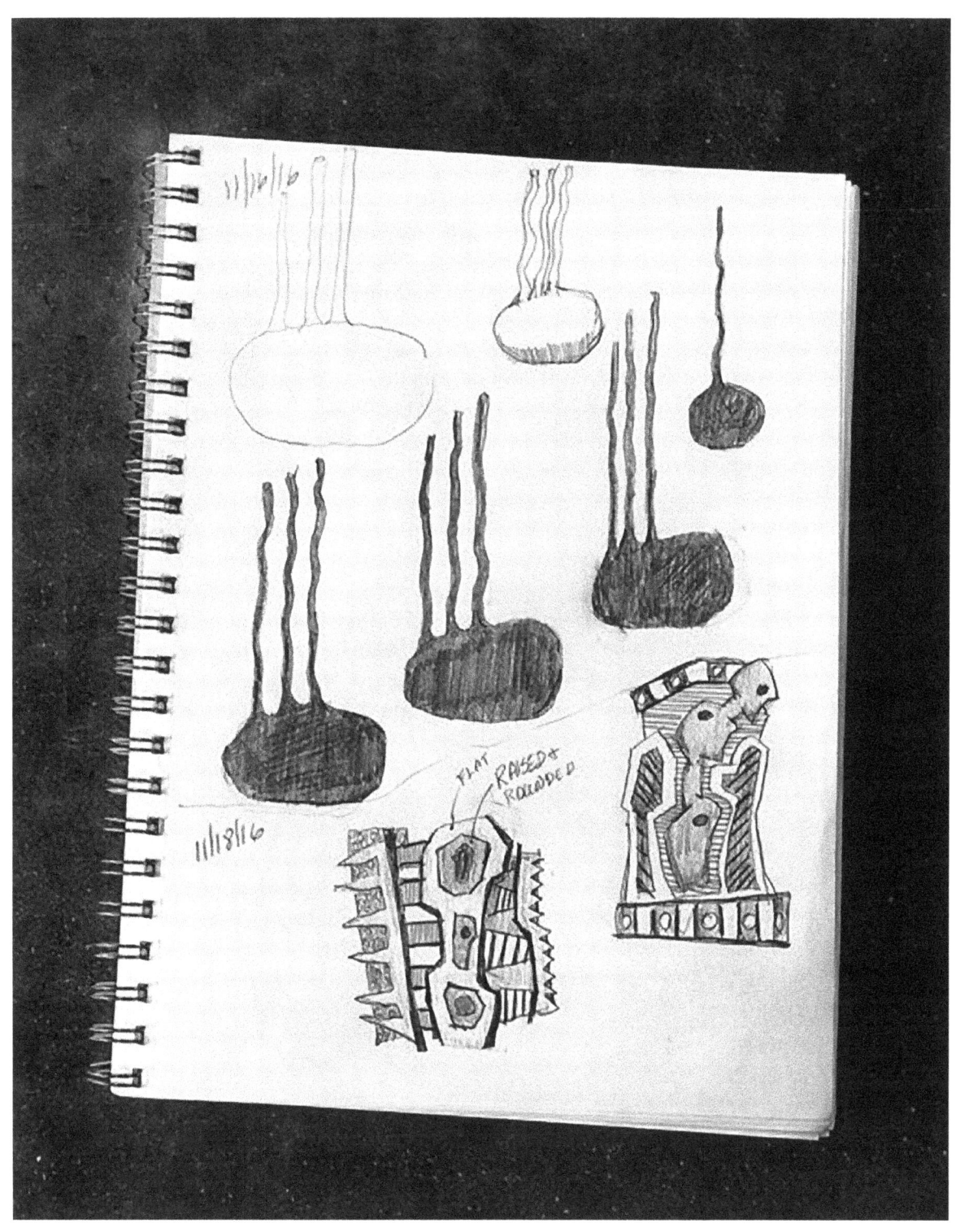

a page from Steve Shellenberger's sketchbook

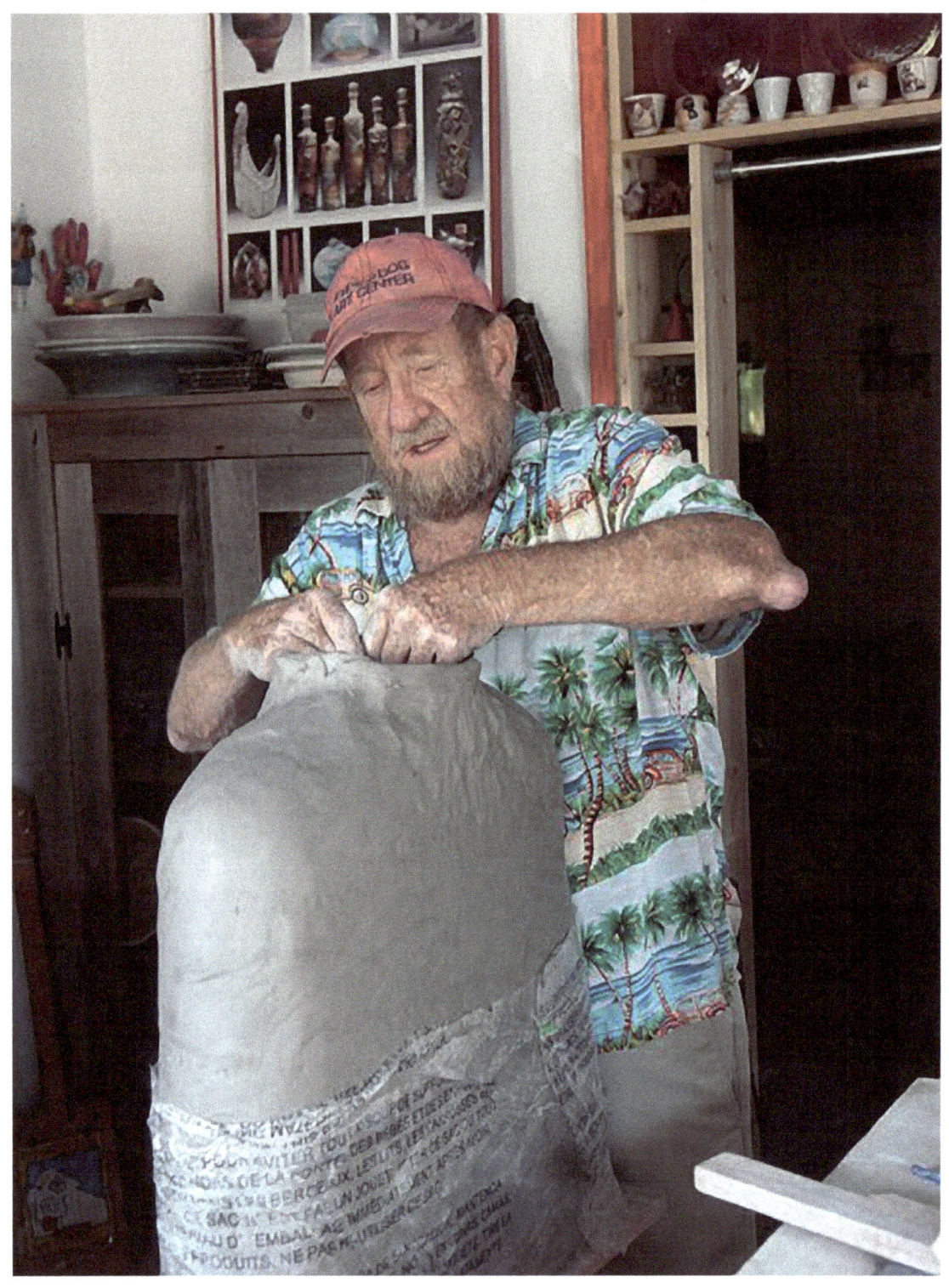

Billy Ray Mangham

Billy Ray Mangham

I wanted to get into forestry. While I was in the Navy, I decided I wanted to be a forest ranger. But the last three months in the Navy, they had this project transition where you could work for the forest and get right into it. So I worked in the forest for three months out in California and they didn't have any job openings, so we headed to Texas. I'd already been accepted into the forestry program in Nacogdoches. We got there in May and I needed to get the GI bill going so I started taking some art classes. I met John Daniel, a really good sculpture guy, and I hit it off with him. There was a lot of good energy - hippie energy - at that time. Everybody was going back to the land and buying land, and doing pottery and building their own houses and stuff. There was a whole group of us down here, so we found good community. By the time the summer was over: I don't want to be a forest ranger anyhow, I want to be an artist.

In early 1980s, there were about forty of us, all different mediums working at Arts Warehouse which was where the *Austin American Statesman* used to be. It was the place where they had their printing presses—big rolls of paper stuffed in there. It was right across from Austin Music Hall. It was neat. We were there a couple of years. When we lost our lease, me and two other potters moved across to east Fifth Street, right next to the freeway. We were there for two or three years. My buddy Dave had bought some land here in San Marcos, Texas and my son and I used to come down here and camp out. I had inherited $10,000 and I thought, I've got to get out of Austin. I asked my buddy, do you want to sell me some land? And he said, yeah, I'll sell you three acres. Turned out he was real far behind on his taxes, so that's why he needed the money. It was perfect timing for me.

I've been working in clay for twenty-eight years. I got a B.A. in ceramics from San Jose State University, and a Masters of Arts and Masters of Fine Arts from Stephen F. Austin University in Nacogdoches, Texas. I worked with different materials. It was that whole idea of pottery for the masses you know. We wanted to make just functional pottery for everybody. And so that was what was being taught, that was the energy level that was going on, and that fit with the whole hippie energy back to the land. So that was where it all started. That lasted about fifteen years. It was all about functional: that was my drive. My first graduate critique, I had my eight little tea bowls sitting there and they said, well tell us about these. And I said, I don't have to. It speaks for itself. I learned, nah, that ain't the way it works. Later, when I started teaching, I realized the importance of being able to talk about what you do. Not so much for the other viewers, but for yourself. For years and years I wouldn't put titles on my pieces. There's this guy, Jack Earl in Ohio, quiet guy. But sometimes his titles were two paragraphs long.

When I started teaching at Laguna Gloria, I started teaching that same thing—

functional. At that temperature, 2300 degrees, your color palette is really limited. You're not going to get any reds, oranges, yellows. You're mostly going to have browns and blues and gold maybe. I just got tired of that and started doing Raku, which is lower fire and you could get really bright reds and all the colors I wanted. But it's not functional, because it's so soft. So that lead me from doing functional ware into more sculptural work. That was kind of the progression. And we did nothing but. We were on the road for twenty-three years selling our work. I did nothing but Raku. I probably did more Raku than anybody on the planet. I was churning it out. Sometimes I had two or three people working for me. We were doing some Raku. I finally learned all I could learn from that after more than twenty years.

I started doing more sculptural work and found out it's really fun. I did this series called "Real People." I had a book that was called "Least Wanted," and it was a book of mug shots from the 1920s and 1930s. I did twenty-six sculptures of these petty criminals. It would just say so-and-so pimp or Commie or Panhandler, whatever. I showed them in the museum in San Angelo, Texas. And I would watch people. They would walk up to the sculpture, look at it from here and get a general idea. Then they'd walk up and look at the title and go *pimp*? And they'd stand back and look at it again, you know, realize there's more to it. I did two guys who were just labeled *psycho*.

I still do a couple of runs every year of high-fired coffee cups. A coffee cup is the mark of a potter to me. If you can make a good coffee cup, then you can probably do anything with clay that you want to do. That's kind of how I judge people. You know when you're working on the wheel you've got maybe a minute to put some soul into whatever it is you're working on, and that's it. So out of a hundred cups, maybe three of four really sing. It's either there or it's not. There are really good potters that can maybe get twenty out of a hundred, or even fifty if they're really good. It's the energy that goes into it somehow. That coffee cup is the most intimate thing, you know. There's not that many things that touch your lips. And it's got to feel right, have the right balance. It's got to functionally work really well. And then if it happens to look good on top of that, that's even better. I get emails every now and then saying, I've had this cup for twenty years and my cat knocked it off the table. Do you have any more? Can you make me another one just like it? People fall in love with them.

I've been working figuratively for twenty or twenty-five years now. But this is the first time I've tried to do something fairly realistic. That's part of where I want to go, trying to learn how to do that. Some of these real-life guys I do now are fairly easy. But some of them I've still got a long way to go on that actually making it look like who it's supposed to look like. Me and my buddy Carl Block were teaching a workshop down in Alexandria, Louisiana in early June. And we were sitting out by the pool and I said, yeah I'm gonna do this Texas musician series. So we started naming them off. Then for the next two days one of us would go, hey, what about so-and-so? Oh, yeah, we're making that list.

My wife Beverly and I founded the Eye of the Dog Art Center in 2008 here just outside San Marcos, Texas. A couple of years ago we were flooded during the big flood that impacted this whole area. It took about a year to come back. But, it turned out to be more of a blessing than a curse. We were down at Port Aransas at the time. By the time we got back up here two days later, all of our friends had already begun cleaning up for us.

Getting the right people together for the right sense of community? It just kind of happens naturally. The right people tend to show up here, seems like. We don't go out of our way to recruit people. Maybe out of a couple of hundred people who've had studios here, there's maybe been just a handful that weren't supposed to be here, and they didn't last very long one way or another. So I had this land and Ty, my buddy, who's now living next door, he was staff photographer for the Austin American Statesman for twenty-something years. He'd retired and moved to Arizona. He came here to take a couple of workshops, and while he was here some land came up for sale. So at the workshop we hatched up the idea for the arts center. He bought that twenty acres over there and moved in and bought a backhoe. So he and I and a couple of other guys did at least fifty percent of the work on that big building over there. He was like an angel. He just came out when we needed him. He was there, he's still there. He's my right-hand man. And then there's this other young guy. I needed a younger guy to do a lot of stuff. And he came down to visit a girl he knew who was here. I said, well, if you decide to come down here, I'll give you a job till you get on your feet. He showed up at exactly the right time. Sometimes people will spend a year or two here and then go back to college, or go to a residency, whatever. We see ourselves as kind of an incubator. People have the facilities and the freedom here to do whatever they want to do.

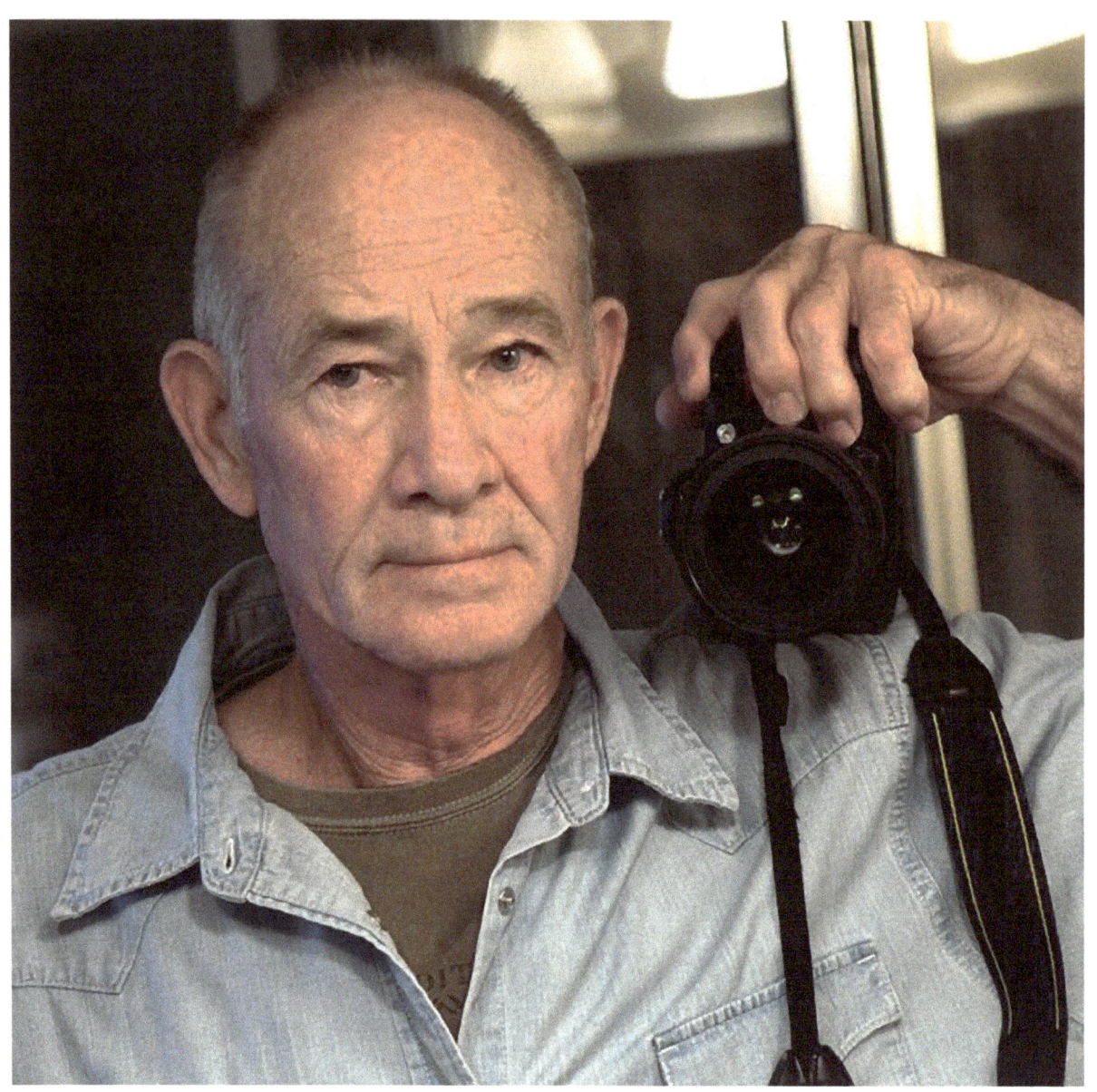

Jim McJunkin

Jim McJunkin

I started out wanting to be a painter and that didn't last long. I was OK in the classroom, but I could tell it wasn't going to work commercially for me. I painted friends, albums covers—made my own version of it, put my own take on it—plagiarism, you know.

My Dad was mostly interested in gadgets. He had a Bolex movie camera and pieced together a way to edit films. Then he had a Voigtlander that he loaned me—his camera. And I just didn't take good care of it. I pretty much destroyed it. I got a Minolta SRT 101 and was fooling around with it. This was during the Vietnam War. I was about to be drafted and I heard that if you volunteered you would get a better job than if you waited to be drafted. So I went down to enlist and when they asked me what my job was I said photographer. I had just seen the movie *Blow Up* and being a photographer seemed like a cool thing to do. The enlistment officer gave me a bullshit kind of look, but he wrote it down anyway. So that's what they assigned me: 84B20, still photographer.

I took that camera with me into the Army and used that along with the cameras they gave me. I had a medium format and a 35mm camera with no light meter. So I had to guess and do a lot of experimenting with exposures. But in the jungle where light alternates between bright sunlight and shadow it was tough. This produced a lot of bad negatives. I took pictures for the Army with their cameras that went into *Stars and Stripes*. And I took pictures for myself with my camera.

Actually, when I got to Vietnam is when I didn't have to look for pictures anymore. They were just kind of thrown at you and everything looked different from back home. It wasn't just the pictures but the whole lifestyle and everything. And it wasn't just the military side of it. Walking through a village with people and sampans, water buffalo and little naked kids running around. Just totally different than where I was coming from. Everything was different, a different culture, and then there was the war.

Even now I take more pictures when I'm traveling. I know I'm missing stuff around here all the time. But I see those things constantly, back and forth down this road. If I didn't take the picture the first time, I get more and more used to it and after a while I hardly see it anymore. That's why I take more pictures when I travel. That's what I was talking about with Vietnam. Of course, people carrying machine guns is really different, and tanks and planes. Just being out of your element really tunes your eye. And it's not just cultural. I can go to another city in the U.S. and see things differently. It's being out of your element, away from what you see everyday. I got into underwater photography for a while and it was the same thing. Everywhere you looked, not just fish, but the landscape was different. Even the same dive at night. It's different animals and the reef comes alive. It's so much easier to see pictures in someone else's backyard.

61

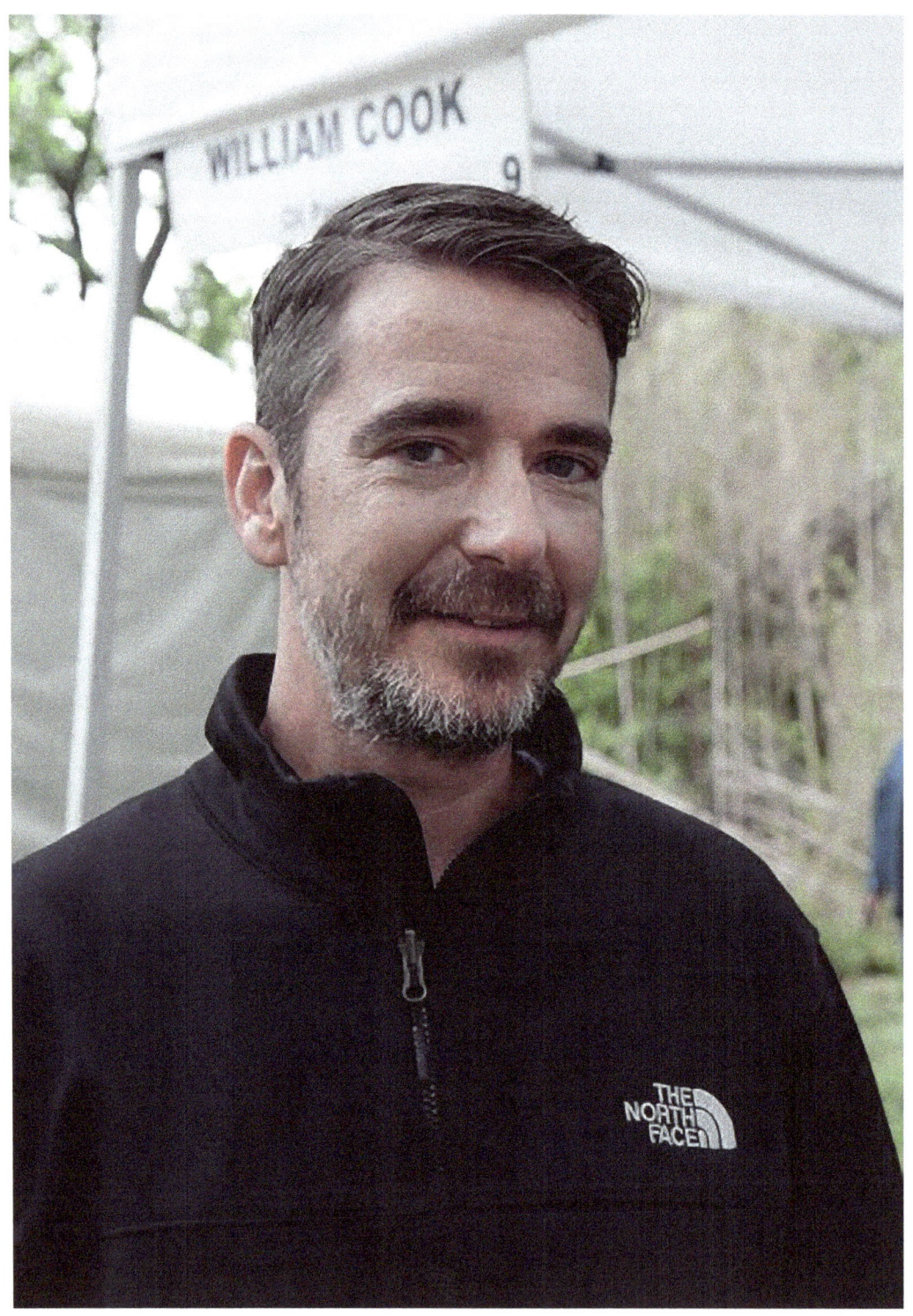

William Cook

William Cook

Early on I was going to be a photographer, but I got a rather rude wake-up call. A friend of our family was a photographer, a guy I trusted. So I contacted him when I was going off to college. He said, do not do it. I'm miserable. I work in restaurants until two in the morning just to get by. So on his advice I went into the more respectable field of public administration. Five years later that guy was traveling all around the world for *Outside* magazine. Guess he was just paying his dues at the time that I called him up.

When I was in high school, I was a big-time skateboarder—a sponsored amateur skateboarder, and we traveled all around. At the time, there were these things called *zines*. My buddies and I would do a whole magazine: articles, drawings, cartoons—a lot of funny stuff; and pictures of us skateboarding all over the state. We'd put those together and Xerox them off and give them to our friends. We called it the *No Scene Skate Zine*. We saw there was a large skate ramp in Houston, and it was the largest in the country. So we built one six inches taller. That made pros come from all over the country come skate with us.

All through high school I took art and commercial photography, and more creative fine art photography. We'd do silk screened T-shirts, anything. We'd just try any kind of crazy stuff. Some came out good, some bad, but there were always just a lot of creative friends around. We traveled around in packs doing our thing.

Probably about ten years ago I had this itch that I wanted to paint, and it kept gnawing at me and gnawing at me and gnawing at me. Finally, I can't take this anymore, and I went out and bought some acrylics. Not even knowing anything about technique or color theory, I just started painting. I had gotten an art magazine that talked about these painting blogs. Karen Jurick ran one. I think it was called *Different Strokes from Different Folks*. She had these monthly challenges: a way to keep engaged in painting and a group to keep you motivated. So I just started doing her monthly challenges. You have to submit your work and there are some professional artists and some beginners involved, and it's good to see your art next to others. I started to read everything I could: biographies of artists whose work I really enjoyed, and it just snowballed. I'd be at work all day, and come home and spend time with the kids, and then paint until midnight or later sometimes. I did some workshops and spent a month in New Hampshire with the impressionist John Traynor.

Now I've decided I'm going to take a year off and just concentrate on painting. When I turned in my notice at my job, they'd just tell me to leave, but they've actually said I can stay on and work as much or as little as I want. So that may allow me to extend my time for focusing on painting. I've set a number in my mind income-wise. If I were to go a year and hit a certain mark, I would pursue this even further. I've structured it with my family. So it will be a year of intense study. I'll try to get into some galleries, do some more art shows. If I really focus, five years from now I'll be a better painter; ten years from now even better. It's kind of ingrained in my soul that I'm going to pursue this until I no longer can. I've read a lot about professional artists and how they've gotten to where they are. Some make it big earlier, but there's always a struggle. So as long as I can make it financially and keep the wheels on at home I'm just going to keep going.

I also belong to another group called *Virtual Paint Out*. This is a blog that was started by a guy named Bill Guffey. It was a way for artists to get together, and for handicapped individuals or other people who can't travel - a way for them to virtually travel to other places and paint. We use *Google Street View*. Bill went to Google and asked if we could do this. And they ended up waiving their legal rights to the street views for this art project in particular. So he picks a location and all the artists go onto *Google Street View* and cruise around until you find a street view you like. You capture a screen shot of the scene and then paint it. You have to upload your painting to the blog. I've been doing it for seven years. Actually, Google has bought fifty of the paintings for their corporate office in London, and the lawyer who helped waive the rights, he's bought a whole bunch. I actually once painted the same scene as an artist in Norway which statistically is almost impossible. It was a scene in Charlotte, North Carolina, a scene in front of an historic hotel. When we discovered we had painted the same scene, she wrote me. I had to use *Google Translator* so I could read what she was saying and write back to her in her native language. So we had a little international correspondence about painting that hotel.

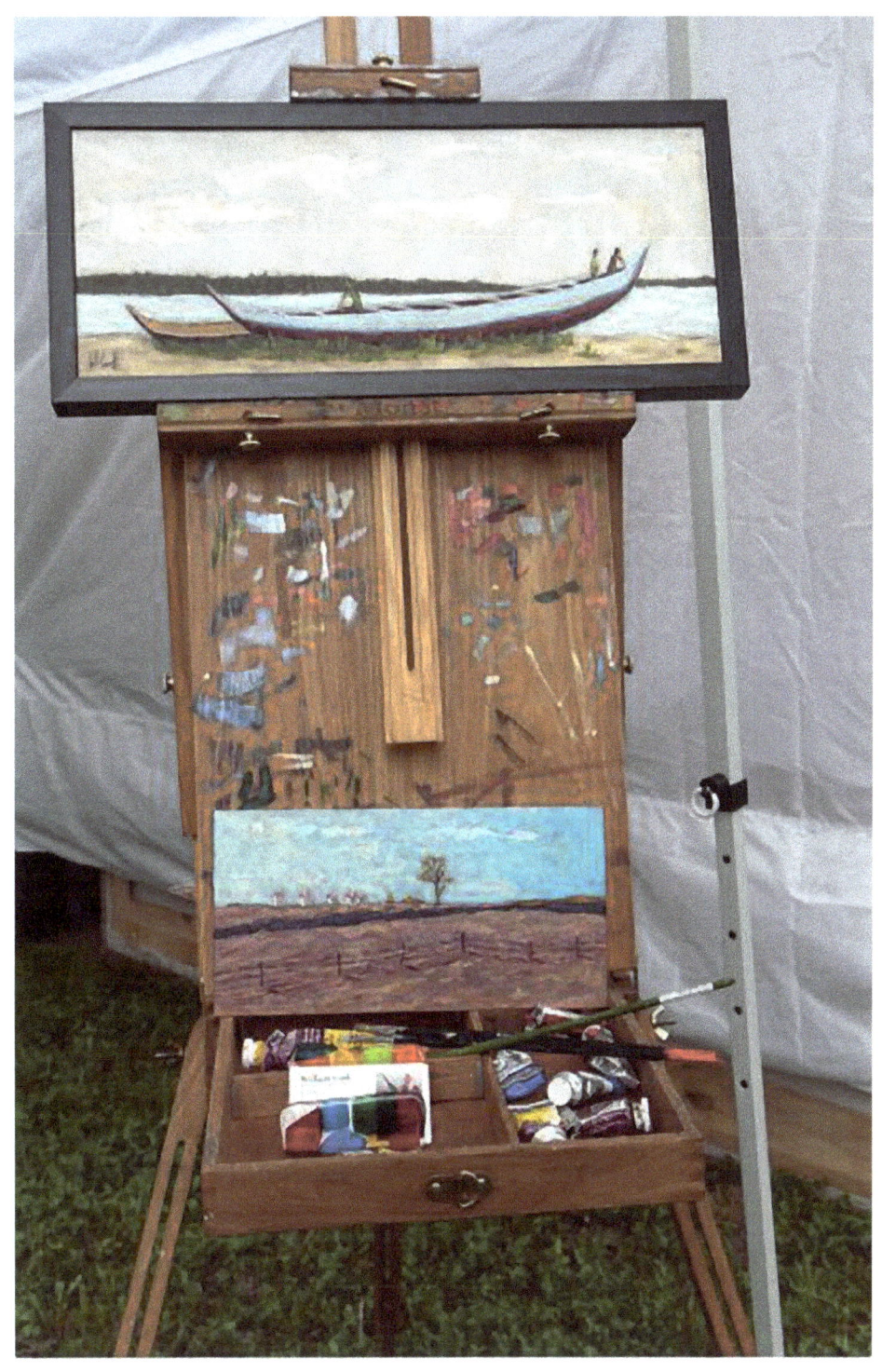

William Cook's portable studio

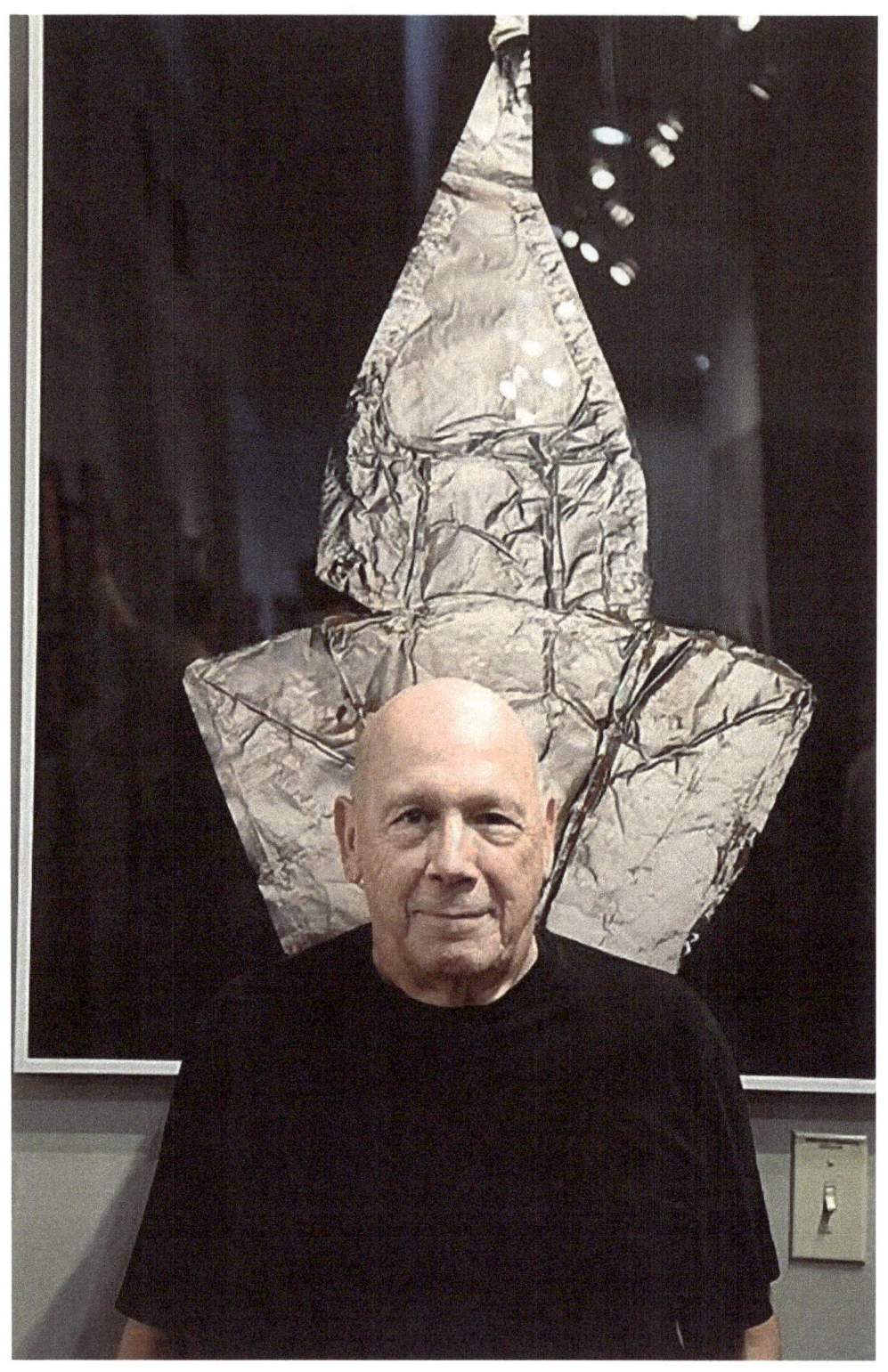

George Krause

George Krause

My father, George Krause IV, wanted more than anything to be an artist. He came from an affluent family that had started the George Krause Hardware Store in Lebanon, Pennsylvania. They sold boats, electric refrigerators, guns. It was one of the first department stores in the country. My grandfather, George Krause III, died at age thirty-nine of a suspicious death, possibly suicide or murder. It was hoped that my father, the oldest of five siblings, would eventually run the hardware business. He wanted no part of it. He disgraced himself and the family name when he declared he wanted to become an artist. He had talent. As a child he had been diagnosed with many ailments. Still sickly, in his early twenties he hopped a freight train headed for Mexico. Thin, blond, blue-eyed, bespectacled and serious, he must have been a strange apparition to the locals. But in small fishing villages like Mazatlan and Puerta Vallarta, the villagers gave him food and a place to sleep in exchange for the drawings he did of them. In 1933, the year he painted his self-portrait in Mexico, the George Krause Store celebrated its 100th anniversary. The shame and frustration for the family ended six years later when my father died of rheumatic fever at age twenty-nine.

My mother, also a frustrated artist, but not quite as talented or passionate as my father, would force me to draw and paint what she thought was art-worthy - many still lives and landscapes. When I was twelve I did this little pastel, a still life of ballet slippers with a rose and a music sheet of Debussy's *Reverie*. It was hell. I grew up in Little Italy in Philadelphia. While my friends were outside playing baseball and football, I had to stay inside and paint that silly setup. My mother would rap my knuckles if I didn't do it the way she thought it should be done. I did about thirty of those ballet slipper paintings. I was just getting into junior high school and the teachers would say, *Can you do it with pink slippers? Green? Blue?* So I did tons of these god-damned things. There was a free art school, The Graphic Sketch Club (now the historic Fleisher Art Memorial) just across the street from where I lived that I attended every Saturday morning. It took some years before I was able to break away from my mother's control and began to make images just for me. I received a four-year scholarship to the Philadelphia Museum School of Art (now the University of the Arts) and over the first three years won the Freshman Achievement Award as well as painting, drawing and printmaking awards. My father is looking down wherever he is and saying, George Krause V is finally doing something HE wanted to do. I'm always aware of that.

At the end of the third year in art school I enlisted in the Army and was assigned to the Counter Intelligence Corps at Fort Jackson, South Carolina as a clerk typist, a position at which I sucked. I probably would have been transferred to combat duty except for the lucky day I noticed one of the agents walking around with this object in his hand, holding it up and looking very puzzled. I recognized the thing as a Weston light meter, the very one I had used in a basic photography class. I walked up and pushed the little button on the side. The low light front lid sprung open and the needle moved. All the officers and the agents yelled, *You're our photographer?*

By 1956 the Hungarian Revolution had begun. Many young Hungarian men, to escape Soviet control, came to America where they enlisted in the American military. If they stayed for five years, they could become American citizens. Some of them had families left behind, stuck in Hungary and they were being forced into espionage. I was asked to photograph the first class graduating basic training. I set up my camera and captured two hundred and forty-nine happy, smiling faces and one guy with his head down. That was the guy that they were interested in getting a portrait of. A couple of days later a general marched into one of the classes and called on this guy to stand up and answer a question, and I took his photograph. Sadly, a few weeks later the young man attempted suicide. There were a surprising number of things in counter-intelligence that needed to be photographed. They built me a beautiful air-conditioned dark room that I could lock from the inside and supplied me with an unlimited amount of film, enlarging paper and equipment. During official inspections, my company commander was happy to hide me with my unpolished belt buckle and un-shined shoes behind the darkroom door with the red light on.

During that time, I discovered a poor black area of Columbia, South Carolina called Black Bottom. The streets, the houses, the faces, the clothes and the spirit of the place was not like any black community I knew back in Philadelphia. The people were so great and were just as curious about the white stranger with the camera as I was of them. Most of them had never been photographed before. The following week I'd go back and bring them the photographs of the people I had taken the week before. My wife told me that she'd walk around town and people would come up to her and say, where's the picture man, where's the picture man? It was really just lovely. I started to see that I had a talent.

It was in Black Bottom that I exposed my first roll of Kodachrome film. It had to be mailed to Kodak for processing, and in the week or so that the film was out of sight, I forgot about it. When those thirty-six slides came back to me in the form of 2x2-inch pieces of cardboard with tiny positive transparent images in the center, I thought it was wonderful. One by one, I held them up to the light bulb dangling from the ceiling. The exposures were accurate and the images were sharp. By the time I had narrowed the selection down to the best three images, I knew I was destined to be a photographer.

Now I have a studio set up here in Wimberley, Texas. I started using the breezeway to photograph. This used to be a horse stable and now it houses a life-size light box, a dark room, wood carving tools and other works of art. I have a wood shop over there and a guest room there.

I have photographed so many santos in various Catholic churches, carved by anonymous artisans. In the 1990s I decided to try and reinvent this dying art form and carve my own versions of Santos, incorporating old ideas and techniques of the past with the new. I carved all these life-size figures, and *God*, and the head of *Jesus*. This is *St. John the Baptist*. This is *Judas*. I had been in this Mexican church and saw this sign that said *San Judas*. I thought, what kind of church am I in? But actually, there are two Judas. One we call St. Jude, patron saint of lost causes. I made my Judas the good Judas. Here's *Santa Veronica*, who just happens to be the patron saint of photographers.

In 2014 I was invited to have an exhibition at the Museo de Bellas Artes in San Miguel de Allende. My idea for the exhibit was to photograph a cross section of the population of the city. I photographed well over a hundred people, many native to the city as well as expatriates and visiting tourists. They were all nude. When they approached me with the idea, I said I wanted to photograph people in full frontal nudity. They said, we can get you some nudes. How many do you need—ten?' I said oh no, it wouldn't be worth it to build this light box and come down there for only ten. They said how many? Twenty? Thirty? They finally got to forty. We'll promise you forty naked people if you come down. So I said alright. I made several trips, and I think, all told, I ended up photographing a hundred and twenty people. Most were in their 70s and 80s. I thought they were beautiful. They said there were eight hundred people there at the opening night of the show. San Miguel is a world heritage site, also it was the year San Miguel was voted by Conde Nast as the most beautiful city in the world, and they asked to leave the show up for three months. It's the most beautiful thing I have ever shown. And people came up to me and thanked me because they said they could be more comfortable with their bodies now.

When I go somewhere to photograph, I can't help but have preconceived notions of what's there. But you don't want to leave with just that. So the only way to avoid it is to start working and let the surprises come, the invention of something. They say when we think consciously, we only use two percent of our brain. So that leaves ninety-eight percent that we don't know how to get to, and that's the secret. If you go there, and you think you know what you want, for me, that limits me tremendously, and I don't usually get something that will transcend or last. But if I go with an open mind and then, all of a sudden, I like to say I have angels that come down and hit me on the side of the head and say, "Wake up stupid. Look at that. It's right there in front of you."

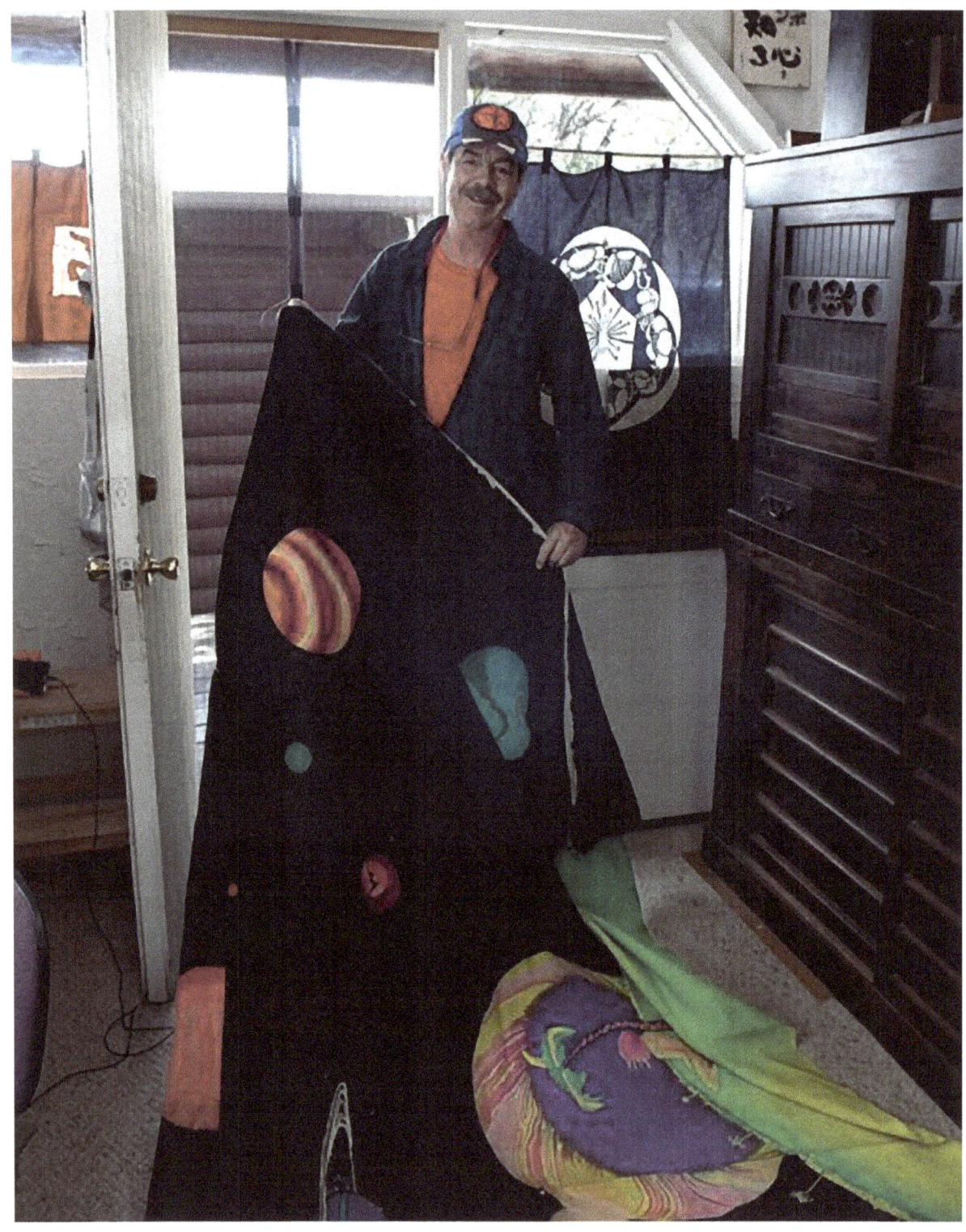

Tim Leibrock

Tim Leibrock

I went to a commercial art school after a couple of years of college, thinking this is more me rather than regular college. Then I found myself in Japan for eight years as an apprentice kimono dyer in Kyoto. The story is that my father was a pilot for a diplomat in Japan in the late 1960s and we lived in Tokyo. And after he retired, after the Vietnam war in the mid-1970s, one of his business associates, knowing that we had lived in Japan, said to me, would you like to study in Japan? I went off to Kyoto and got off the train. They were expecting a young woman and exclaimed, what are you doing here? They didn't give a hoot about the English-speaking world, so it was the best darn immersion experience. I got totally immersed in their culture and studied a 1400 year-old dye technique. I stayed there eight years. I left two years shy of an actual finished apprenticeship because I knew I wasn't going to stay in Japan and be a kimono maker. Back in the U.S. I'd been struggling, working at art for a while. Eventually, the husband of a colleague of my wife, who had a construction company, said, do you want a real job? And I said do I get a paycheck? So I did construction at age forty-five until age sixty to pay the mortgage and all the bills. Then my Mom died, and she left enough for us to buy my brother's share of the house here and move to Wimberley, and I didn't have to go to work every day.

My mother was an artist and to get even with my father she always kept my brother and me supplied with art materials and said, amuse yourself. And she never scolded us for doing things like scribbling on the walls. My Dad didn't encourage this. He wanted us to be, you know. Soldiers. And my Mom messed that up. She wasn't going to let us be soldiers.

Since I've gotten here to Wimberley, I've been doing colored pencil paintings and acrylic paintings, because those are the fundamentals. I just started again to dye natural fabrics. I'm really excited to pursue fabric dying again. I'm getting all set up making new tools. I have to make my own tools to do that work. The most immediate application for a market like this is to sell silk squares and silk runners… wearable art. Textiles. I feel like it's a sin for me NOT to do them because I was given this extraordinary opportunity in Japan, and my teachers are still alive and they're encouraging me. So I look forward to embracing that again. People in the Wimberley Valley Art League have helped me ratchet up my energy and my enthusiasm. It may be a dyeing art, but it's not dying in Wimberley, Texas.

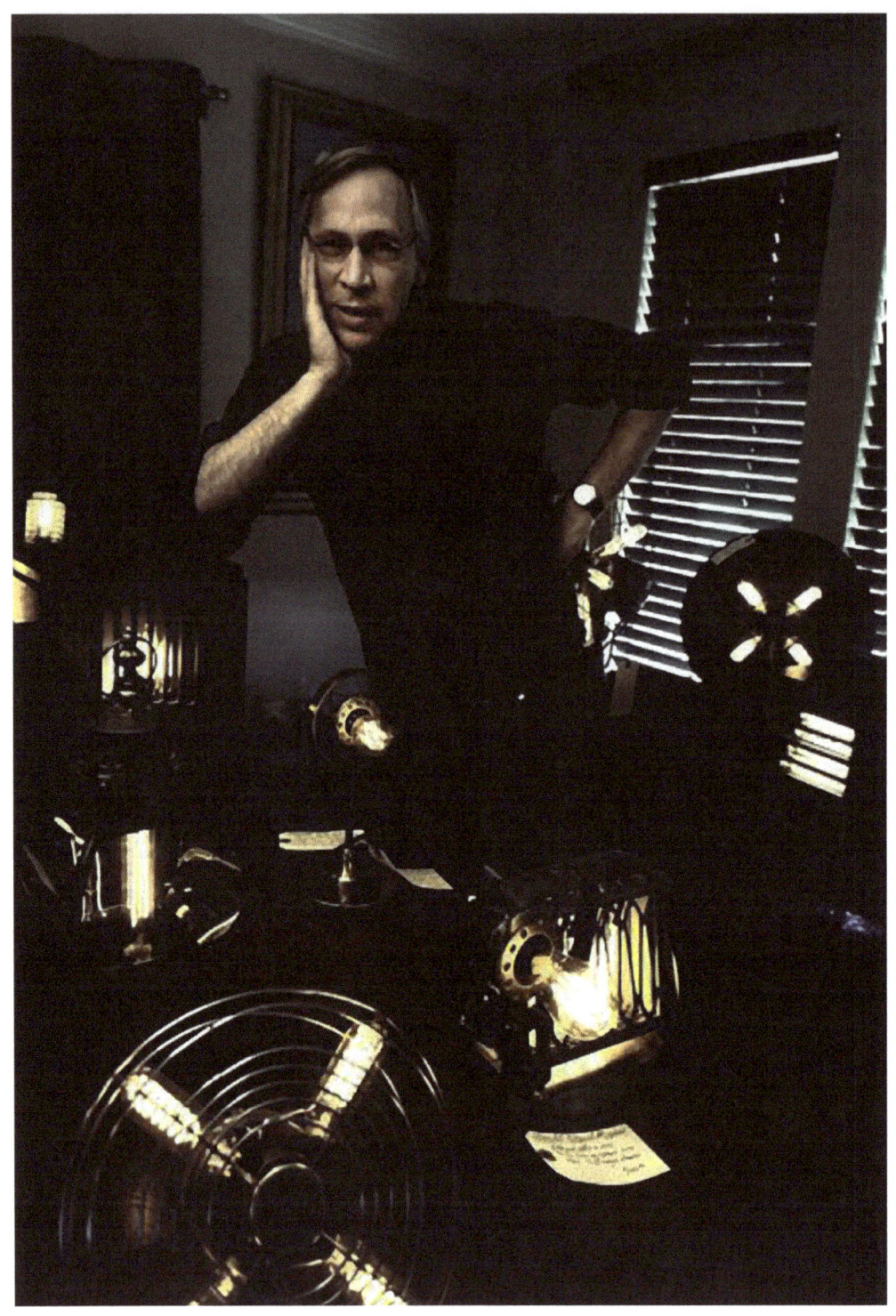

Kent White

Kent White & Jeff Smith

(Kent) Prior to this I was the CEO of a small credit union in Oregon, and I also worked for software companies. I found myself waking up and thinking, I'd kind of like to stay home and make some illuminated objects today, but NO I have to go to work. Banking treated me well. I was competent and fairly content, but it was never the sort of thing where you spring out of bed and think, hot damn, I get to do some more banking today! When you ask kids in kindergarten what do you want to be when you grow up? No kid ever raises their hand and shouts, I want to be a BANKER! It's just not terribly exciting. So one day I found myself out of work and realized, OK, let's take a little inventory here. I had this property, I had this shop. I'm looking for a job, and know it's going to take a while. I'm an older guy, and it's damn hard for an old guy to land a job. I thought, I've got a little savings and I had this space, so let's take some time and get this started. Give it six months or a year and if it works, keep going. So I found some sources for the things I needed. This seems like a little ole shop, but we manage a worldwide supply chain. We've got stuff coming from all over the planet to make these things.

Jeff and I know each other because we are both musicians, and we met at an open-mic event at a place called Baker Street Pub in south Austin, Texas.

When I started this, I had no idea if people would like these things, or if there would be a demand for them. So we did the Pecan Street Festival and were quite surprised by our success. Then we did the Cherrywood Fest, where we did twice as much business, and I thought, I'm not going to be able to pull this off by my little old self. I knew Jeff had a background where he'd been around electrical items and knew his stuff, plus he's also just an amazing guy, meticulous, and thorough, and creative. And I think we're just a perfect fit, the light brothers. It takes a lot of detail to think through these objects. You have a vision when you're looking at this stuff. You see it, but then you have to envision how it's going to be as a final piece. What I had already, was a lot of detail-orientation. I had been in information technology and sat at a desk for twenty-five years and did the most detailed computer programming. So now the detail is, instead of programming, it's building that thing over there. I've taken all the importance of paying attention to every little single detail to make sure something is going to operate properly and safely as well. The most important thing that we have learned is that there is always a solution. If you find something you really love doing, you'll put your heart and soul into it.

The thing that's always intrigued me about all these objects is that they are really kind of from the era of electrification. Prior to that, or literally from the stone age before artificial lighting, you burned oil or wax until really not that long ago. The most advanced thing was a kerosene lantern. Then guys like Thomas Edison came along (by the way, he wasn't the inventor of the light bulb; that's a shared honor), but he was the guy who industrialized it.

This little light bulb transforms everything. Not just because it produces light, and fairly cheaply, but once it was out there, we had to figure out how do we get power to it? We need networks and grids and power sources. It completely transformed the world, especially when the people who were making the electricity realized, we're making this electricity all the time and people only use it at night when they turn on the lights. So we need to find some way to keep the demand for it up. Bet we could run machines with it. If you can run machines, we can put those in factories and factories can make stuff that people buy, so that's cool, that'll eat up a lot of electricity. So this little light bulb opened up the floodgates of all the things that became part of our electrical lives. So to me, it marks this big turning point, and it allowed the development of really simple things: a fan, a radio, things that tie the world together. It's really momentous. It created all these objects, and illuminating them like this just ties them back to their origins. They wouldn't have come into the existence if it weren't for these funny little light bulbs.

Most of these things are kind of obscure objects that might just be lost in a junk heap somewhere. And the interesting thing about this particular kind of bulb is that it puts out a light that is just especially attractive to the human eye because it has the full spectrum of color. We have them made for us, and we can specify this shape bulb, and this kind of element, spiral or straight, or squirrel cage. We do a special amber tint on them, and a little bit of a mirror finish, so they look nice and interesting, even when they aren't lit. They're as nice off as on.

The moment when I decided that this is what I want to do, I was at some eating place here in Austin, Texas where you'd see the exposed bulbs. They really looked beautiful. And then I'd be out shopping or looking at stuff, and I'd think, you could put a light bulb in that. So I started just gradually collecting some things. I started making them as gifts for my family, tied into an interest that person had. My son is a musician, and I had the idea of a microphone. His wife is an attorney, so the scales of justice came to mind. My younger daughter does films, so a movie reel. My little daughter dances, so I found a wire dress form and illuminated that, so something for everyone. They really liked them a lot. And then their friends started asking, wow where did you get those?

(Jeff) My grandfather would always have old phones around, one in every room. He would rewire them and make them work in the house. So I learned the wiring from my Dad and grandfather. Eventually I started doing Heath Kits. This was a fascination for a ten-year-old.

The phones are a really good example of how this all came together. The first one I found was a really old, old candlestick phone, no dial: the kind you just pick up and talk. On the inside on the earpiece hangar was a switch. So I thought ah ha! If there's a switch we can use it to turn on the light. The most important thing is to respect these objects, so we try and incorporate their original functionality with whatever we do to it. It's not a matter of just finding something cool and sticking a light bulb on it. We want to retain its original functionality so that it becomes something that is a tribute to where it came from.

It's so exciting to make and show these things. When people see them it's like everybody becomes six-years old. Because it's so pretty and interesting and a bit odd, and you can play with them. People become really intrigued by them and they have the nicest things to say! They are just so gracious. It's unbelievable. I just really, really am genuinely blown away by it. And frankly, it just inspires me to want to do more and more and more.

(Kent) At the most fundamental level yes, these are sources of light. But when you think about a source of light, there are a number of sources of light you can use. The very first electric source of light was an arc light: super bright, super cold light and they just didn't work in homes. People didn't like them. They will light up anything, not a problem, but people just didn't like the light. It was harsh. That's one of the reasons why Edison-style bulbs took off: because it's so much like candlelight, like what the human eye is used to. When you put them in a room, they instantly become a focal point for the room almost like gathering around the fire. Humans just naturally gravitate toward them. And they're in objects that are cool and fun to look at as opposed to just a table lamp. Yes, they are sources of light, but they are also sources of inspiration. The story of light is the story of darkness, and brilliance and constancy, and it really sits at the center of our thinking and being and dreaming. Everything is lit up all the time, of course. If the lights go out MAN an hour is WAY too long to be without light. We just don't like it. When there is no light It feels primitive and creepy and spooky, and you can't get things done.

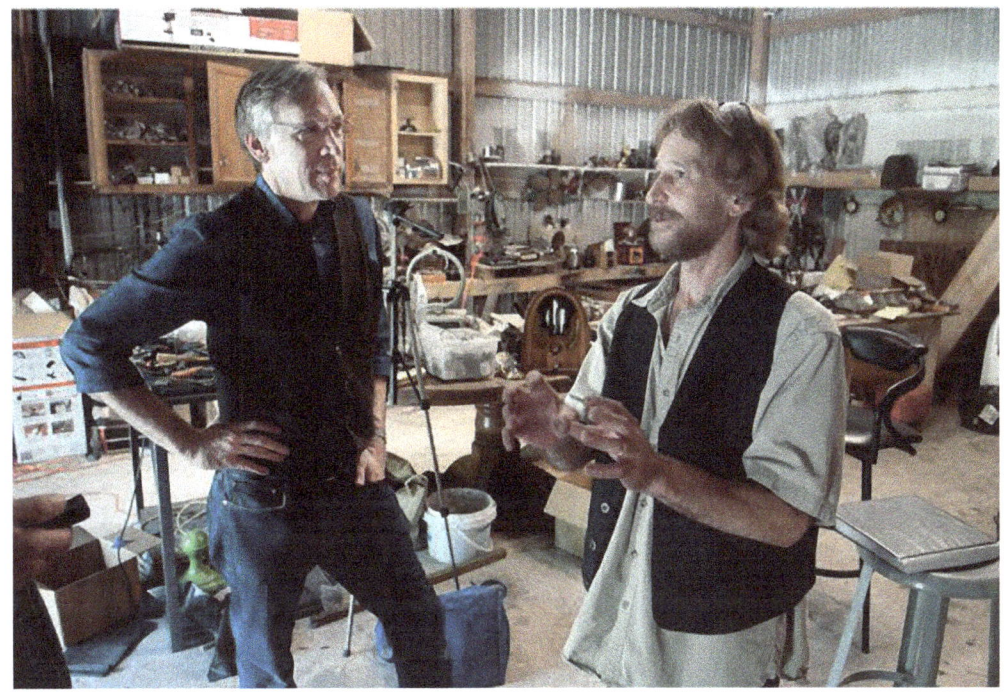

Kent White and Jeff Smith

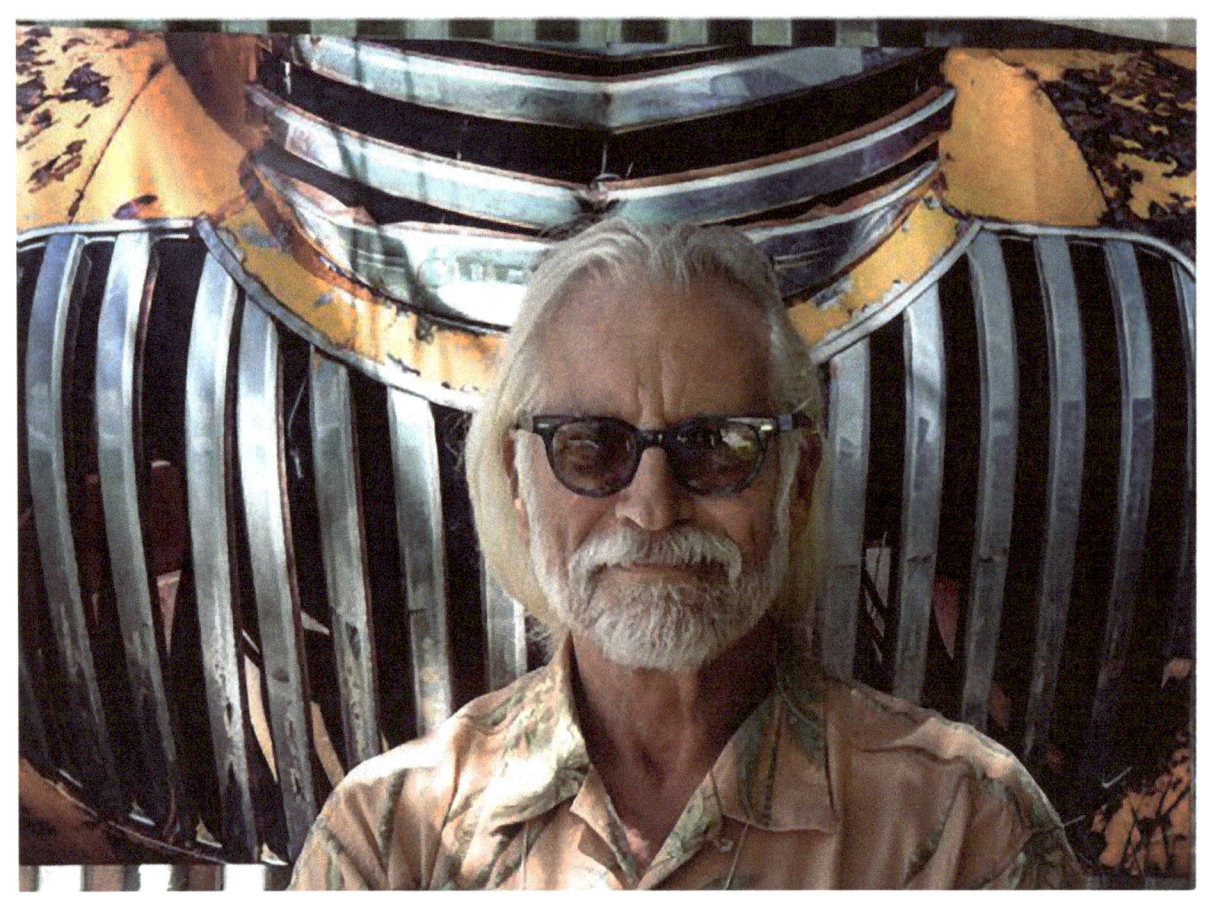

Ron Bullied

Ron Bullied

I remember the first new car my Dad brought home was a 1954 Chevrolet. He was so proud of it. I was six and I thought that's about as cool as it gets. We had cars. He liked cars, so I liked cars. When I came to Texas, I started to explore the backroads. It was a matter of driving around the back roads and you start to see these things. I took a couple of long road trips, and you'd see something in a farmer's field or behind some gas station in a little town, and sometimes even trespassing was required. I rarely got a whole car to work with, so you end up with a perspective of it whether it was textures or colors or just a trip down memory lane.

There are other connections to cars. Names like R.E.O. Speedwagon. When I took this picture I started to do a little research on the name of that band. The car company Oldsmobile started up and then General Motors came in and took over. One of the kids in the band had a truck and it was called a Reo, a Reo Speedwagon. I guess they thought what great name for a band—R.E.O. Speedwagon.

Anytime anyone has a look at these, they have a story to tell. Most of us grew up in the age of the car, before TV. People will walk past here, and they'll stop and say, oh, I remember my Dad had a Ford like that. Or, my grandpa had one in the garage for twenty years, and I kick myself for not keeping it. Everybody has a car story. My Dad bought a 1966 GTO for my mother. I talked him into it. She didn't like it because it was much too powerful. But it worked out great because then I got to drive the GTO. My Dad was very angry at the Firestone tires that I burned off the car. He blamed Firestone for that.

Back in the day, I started with photography. It was always photography. The days of chemicals, and darkrooms and trays of stuff in your basement. I went to the Banff School of Fine Arts in Canada for two years. It was right at the beginning, when they offered photography as a course of study. So I lived up in Banff. There you end up taking a lot of mountain shots and elk and deer, whatever. The distinction was I was with probably forty other student photographers. It was a very good way to start to see things. The two years there, more than anything, taught me to see. That's helped me to isolate. Because, sometimes you don't have a whole car to shoot, or there is something over here that pulls you in. It's just a matter of lighting and perspective and composition. It's interesting if you go out with five other photographers and all of you take the same shot, they will all be completely different. And some will be disappointed because they didn't see it that way. Sometimes we are so intent at capturing something at the beginning that we don't focus on what drew us there. There is always one magnet that pulls you in, and that's what I want to capture.

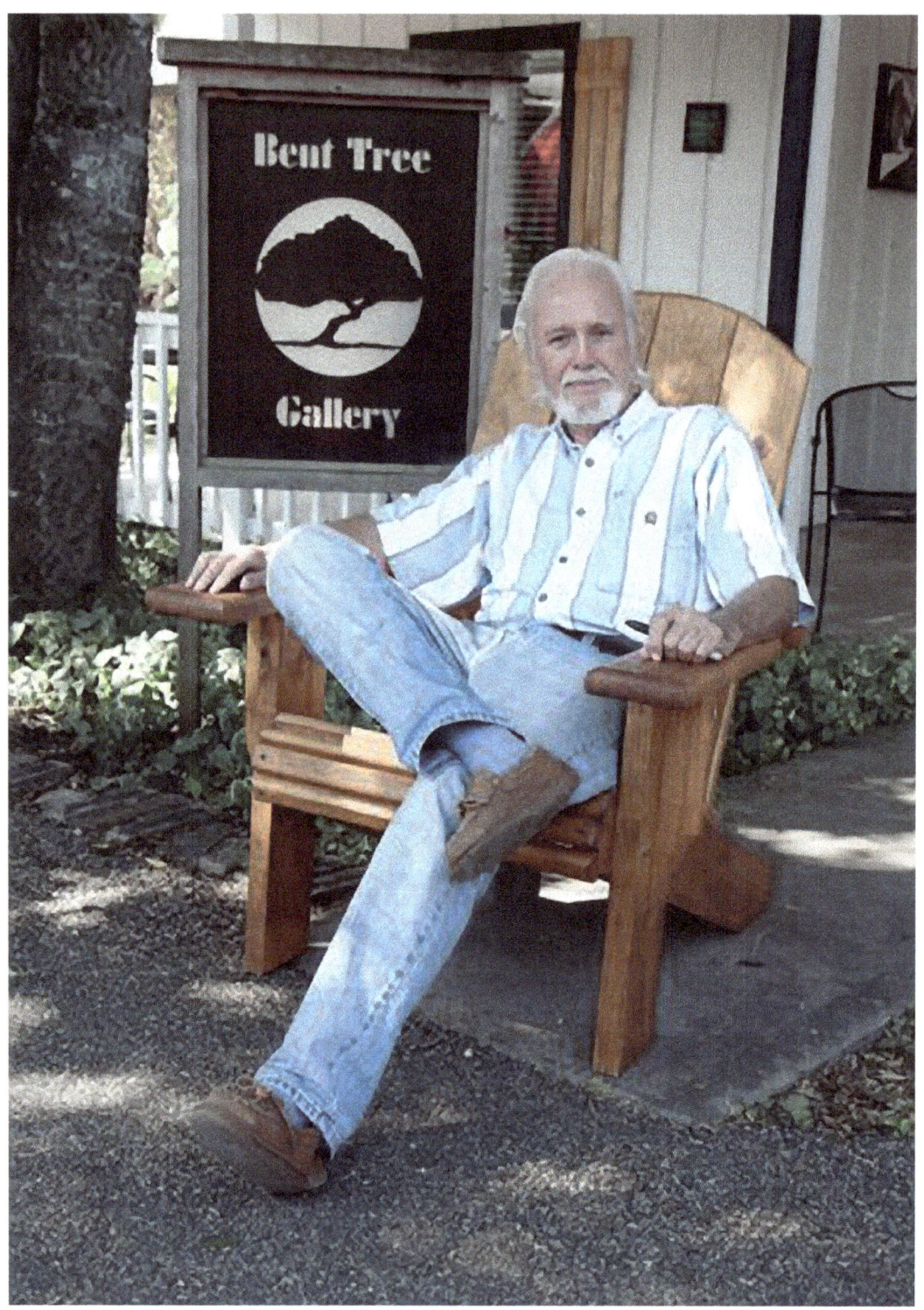

Stan Allen

Stan Allen

I don't know what I would do if I didn't have art at this point in my life. I used to install computer systems for companies and traveled all over the world. There was a program called *Snappy*—a device that would capture an image off of a videotape. So I played with that and tried to get a digital image. Then when the digital camera came out I thought, ah ha! This was a way to capture that image so I could play with it on the computer. I got interested in photography and I bought the first digital camera ever made, a Sony Magnava, and I started fooling around with it. I lived in Dallas, Texas at the time and used to watch this TV show, *Texas Country Reporter*. Just before they would cut to commercial, the host would be standing in some scenic location and when they would go to commercial the digital image would transform into something that looked like a painting. I thought, if they can do that, I can do that. When I hit a brick wall in my business, I went to see a shrink and I said, I'm kind of interested in art, what do you think I ought to do? And he said, go for it!

I ended up at Artists Showplace in Dallas. I was part of the original group, a big co-op type thing. I think they only let me in because I had a forty-four-inch digital printer. That was when I was fifty-nine or sixty years old. My daughter had put some work in and got recognized by Dallas art critics. So she wanted to try Taos, New Mexico. We went to Taos to talk to some galleries, but the group she was interested in didn't accept her work. So we thought, what the heck, we'll start our own gallery, and started the Bent Tree Gallery of Taos. We needed a place to live and rented a little adobe up on Rim Road that overlooked Donald Rumsfeld's and Julia Roberts' houses. It was great. The gallery was on Ledoux street. One big thing we did was a show called, *Taos Does Dallas*. We got four or five works from each gallery in Taos and took them to Dallas for a big show in the Artists Showplace. We had that gallery in Taos for about two years. Now it's a wine bar.

Then we did something I'd wanted to do since I was in my twenties. We sold our house in Dallas and took off in a forty-foot diesel pusher and just traveled around the country. My wife Myra had said, OK Stan, I'll give you two years. So off we went. We spent a couple of summers on Vancouver Island which was great. One day we were sitting in Taos in two feet of snow in January and we decided it was time to make a change. The price of diesel was way up, and the price of homes was coming down. So we decided it's time to come back to Texas and find a place to live. I'd never been to the Texas hill country. Myra said, I've heard the artists at Artists Showcase talking about a little place called Wimberley. We pulled into Wimberley, and it was right at the end of January. It was 75 degrees and we drove into town and got stopped by a herd of deer going across the road and we said, OK this is a fun place.

My work was rejected by the Wimberley Valley Art League in the first show I entered. I went and got my piece and asked for my money back and said, I don't need to be in the Art League if I can't show my art. So once again we started up our own gallery, Bent Tree Gallery here in Wimberley.

Winifred Simon

I'm really kind of shy. I'm not sure I'm even qualified to be in a book with a group of fine artists. Wimberley, Texas is such an artistic haven. In my experience, everyone here is so supportive of one another and so willing to share. To have so many artistically-minded people in the same place is rare and it seems that most of them are producing art. It's not a tense environment with a competitive spirit. It's quite the opposite. Everyone is positive and helpful. Every day I'm so glad I live in Wimberley.

It's the same in our neighborhood. We have pot-luck dinners here once a month, so we can keep tabs on one another. We can't have everyone on this road come, because that would just be too many, but we usually have about twenty-five. We're surrounded by good people. Most everyone on the road is a Master Naturalist. We all look out for each other. We moved here from Austin. Shirley and I owned a gift shop there for twenty-five years. We were so glad to move out here. It's the perfect place. We're surrounded by nature.

I've been a photographer all my life. I got my first camera when I was a young girl. When digital cameras came along, that was a godsend. It was like a little miracle. In the old days, you could do a little manipulation in the dark room with black and whites, but you couldn't do anything with color. Plus, you would have to devote four to five hours to work in the darkroom. Now you can sit down and do something in ten or fifteen minutes with an app. I guess it's good to be open to new things. I could never have imagined that my favorite camera would be my phone! It's good for my mental health. I can wander around and take pictures wherever I am. It makes my life so much more interesting. While I'm waiting for an appointment, I wander around looking for patterns. I still process my own work and print it upstairs. I do all my own matting and framing here too.

Before you go I want to show you something. I have a hummingbird that's sitting on a nest. I'm not sure the eggs will ever hatch. I think it's been too long, but it's so much fun to watch her. She doesn't want to abandon that nest. Just look at that perfect little nest!

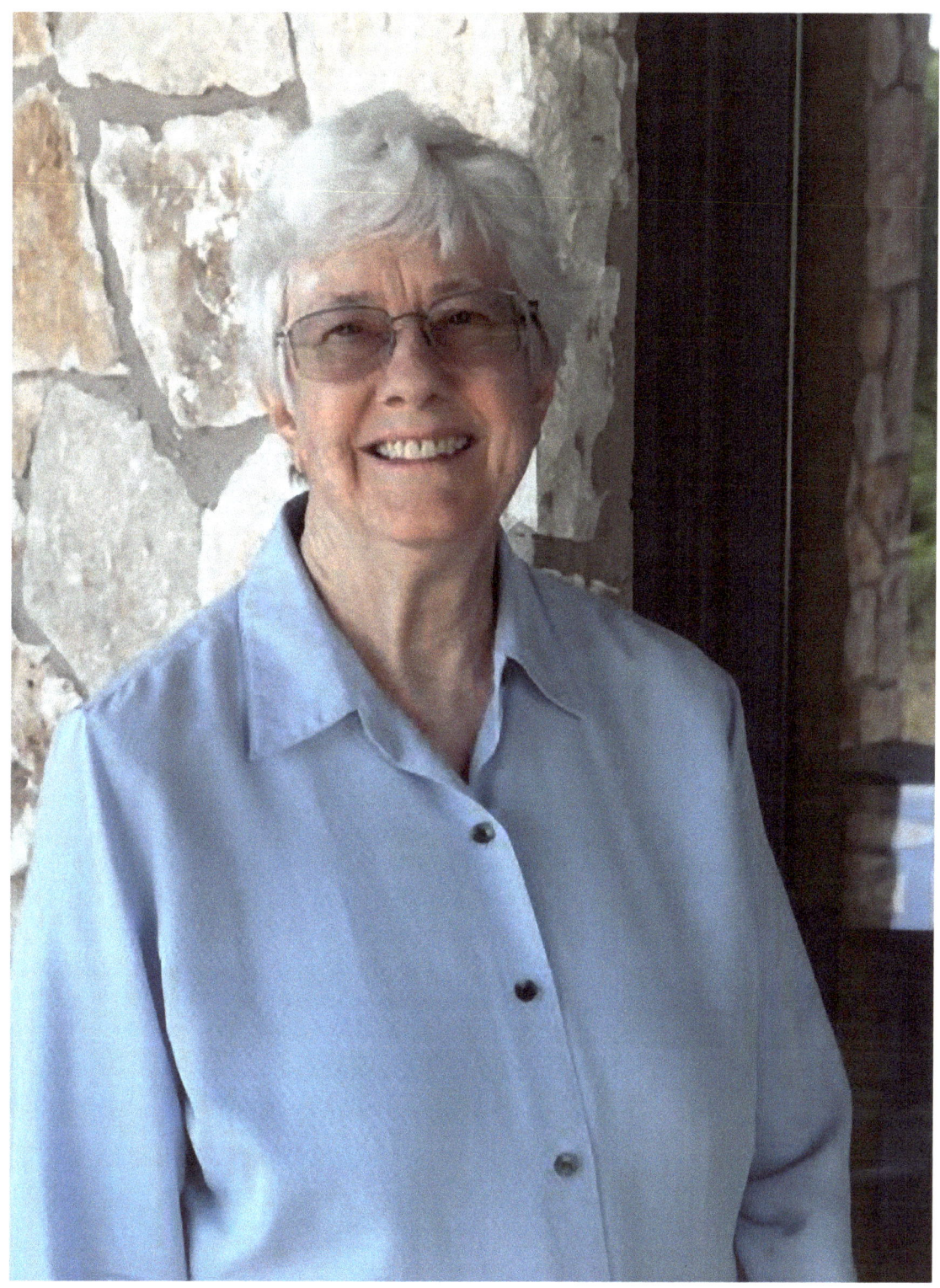

Winifred Simon

Wendell Fuqua

I was not artistic as a kid. Well, I won a couple of photography awards in high school. I was a good photographer. But, I really wanted to be a writer. My first degree was in Journalism. I went into video production out of college. That was my career. I loved video production. I also did some freelance script writing when I lived in Virginia.

I have been doing wood carving for five years. I got a bachelor's degree in art about forty years ago and concentrated mostly on print making: actually silk screen prints. I wanted to get back into silk screens after I retired, but silk screening takes a pretty elaborate set-up. You need a lot of space and a good ventilation system. I can do wood cuts at my kitchen table. I actually started out at my kitchen table.

I'm self-taught. I read a lot, so that's how I learned the process. There's a guy on the West coast, Tom Killion, who uses a Japanese-style process. His work is very distinctive and beautiful. He does scenes from the high Sierras and the California coast. When I saw his work I thought, that looks like fun. I think I'll do that.

I'm very happy with what I do now. Carving wood is a very meditative process. I start with a very smooth piece of plywood from Japan and use a set of knives and a chisel and carve my blocks. One piece of my art can take as many as a dozen separate blocks. I usually work from a photograph or a sketch. So I'll start with a photograph and then I'll sketch it. After that I transfer the sketch onto the block and start the carving process. I'm not really an experimental artist. I know a lot of other artists are, but I think of myself as more of a craftsman. I enjoy the whole process and the challenge.

I do a lot of camping and hiking, so this is my camping and hiking tax write-off. I meet up with a group of guys from the East coast, that I got to know when we lived in Virginia. I take photos on the trips and use those in my work. We're usually moving too fast for me to sit down and sketch at the time, so I work from the photographs. We've been hiking and backpacking for more than twenty years. It's getting harder to get all the guys together. We're getting older. We don't do as much backpacking as we used to. Now we generally do car camping. We pick a place and all meet there. Our last trip was to Palo Duro Canyon, up in the Texas panhandle, and our next trip will be back to Virginia. We've been to Arches National Park, Big Bend and Enchanted Rock. I've yet to tap all of Big Bend. I gotta get back out there.

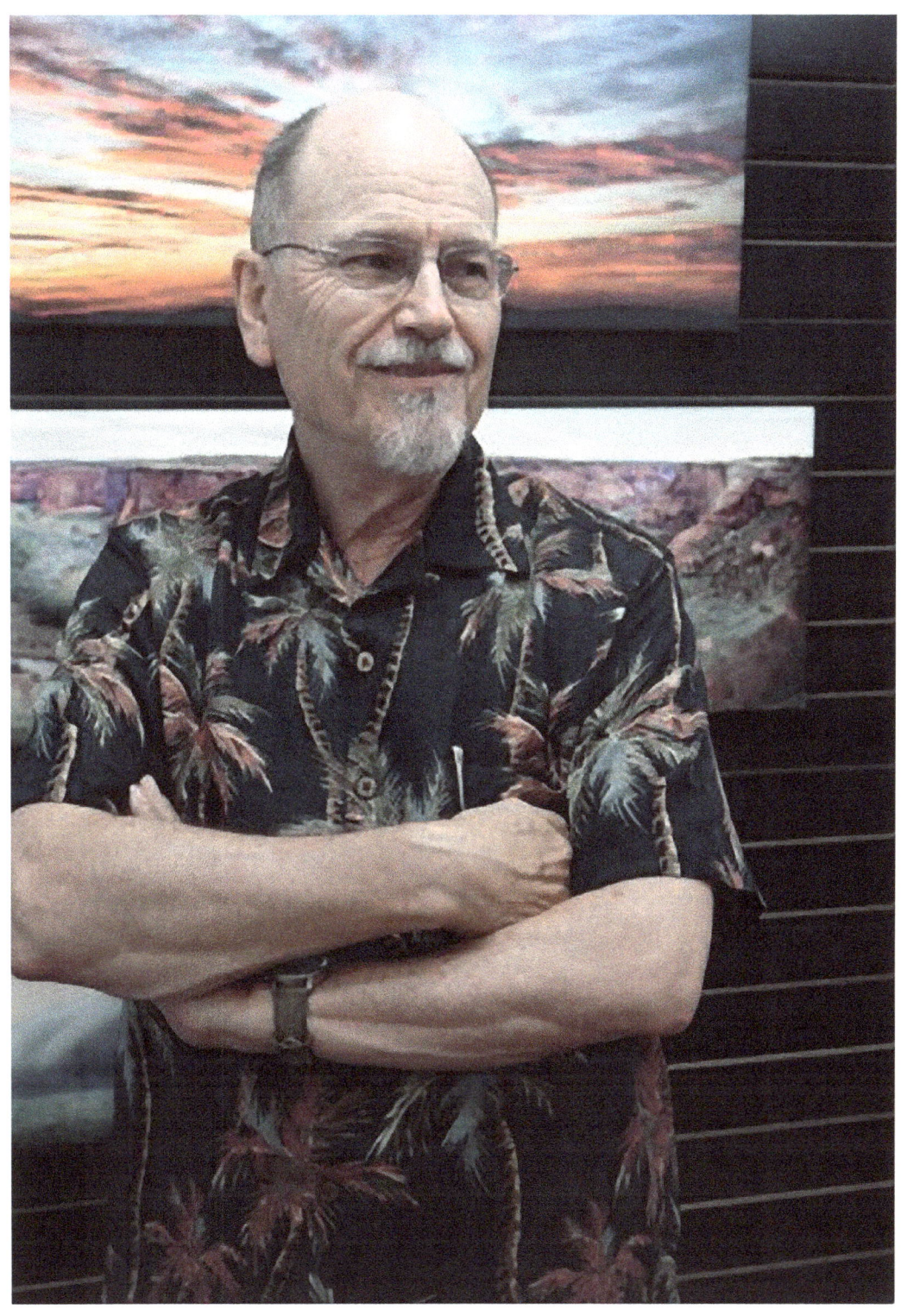

Wendell Fuqua

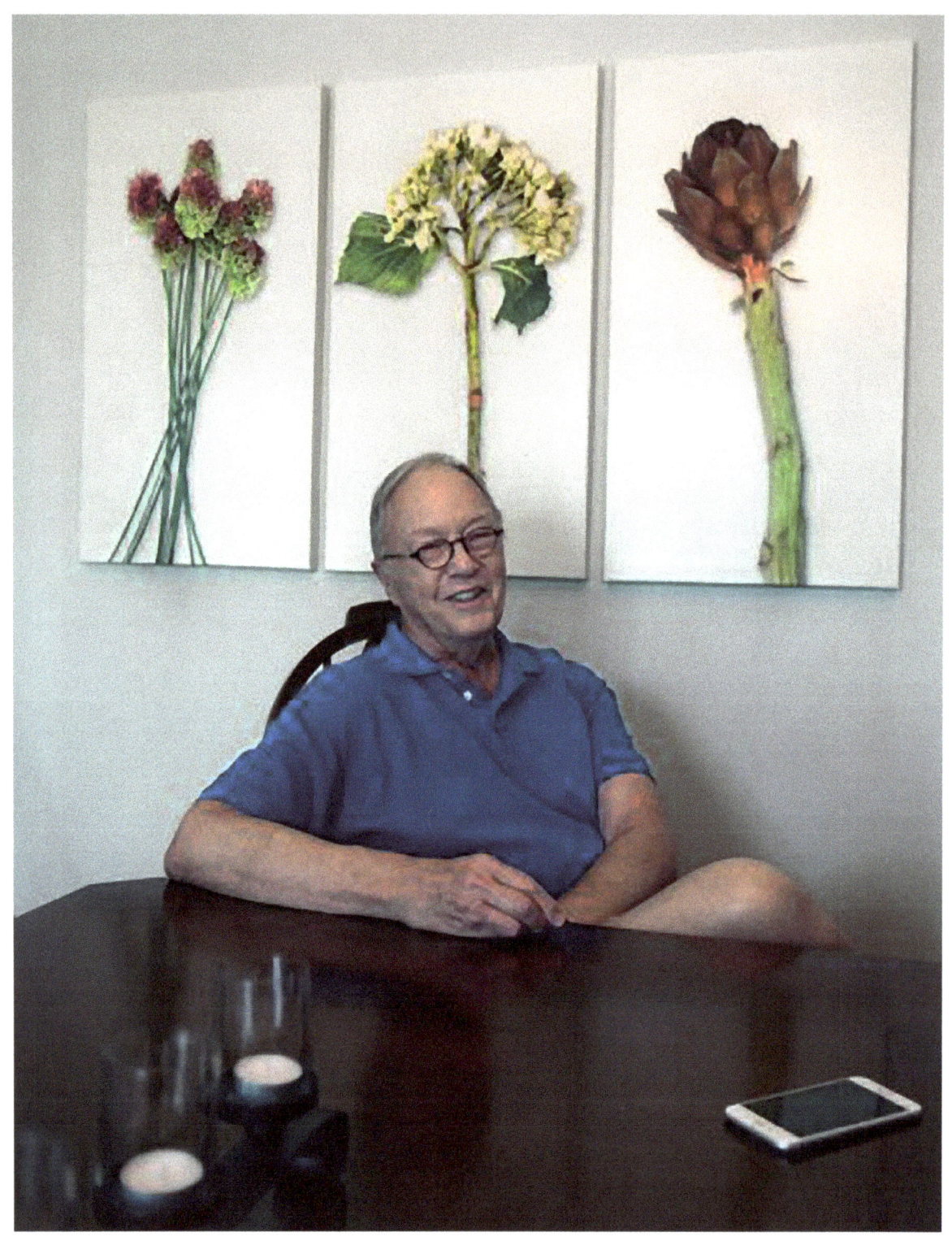

Tom Bender

84

Tom Bender

I don't have any art education, but fortunately I've had wonderful photographer mentors all my life. The first was my high school girlfriend's older brother. He had a dark room in his basement. This was in northern Nebraska. He took me under his wing, and we spent tons of time together. He was probably a senior in college, so he wasn't around all the time, but when he was, I was invited in.

In high school I painted something that my mother wanted. It was on a bed sheet from a single bed. It was a Nativity scene done with tempera paint. It covered half the front porch. I'm a minister's kid and we didn't have any Christmas decorations for the parsonage. She said we had to have decorations, but they sure didn't want any lights and ornaments. We didn't have any money, but they did buy me those tempera paints. I spent weeks and weeks and weeks on that thing. I received my first critical acclaim for that piece. That was the first praise I got for anything I did creatively.

I won a scholarship to junior college, but they didn't offer art, so I turned it down. I've really only had one real art class. I learned about perspective in that class. Learning about perspective was like magic to me. I'm a stickler to this day about making sure the perspective is right, especially now that I'm painting.

I decided I wanted to start painting again for two reasons. About three or four years ago my wife, Pat, asked me if I was ever going to paint again. I had painted one painting about fifty years ago when I was in the Air Force, working as a weather observer. Then I got shipped out and I guess I never found those paints again. Anyway, I promised Pat that I would pick it up again. Within two weeks I owned a set of oils. She was going to force the issue. She made me keep my word. I let the paints sit there for two years and then finally got started. I got a piece into the Wimberley Valley Art League show and during the reception Betty Rhodes came rolling up to it in her wheel chair. She asked if I wanted her to critique it. She gave me all kinds of good advice about using the color purple, and depth and shadows.

Now I paint with Betty in her studio every week, along with other artists. The first time I went I took two pieces for her to critique. She asked me if I wanted to sit or stand to paint. I hadn't planned to paint, so I didn't take any paints or brushes with me. She handed me a brush and a blob of white paint and a blob of black. She asked if I had a piece of paper, so I pulled a piece out of my notebook. She pointed to a picture of an apple and said, paint that in black and white. I struggled with it for three hours. I was so slow I didn't even get the stem on the stupid apple! When I went back, I completed a painting of some pears. It's hanging over there on the wall. When I walked in with it, Pat burst into tears.

Lilli Pell

I helped organize the very first Studio Tour for the Wimberley Valley Art League. Along with my co-chair we decided our criteria was to include only studios that had never been open to the public, places that people had never seen. We invited George Krause, Ellen Berman, and Bob Gottschall, artists like that. Most people don't really know who is in Wimberley, Texas. There are so many magnificent artists who live here. You might not ever see them or their art around, but they're here. I feel like I'm in important territory around here.

I was just typing away last night, thinking about my philosophy about my art and about my students and about the entire art community. One of my concerns about my art is it's just very classic and traditional. It's not edgy, but it expresses me and what I value. It's about where I was born and where I've lived and what I value about Texas. I love Texas. My ancestors have been here since 1870. I'm a sixth-generation Texan and now with my children and grandchildren we're up to eight generations.

I also love nature, so that's what you see in my work. I spent part of my childhood on a farm, so I love painting farm animals. We lived there from the time I was around five. I used to help gather the eggs. I loved that. My family and I had such fond memories of that time together. It was a special time and it left an impression in all of our hearts.

I'm very happy to be back teaching again. I usually have around twenty to thirty students, so that means I might have around eight on any particular day. I wasn't sure how many would come back, but I'm so pleased that they have. Some of them haven't painted since my diagnosis and treatment started. I missed them all so much when they weren't here.

I just love what I do. I'm so fond of my students. They enjoy being together. They like each other and they like being with others who have that artistic spirit and attitude. Some of them have had art in their souls all their lives, but they've never painted. They're finally getting to do what they've always wanted to do.

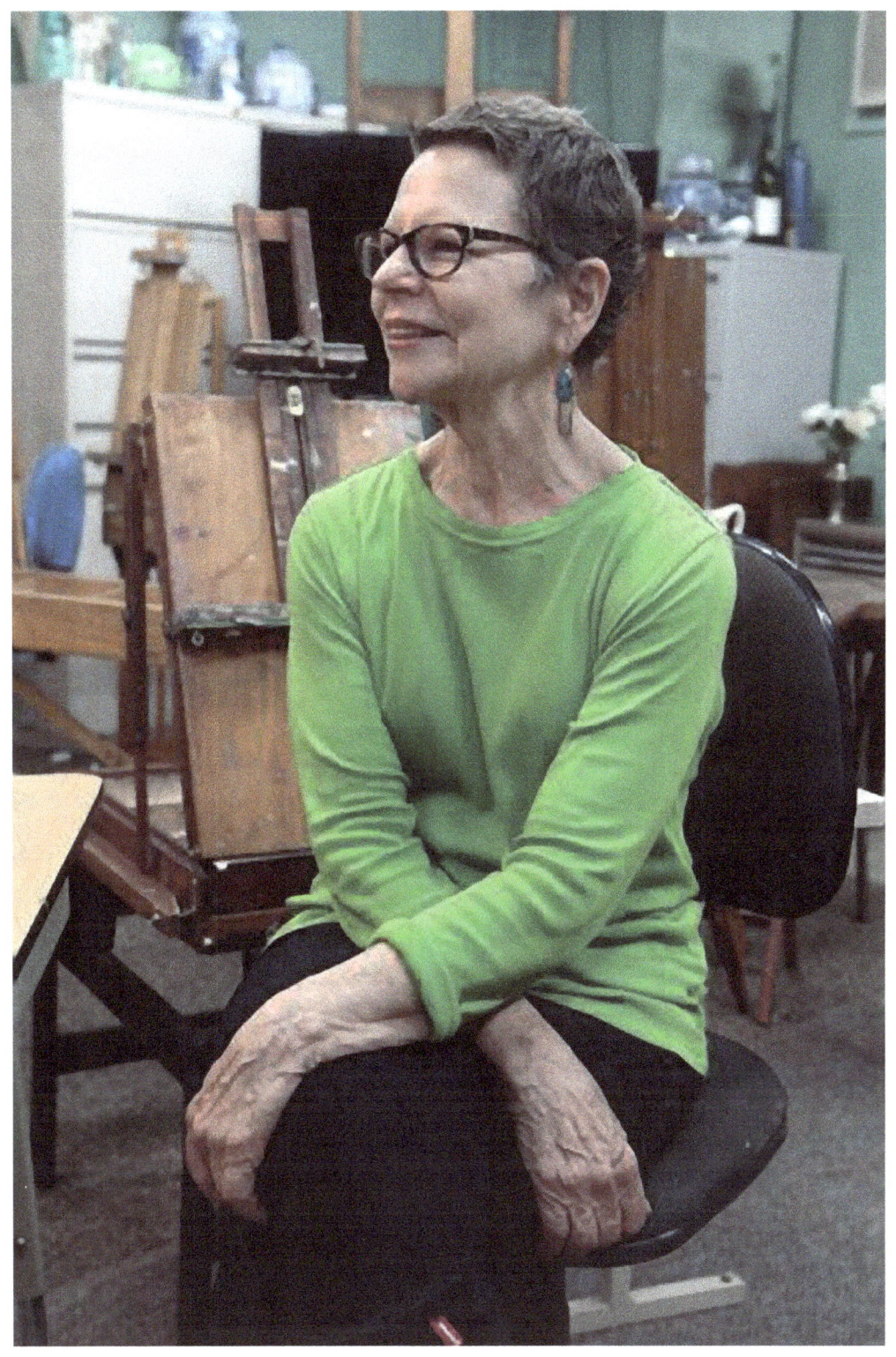

Lilli Pell

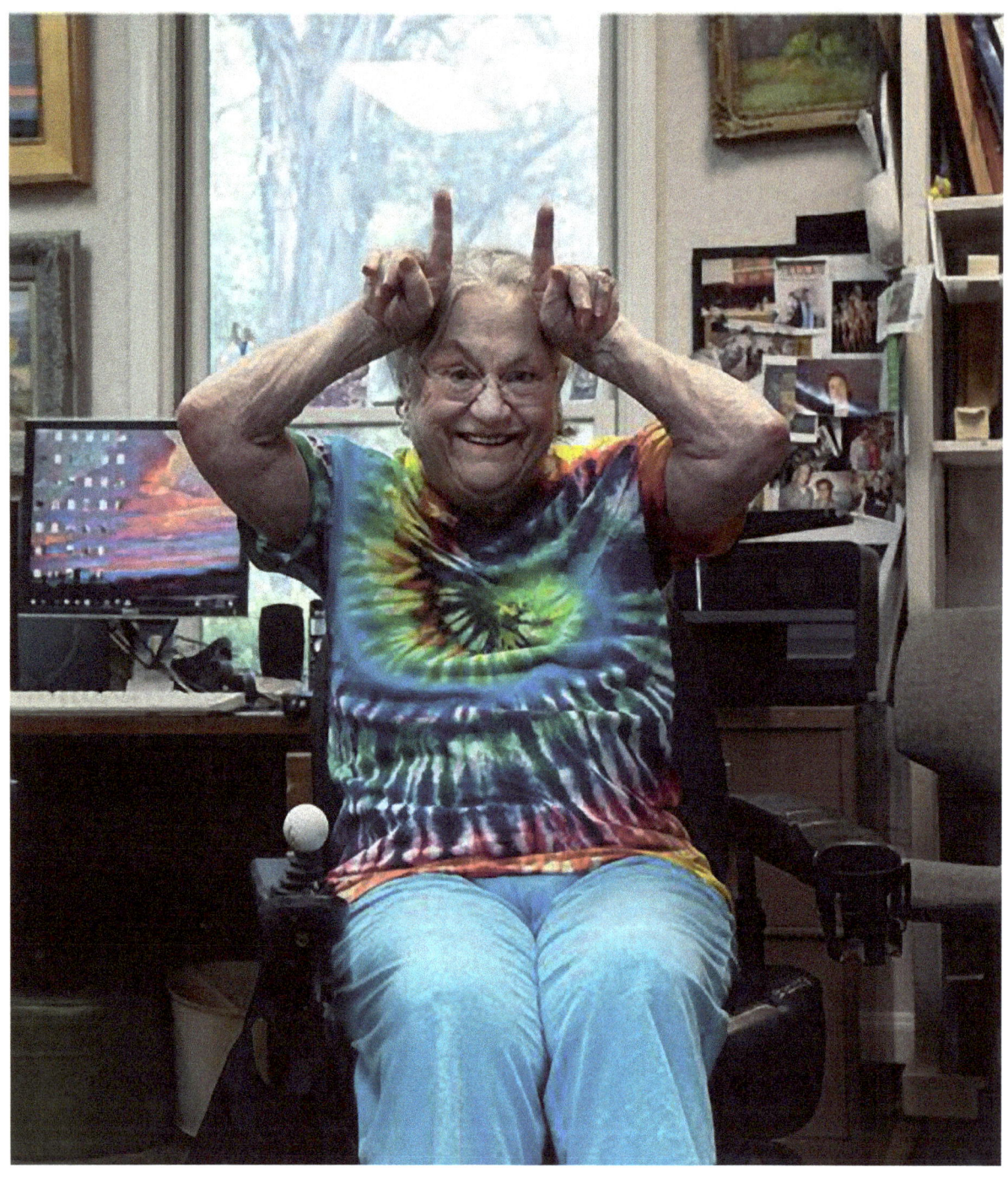

Betty Rhodes

Betty Rhodes

People ask me what I like to paint. I usually tell them just anything happy. I love to use bright colors that make me smile. I hope they make other people smile, too. I like to paint dogs and farm animals with attitudes. I get a kick out of watching people smile when they see my animals. Some of the paintings have even won awards and been featured in magazines. I paint goats, chickens, donkeys, you name it. I paint Texas Hill Country landscapes, florals and abstracts, too. Just whatever strikes my fancy when I get up in the morning.

My husband, Barry, likes to tell a story about when I started painting the animals. I walked into a gallery to ask about showing my work there. The owner asked if I could paint farm animals, because that's what would sell. I said, of course I paint farm animals. I'd never painted a farm animal in my life, but I went home and started that day!

Speaking of Barry, you know I met him while I was dancing on a bar. Somebody told me to go through Bandera, Texas on my way home from school, because it was a nice little town. I didn't have a penny in my pocket, and I had car trouble along the way. I saw a nice hotel that I wanted to stay in, so I checked into a room and started trying to figure out how in the world I was going to pay for it! I went downstairs to the bar and told the Gypsy bartender about my dilemma. He said if I danced on the bar, I could earn enough money to pay for the room. Pretty soon, in walked a tall guitar player named Barry and we got busy entertaining the crowd. The rest is history.

I studied art in school when I was a little girl, because I loved it. But in those days, they couldn't afford to pay a real art teacher, so I didn't learn much. I did go off to art school in San Antonio, Texas later. That's where I really learned to draw and paint. It was at the Hunter's Art School.

I owned a couple of galleries in Dallas when I lived there and worked as an interior designer. I've also shown my work in other galleries around the state. It's been a fun career.

I love my studio. As you can see, it's crammed full of my art supplies and my work. I love this old easel and I use my computer to look at the images I paint. I teach art students here. Some of them want one-on-one instruction, and some of them come to my group classes. I've taught so many artists here. Many of them have had successful art careers and I think all of them have had a good time here. We like to have fun in here and we do a little swearing while we're at it. I tell them to yell *shit* when they walk through the door of the studio to get us off to a good start!

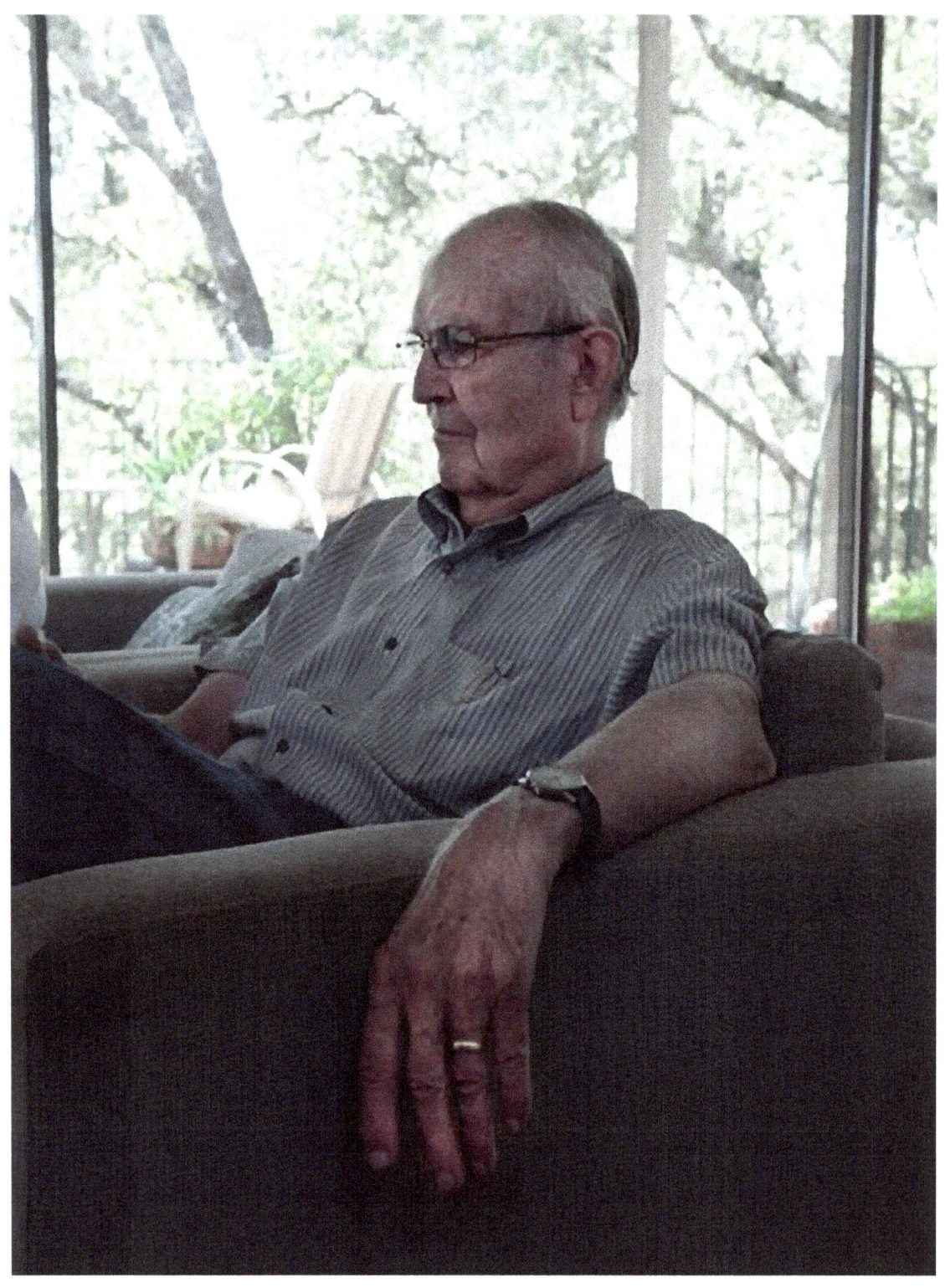

Bert Ray

Bert Ray

All of us in the arts have a lot to be thankful for. Art, the big word *art*, covers a lot of things. We don't have to divide art into cubbyholes. There are so many fun things out there to try your hand at. When you think about it there are an astounding number of incredible artists in this little place. We need to revel in the glory of this environment and living in a place dedicated to creativity. After all, art is to make us enjoy the world.

I'm an architect, so when we were thinking about building our home, I wanted to be up high. I got a topographical map of this area and colored in everything above eleven hundred feet. I figured that would get me up high enough to see the sunsets. So we only looked at property at that altitude and here we are. We've lived here twenty years. Julie and I went to junior high, high school and college in Austin, Texas, so we're both Hill Country kids. We were living in Houston when we decided to retire. We decided to look around and stumbled onto Wimberley. Now you would have to drag me back to Houston. I jettisoned all my friends there when I left.

I made most of the furniture in this room. I made the lamps, the stereo, the planters and the sculpture. I figured it was cheaper than buying it. I'm too cheap to buy furniture. It's all kind of corny. It's just thin veneers on top of high-quality plywood. I use very thin slices of exotic wood, so I'm not savaging the rainforest or chewing up the jungle. I can make one tiny piece of exotic wood go a long, long way. Part of the fun for me is the technique. I try to make something that looks incredibly complicated easy. Half the fun is figuring out how to do it. I'm a closet engineer. I make most of my machinery and gadgets. I have lots of gadgets, jigs and contraptions that I've built. You won't find any store-bought tools in my workshop. I made them all. It's all very primitive, but that's what I enjoy.

I've always liked putzing around. I'm just into making stuff. The idea of designing and creating things has just always appealed to me. This dining room table is made of native Texas woods and turquoise. Here's a corny story: I once told someone I used all Texas materials to create this table and they challenged me on the turquoise. I said it came from New Mexico which used to be part of Texas. I think we should have kept New Mexico, so I'm sticking to my story.

I love to use Mesquite. It takes a good finish and it's not toxic. The trees are gnarly, but I need straight grains for my kind of work and that's very hard to find. There's a place near Bastrop, Texas that sells native woods, so Julie and I took a drive out there one day. The place is way out in the boonies, up an old gravel road with a bunch of barns. We drove up and a fellow came out to meet us and asked if we were looking for something special. I said I would tell him if he promised not to laugh. I told him I needed an eight-foot long piece of Mesquite with straight grain. Of course, he laughed! After going through a zillion dusty old planks of wood, we actually found one. Now there's a project at Texas A&M to breed a strain of straight grained Mesquite. If they're successful, that guy would have to quit laughing at me.

I love the idea of artists sharing their knowledge with one another. I was invited to a meeting of woodworkers the other day. They want to start a group to teach woodworking, maybe even have a facility with tools available to students, that sort of thing. I don't want to teach. I could give a presentation or demonstration, but I'm not really interested in teaching.

I really don't do woodwork. I paint with wood. I'm not a woodworker, I'm an oddball. If a real woodworker saw my gadgets they would probably roll their eyes. I don't know anyone else who does what I do, I'm pretty crazy. Crazy is fun.

I enjoy nitpicky stuff. I spend a lot of time planning the projects and working everything out. I work out the patterns and details ahead of time. I just like to experiment and enjoy the geometry. I like to draw stuff and then I use *Photoshop* to make the changes. After that I make a rough study in cardboard. Once I work all the kinks out, I'll start on the actual piece. I still use the first version of *Photoshop*. The *Photoshops* of today are incredibly complicated. Of course, I'm old and cynical, but today's products are too complicated. They want to sell you something new every couple of years with new features, whether they're features you need or not. I have no patience for that sort of thing, so I'm still using my original *Photoshop*. I love *Photoshop* for mischief, too. I'll show you sometime.

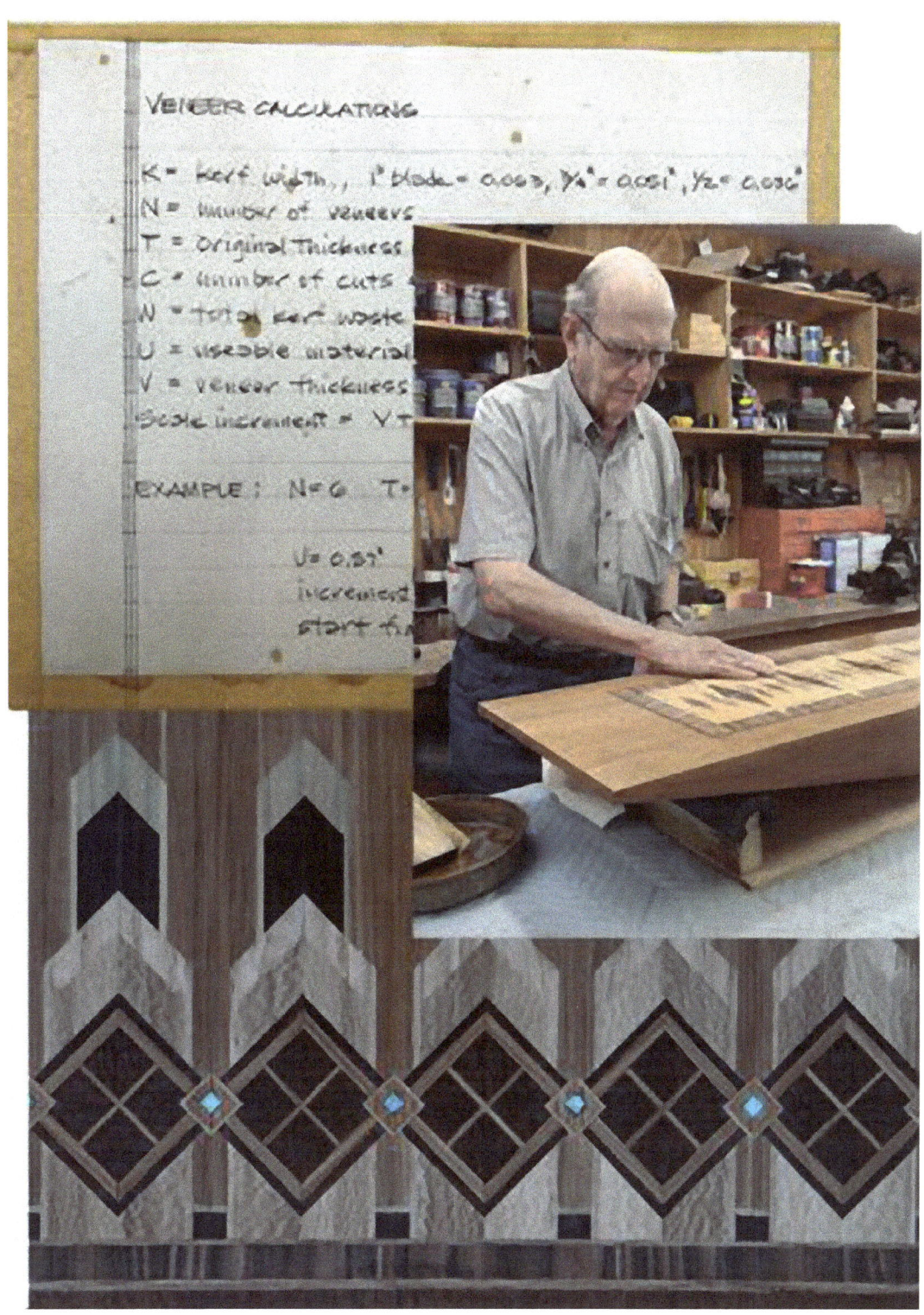

Bert Ray composite

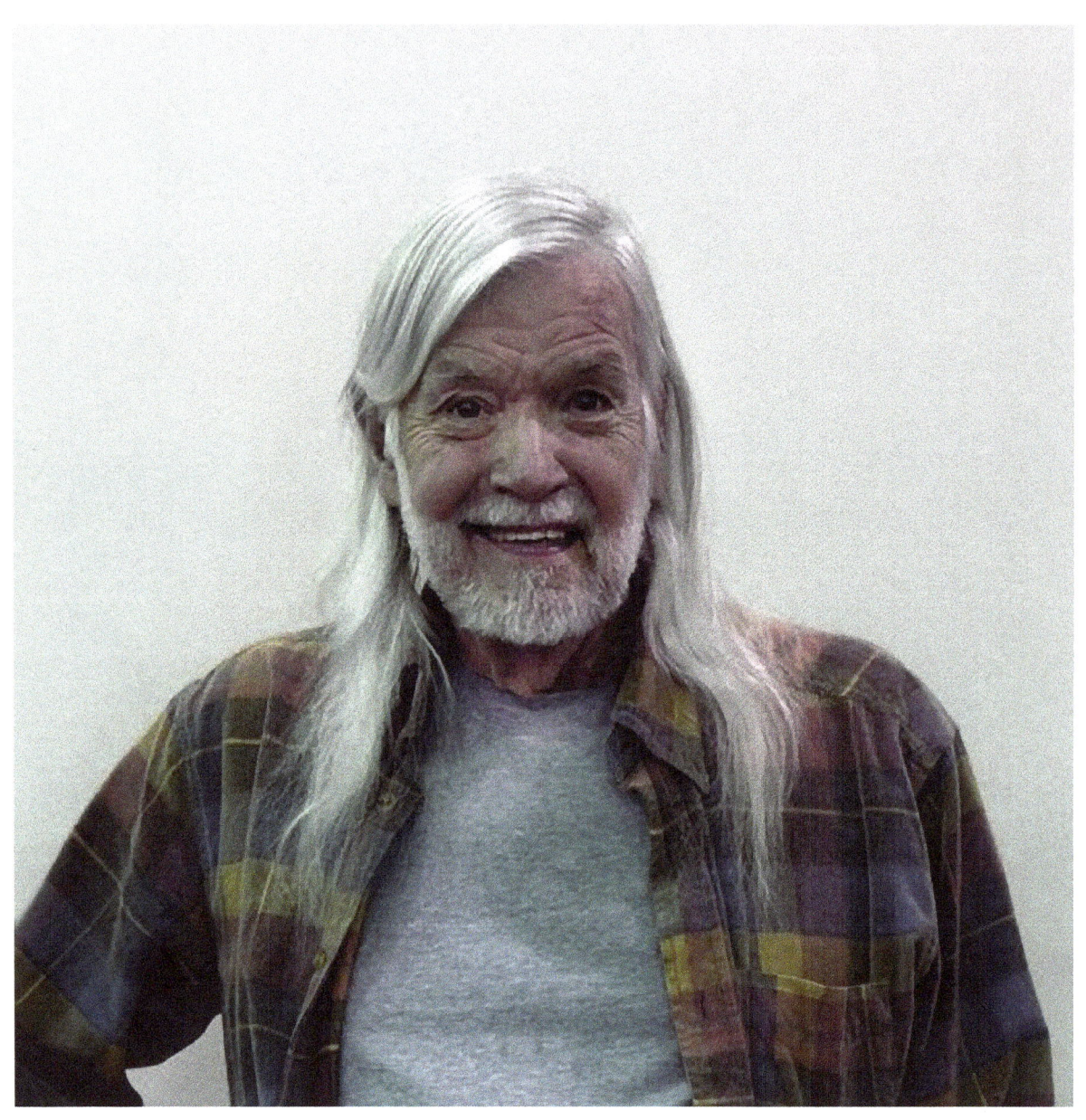

Herb Smith

Herb Smith

I've loved photography since I was a little kid. I had a darkroom by the time I was twelve. I grew up in Detroit, Michigan. A neighbor two doors down was a Principal of one of the schools there. He had a boy's summer camp in Wisconsin that I attended for seven years. I really got into nature and ended up with the nickname *Nature Boy*. They had a darkroom and encouraged the campers to do photography, so I did, and I just loved it. I ended up creating a dark room down in the basement of my parent's house, kind of alongside the furnace. I did a lot of photographs, the kind a twelve-year old would make - my dog, my brother, my sister - whoever would hold still for me.

I took some trips out west, first in 1952 with my parents. I took a lot of photographs then. And then I took trips with a group of guys for the next two summers. I was pre-med in college but by my junior year I was not so sure I wanted to be a physician. I went to Albion College, a small liberal arts school in central Michigan. As part of my biology major I took a problems course where you did research and wrote a paper. Most of my paper was illustration rather than words. The pre-med advisor said, have you ever thought about medical illustration? I said, no, what is that? So I ended up visiting a medical illustrator in Detroit, then visited a medical illustrator in Chicago. I decided that's what I wanted to do - medical illustration.

To that point, I hadn't taken any art, just science. The admission to the program was based on your grades, mainly in science, and the art part of it was based on a portfolio. I didn't have a portfolio, so I took as much art as I could that last year-and-a-half in college, and didn't feel like even that was enough. In a small Methodist college in Michigan you couldn't draw nudes. And that's the best way to learn how to draw the human figure.

I had planned on going to Europe with my roommate and a couple of other guys, bum around Europe, you know. My roommate said, have you thought about art school in Europe? I checked it out and ended up going to the Glasgow School of Art: a wonderful old school. You start off drawing from antique casts, move to nudes, really classical drawing. That's what I needed. It ended up being the best year of my life. School was great. I learned a lot that way, but I was also able to travel. That year I spent about five months traveling the continent. During that period I applied at Johns Hopkins and I ended up getting in there and got a Master's in Art As Applied to Medicine.

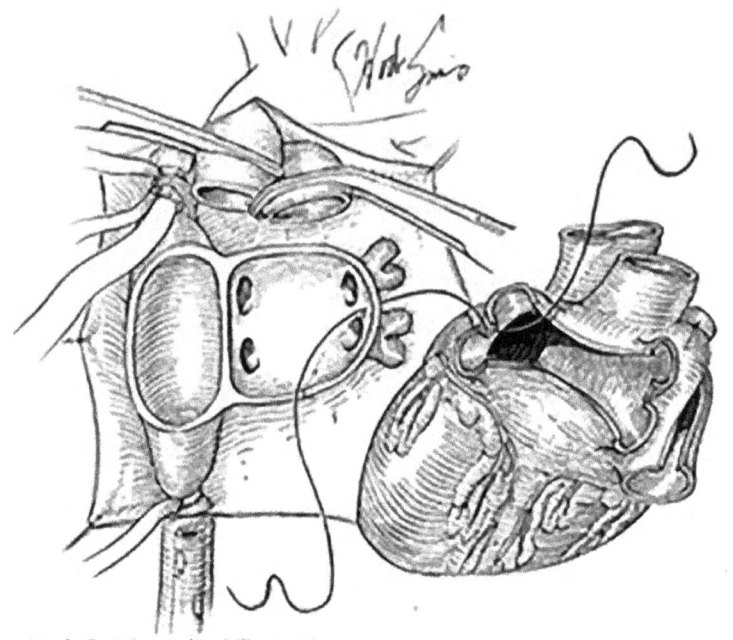

Herb Smith medical illustration

My first job was at the National Institutes of Health. Two years later, I was recruited by Dr. Michael DeBakey to come to Baylor College of Medicine in Houston. I ended up as the Director of the Department of Medical Illustration and Audiovisual Education for thirty-seven years.

I was very fortunate to be able illustrate for Dr. DeBakey and Dr. Denton Cooley, both of whom were outstanding surgeons. Denton Cooley did the first human heart transplant in the U.S. I had a team and we were filming it. I had my cinematographer and one of my medical illustrators with me. I had grabbed my camera. I had never taken a photograph in all my years at Baylor. But I thought this was history in the making, so I grabbed my camera. The hospital insisted we had to use the hospital photographer for the photographs of the surgery. That was fine with me. So Cooley gets the diseased heart out and was holding it in his hands and said, OK Fred get a picture of this. And Fred said, I'm out of film. So Cooley said, does anybody else have a camera? I spoke up. Well, I guess I do. I was right behind him watching the surgery to illustrate it later. I didn't have the right lens or anything, but I thought let me try. I was able to back up far enough. The boom we had for the cinematographer was right behind me and over my shoulder and I couldn't back up very far. I was really trying to get it into focus. I ended up making the picture (the only medical photo of my career) and it ended up as a double-page spread in *Life Magazine*. I was thankful I knew how to trip the shutter.

By then Denton Cooley was doing a lot of heart transplants and he used to really belittle Debakey's artificial heart program. But then the transplant patients all were dying in short periods of time. I think Cooley thought, well maybe we ought to start looking into this artificial heart thing. He colluded with a surgeon who headed up DeBakey's artificial heart lab at Baylor. The guy in charge of the lab thought that Debakey wasn't giving him enough recognition.

So one day Cooley had a patient who was going to die if they didn't do something radical. So they took DeBakey's heart and the only thing Cooley did was to replace the aortic valve in the heart with a different commercially available valve. They put it in the patient, but sadly he didn't live very long at all.

And then it hit the proverbial fan when Debakey learned about the surgery. He was coming out of a National Institutes of Health meeting that was actually about his artificial heart program. When he walked out of the meeting people were asking what's going on in Houston? He had no clue. So he kind of went ballistic. It was a very strained relationship, but for a short period of time, because then Cooley resigned, he really had to. The two didn't speak for forty years until they reconciled in 2007. The split saddened me because I had tremendous respect, and enjoyed working with both of them. I was able to continue to work with Dr. DeBakey, but work with Cooley became very limited.

Well, I never left my interest in nature. That's a common theme for as long as I can remember. Even medical illustration was science and biology, anatomy, that sort of thing.

I want to continue doing photography, but I also think about sculpture. That was my favorite art medium. I would like to do that when I get too immobile to walk around and photograph. My sculpture would probably tend to be abstract, purely abstract. Most of what my wife and I have collected is abstract art. I'm very conscious of composition. To me composition is everything. Basically, you're designing. When I'm photographing, I'll spend a lot of time trying to compose a shot. The technology of taking a photograph, you just take for granted. It happens automatically. I'm always amused when someone says, oh, I love your photography. What kind of camera do you use?

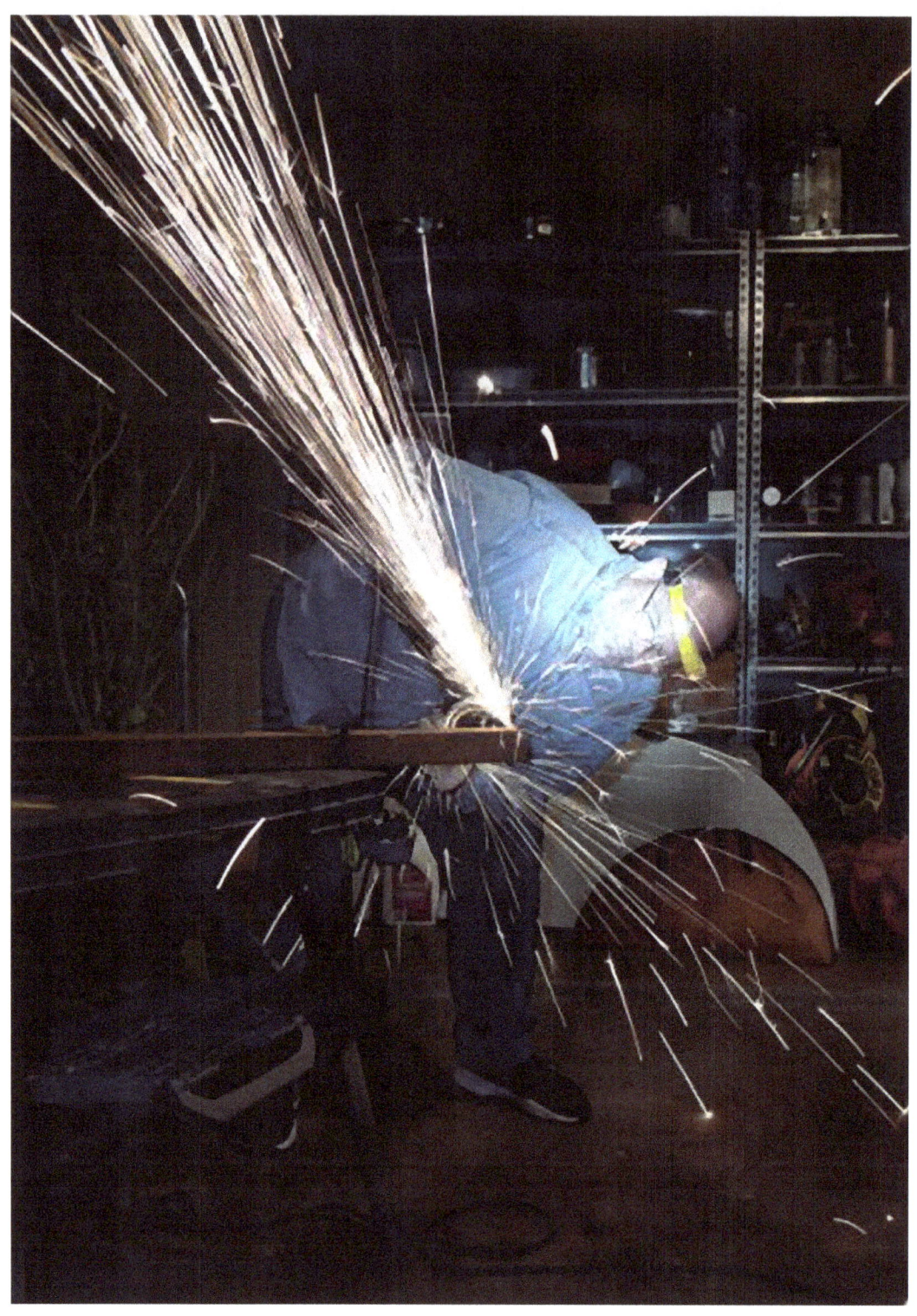

Solon Williams

Solon Williams

You're the only person who has ever afflicted me with the title of *artist*. I like to just think of myself as retired, as somebody that likes to have fun and do things: fish, hunt and cook.

I was in a choir once, but I got tired of going to practice. About twenty years ago, we moved back to Houston, Texas. The kids were in college and I thought I'll start another hobby. I bought me a welding torch. I'd taken some welding classes because I'd worked in a chemical plant. I thought that would be fun to do. I took some metallurgy classes. The second project I did, I decided to make a bed, you know with a headboard and a footboard. You think I'd be smart enough to figure out that a half-inch rod doesn't go through a half inch hole. So after five-hundred-something holes I learned that I had to ream them all out. That makes more noise than grinding does, but it doesn't make very many sparks. We'd inherited a brass bed, but it was the wrong size, according to my wife. So I had to shrink it one notch down.

I think about this as my therapy. I take my time with it, have fun, and not be in a rush. I'd done wood working on-and-off forever. You know, in refineries and chemical plants, there's all kinds of craftsmen making things. And when you go watch them you think, Jiminy Cricket that's neat looking. They make it look nice, but it's one-hundred percent functional. The trouble with woodworking is if you mess up, you've messed up. With metal you can weld it back together and grind it down. If you're gonna paint it, nobody will know the difference. Also, there's Bondo. You weld the parts that's easy to clean up, and the rest you use Bondo, and people think you really know what you're doing.

I'm an engineer, a chemical engineer. I built a gate, two sides swinging, hopefully match up in the middle. I was so excited when I put it together I almost peed in my pants when it matched up. The things I usually make, I had some reason to make it. But if you're going to have something around you, you want it to look good. In our side yard we had some plants die, so we erected things to fill those holes. So that worked out. It's part mechanical, and then you think about the *feel* part: how do you make it look good?

I made a doll house for my granddaughter, with a spiral staircase and everything. That doll house! It seems like it's harder to do that than to build a real house, except there's no plumbing or electrical. My granddaughter still has it. She's making apartment complexes now with boxes. She'll color the insides of them. She'll make furniture out of clay and flour and paint it, and she'll paint pictures on the walls. She found some dolls to put in there and looked around for ones that looked like people in the family, and she'd put them in there. Except she had me sitting on a toilet. But she had a desk in front of it, so …

Jim McDonald

We all know what we like and what we don't, and we'll take those prejudices to our graves. We all have our ideas about what is art. They say it takes ten thousand hours to be proficient at anything, and that's a lot of solitary time. I hope that eventually what I produce communicates to the universe. So I take making art very seriously. But I have fun with it. I have serious fun. How do you do that *serious* fun?

I have this story: it's kindergarten and the first day in art class. All the kids have got their crayons and they're all working like crazy. And the teacher is going around saying oh that's great, that's really good. She gets to little Joanie who's drawing up a storm. The teacher says what are you drawing? And Joanie says I'm drawing a picture of God. And the teacher says well Joanie, nobody knows what God looks like. And little Joanie says they will in a minute. That's the essence of how you paint loose. Little Joanie would say paint what you feel. Whatever happens next is the right thing to happen.

I'm never more alive than when I'm painting. I paint from memory. I do that for a reason. I don't want to be prejudiced by a photograph or a line drawing. When I start a painting, I start with a blank canvas. I pull up in my mind's Rolodex some scene that I saw, that had some ummph, that had enough punch to it that it caught my attention. Months later, I still have that vision that I can pull that up in memory. I can't remember everything about this scene, but I know what grabbed me, so I paint that. Everything else, the minutia, goes away. If I'm trying to paint from a photograph or a line drawing, I will not get there.

If you walk away from the work and turn your back it's like cleaning your palette. I'm more objective at that point than I would be if I were staring at the canvas. Then I turn around and I can see what I need to do next. Painting is like drilling a tunnel through a mountain of unknown distance. Every day you're working so hard and maybe make a quarter of a mile through the mountain. But you have no idea how much farther you need to go. And the next day you come back and do your quarter mile. And then one day, pow! You break through and it's so, so sweet. When you're painting you get to a point you're painting, painting, painting, and all of a sudden bingo it's there. That's when you quit. When you hear *Bingo* you quit.

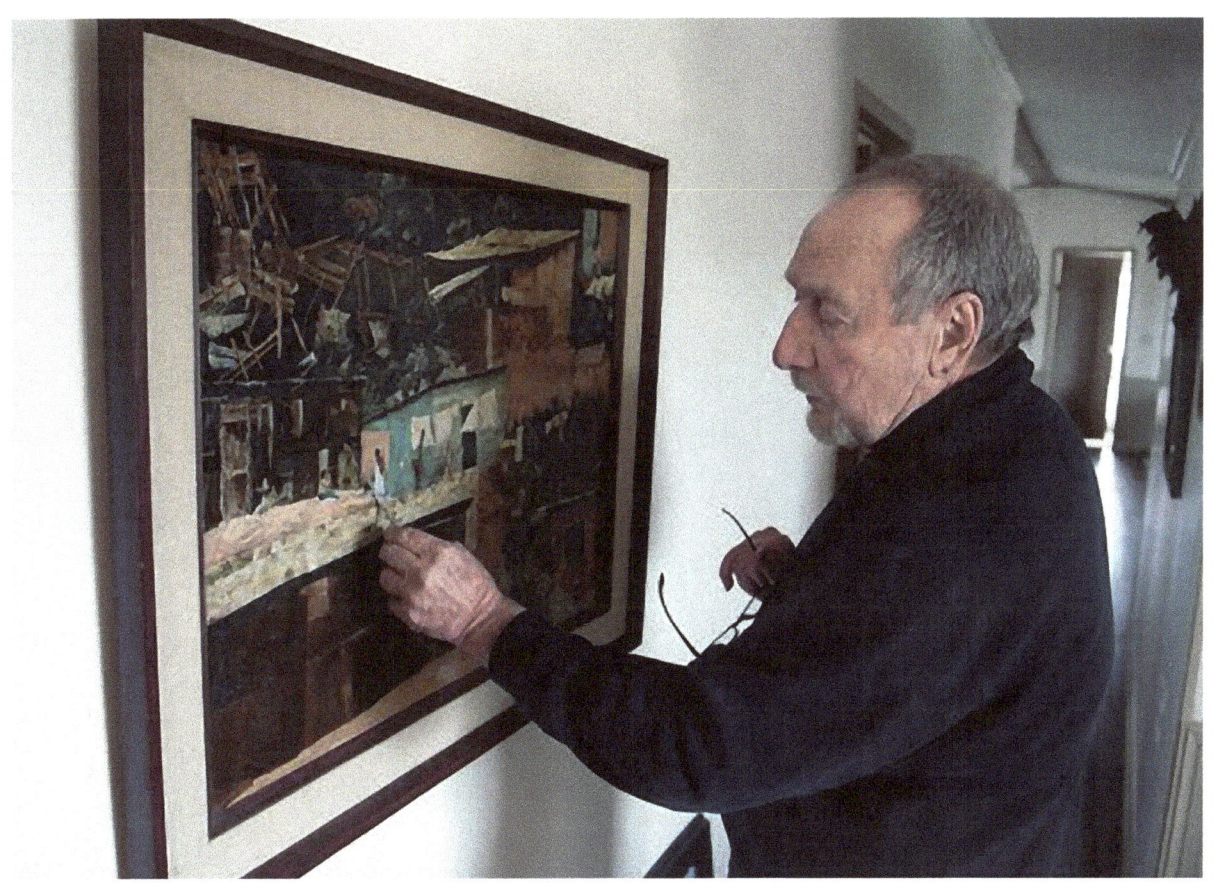

Jim McDonald

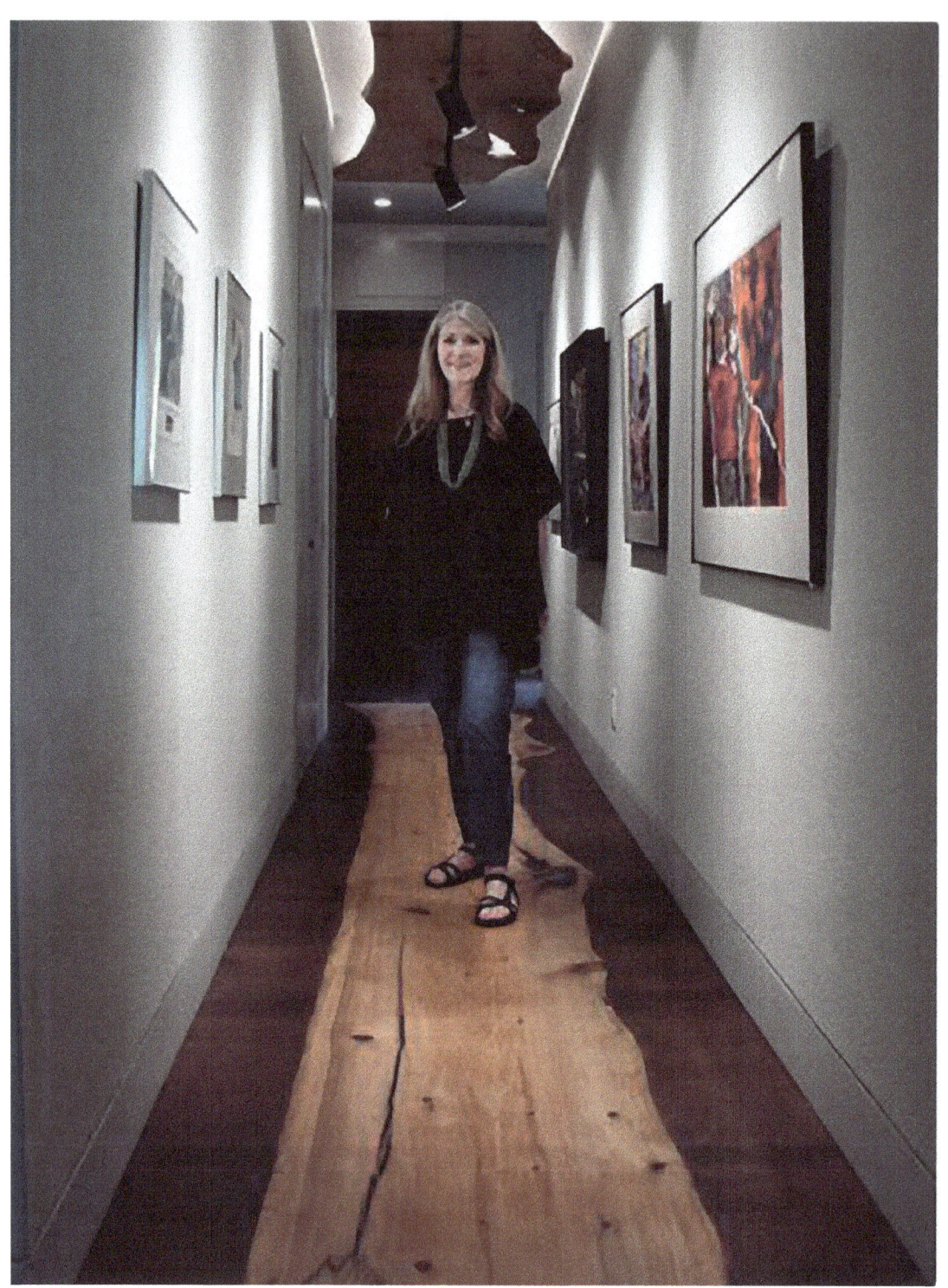

Pamela Lamoureux

Pamela Lamoureux

These drawings were on my drafting table when our house was destroyed in the Memorial Day flood in Wimberley in 2015. The water must have pushed the drafting table up to the ceiling and smashed them together because these are all of my art that survived the flood, even though they were pencil drawings on paper.

Recovering from the flood stifled my art work at first, then there was the depression associated with everything you owned being destroyed. I had lost all my art supplies. I went to the art supply store and piled up art supplies to make my list to be reimbursed by the insurance company. The worst part was I found out insurance only pays $1500 total for any home business. That included my real estate business and my art combined. So it was a major setback. Now I'm kind of getting back on my feet and people have been so generous to give me art supplies. All those supplies in my studio have been donated to me by friends. We found so many creative things in building back our house, that took the place of art for me for a while. Now I'm just getting back on my feet with painting. My drawing has been very healing.

We were in the house at first during the flood, but we couldn't see the water coming up because there was no moon, it was pitch black. We waited until midnight and we were listening because the flood is usually real quiet. The noise you usually hear is the creek and when the creek is covered over by the rising river, the creek stops making noise, and then you know the river is coming up. We were getting texts from our family and friends saying get out, get out. I took all my shoes and put them up on my bed and then took our two dogs and our computers and at the last minute we took the second car. We went to Don's (my husband's) brother's house and ended up living there for two-and-a-half years.

I don't know how you get started as an artist. I remember as a little kid I'd take the encyclopedias and just copy people out of it. I was doing that real early. So I've always drawn, but I never thought of it being a career. When I went to college, I took business classes. I kick myself now because it never occurred to me to take art classes. I came from a home with a single mom and she couldn't pay my way through college, so I knew I had to get a job that could produce income so that I could take care of myself. I dropped out after two years anyway and went into business and real estate.

I absolutely have these two sides of myself—my artist side and my logic side. When I'm painting, I used to stay up real late at night. I'd keep the TV on like *Nic at Night*—old sitcoms where you didn't have to look at them because you knew exactly what they looked like. That would keep my logic brain busy so my creative stuff could just flow. That worked for me. Music doesn't work for me. I need to distract my logic brain so it doesn't say no that's not how that's supposed to look. What I like about real estate is the matching up of people and places and the research. It seems to me to be totally different. It's creative when you're trying to make a deal come together though. The art is more healing. Art for me is just meditative, healing, where I need to be. Real estate is fun with people because I only deal with people I know and like. The art is very personal. It's nice to have the real estate to balance.

When I moved to Wimberley, Texas I met Gayle Stoops, and she had just moved to Wimberley, too. And she wanted to start an art league. So Gayle and I found Nicky Johnson who had helped start the art league in San Marcos, Texas and the three of us founded the Wimberley Valley Art League in 1989. Then we talked Lois Roper into helping. Gayle was the one who started finding classes to go to in Austin and that's when I started getting immersed in art and getting more serious about actually selling art. At one point, there were ten of us painting together in Austin. We had arranged to have this space every other week. The great Wimberley artist Jerry Seagle managed us to keep us quiet to get work done. We all did some of our best work there. We rented an old building behind a barbeque place in south Austin that was a VFW hall. They let the Boy Scouts use it one week, and we got to use it the next week, five days in a row. We worked together in that space for years.

My friends talked me into entering an art show in Austin. I entered a watercolor I had done. A friend of ours had her mother come sit for a few of us. I did a watercolor of her and it won an honorable mention, and a juror actually did a critique of the work in the show. When he came to my painting, he said whoever did this knew this person really well. I didn't know her at all. He said you can just see that she's calling you in with her hand because that's the focal point. But she's not finding the words because there's no mouth. And I thought dang I forgot to paint her mouth. I was so embarrassed. Then he finally said whose work is this? You knew her really well, right? I said, no I just met her, but actually she was trying to tell us her children's names, but she couldn't remember them because she has Alzheimer's. So I captured Alzheimer's without realizing it. That's when I realized that I don't need to plan ahead; I just need to feel and do and let other people tell me what works and what doesn't. So that's what I always do now.

After the flood all the art supplies I had left was just a pen and paper. I just drew and drew and drew. I still do that every night. I did a series of bird watchers. I had found a feather. I was going to do an abstract. I always start out with a non-objective abstract. And then it turns into something because I like some part of it. This piece turned into circles that turned into eyes. Then more circles turned into a bird. I did a whole series with that idea. From that series I got a show in New York. That was exciting. Galleries seem to find me. They see something and like it. That show was in a gallery in Chelsea for six months.

Having studio space is huge for me. I started on my kitchen counter. I'd do watercolor on my kitchen counter and my drawing studio is here on my couch. Studio space can be anything. For me, what I needed was just a window and floor space so I could set up a table. I mainly paint flat. I prefer that. So I needed table space. Before that, my office and studio were kind of together and they needed to be separate. I need to be able to go into my left brain when I go into my studio and then have a separate space for my right brain when I work in real estate.

My inspiration? I just start scribbling. For some of the drawings I'm dripping ink and taking two sheets of paper, pressing them together and making ink blots. Then I just start drawing into them. I did a series that started with needing a drawing really quickly. I had a show coming up. I started scribbling up in the corner. The scribble turned into hair, and then her face came about, the eye came around and the scribbles turned into a big ball of yarn with another face in it screaming. Then over in that corner was some dark space and then a bird emerged pulling on the string. That became my series "Unraveling of Self." I could have never thought of that in advance.

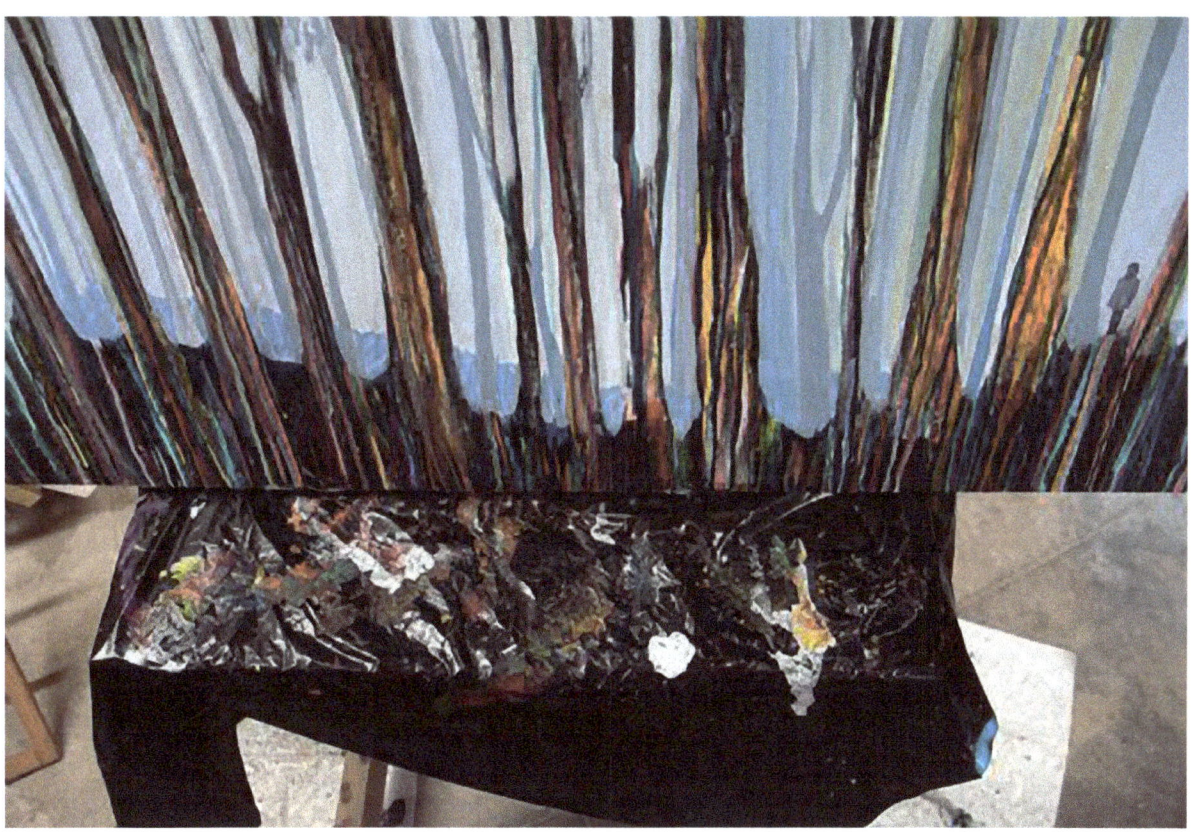

In Pam Lamoureux's studio

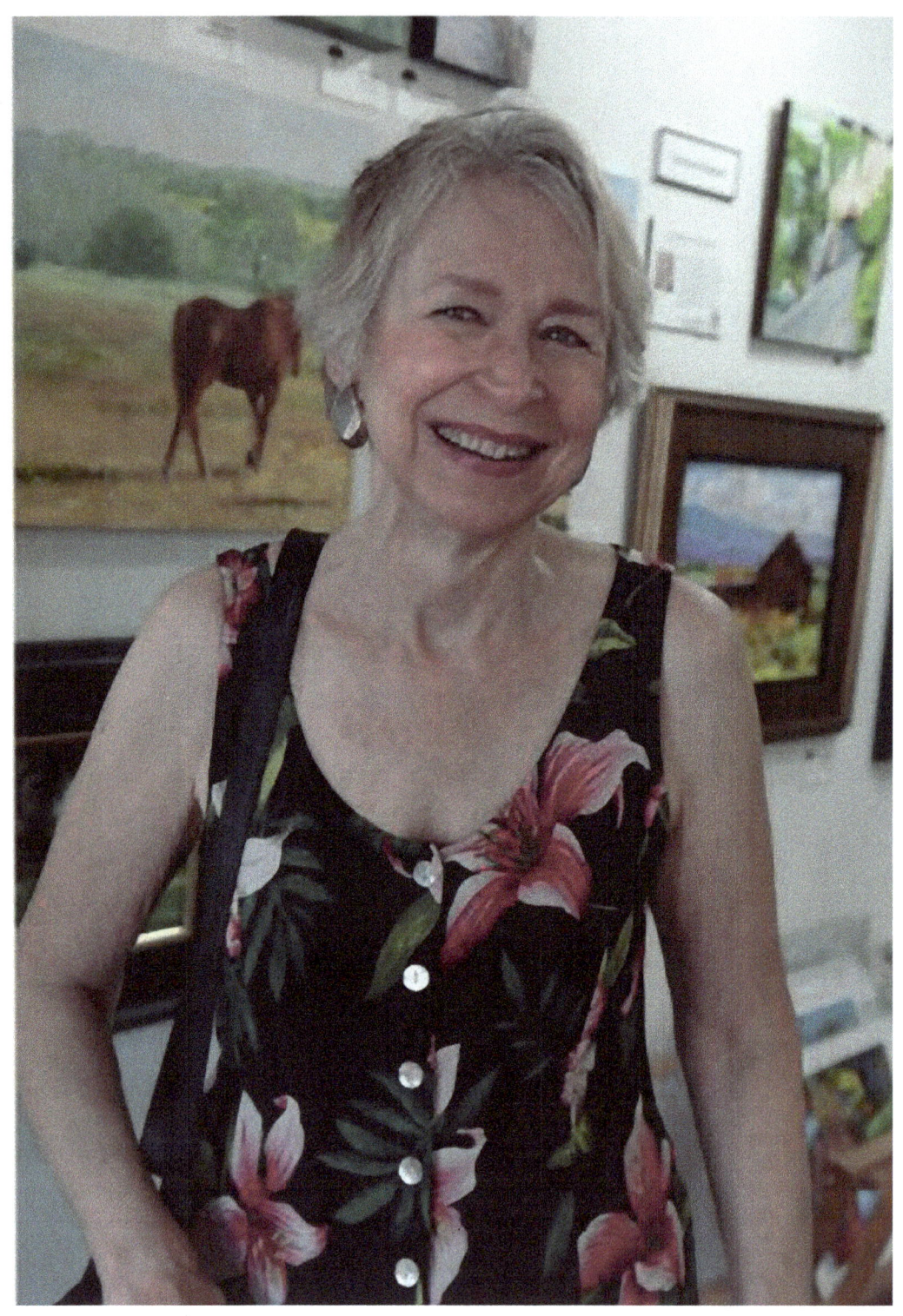

Connie Schaertl

Connie Schaertl

My interest in art and particularly in figurative art, I think goes back to my grandfather reading me the funny papers and me having the visuals to go with what he was reading to me.

When I started reading myself, I always had books that had illustrations in them. I loved the illustrations. So illustration was always important to me.

My grandparents lived in Seneca Falls, New York. You know, "It's a Wonderful Life." It was really a special place. My father was in the Air Force, so we moved all over the place. I think maybe the fact that we moved so much is what drove me to read as much as I do. And that goes to my influences with my art. I read a lot, and it's mostly novels. I listen to audio books when I paint. I'm inspired by things that trigger stories. I see something that will trigger the shape of the story, and I especially like it if it's slightly humorous. There is no one narrative. It feels like life is too full of narratives to just stick to one. I have done a lot of art with a restaurant or bar theme. That's not necessarily about the story, that's about enjoying being in restaurants. It seems that some of the best times I've had, especially in the last twenty years, have been with family or friends in restaurants. It's that kind of shared experience that draws me to restaurant themes.

My first art cheerleader was my middle school art teacher. She actually bought me my first art supplies. My parents didn't really think that art was of any value, my father especially. So that teacher was a good cheerleader for me, and I ended up going to school to be an art teacher in Buffalo, New York. I wanted to be an artist, but my father insisted I had to do something to make some money. I resented it at the time, but I understand now. You want your kids to be able to support themselves. I was not cut out to be an art teacher, though; the kids scared me. I've never been able to talk about the structures of art, the academics of art. It's from my gut that I paint. It's hard to tell somebody how I do what I do. So being an art teacher was never really something I wanted to do.

I dropped out of college because I got pregnant. I gave the baby up for adoption and back then that was the end of the contact between mother and child. But now, fifty years later, my son has shown up again in my life. In February this year he tracked me down through my brother's and my cousin's DNA. I'd given up on ever finding him. He's wonderful. He calls me at least once a week. He lives in Montreal with his partner of thirty years and they're both so great.

When I decided that I was going to go into art as a means to make money, I went into commercial art. I did illustration and fashion illustration. And then I worked for a publishing company that had a weekly newspaper and several quarterly magazines, and I got to be the art director for some of those magazines and do some of the illustrations for the stories.

I probably started thinking of myself as an artist just a few years ago. I always felt like I couldn't really claim to be an artist because I didn't really feel like I was creating something new. At some point I realized yes, I'm not just copying what I see, I am creating. I am an artist. I don't claim to be a great artist, but I am an artist. One of the first restaurant paintings I did, "Sweet Closing Time," was a moment when I thought I had become an artist. I was telling a story. That's still one of my favorite paintings.

I was concerned about setting up a studio space to capture the light. It was a room that already existed in my house. It had cathedral ceilings and was a fairly large room. I originally had my computer in there so I could see my reference photographs and paint. But everything has been changing over the years, and the space has gotten incredibly congested with stuff. I have an awful lot of duds in there. Some that I may be able to save and others that may need to go on the burn pile. That studio is the place where I reconsider as well as paint new things. You can see if a painting is just not working. Sometimes you can't figure out exactly what is going wrong. It's just not there sometimes. But you can go back months or maybe years later and see exactly what the problem is and fix it. Sometimes it just takes half an hour, or sometimes you redo the whole damn thing.

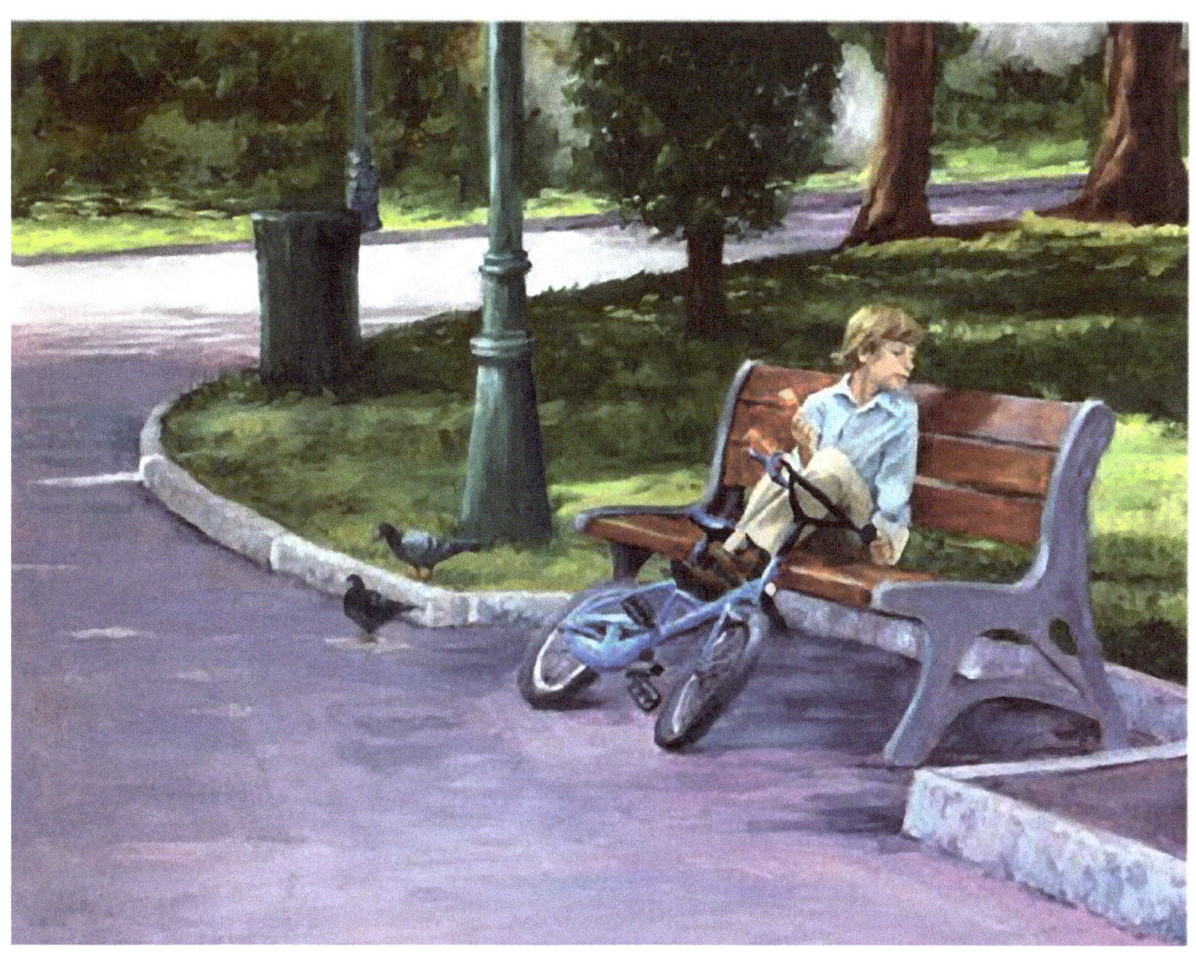

"White Male Suspect with Possibly Stolen Bike, Loitering in Park, Ignoring Pigeons"
14 x 18" oil on cradled wood panel
Connie Schaertl

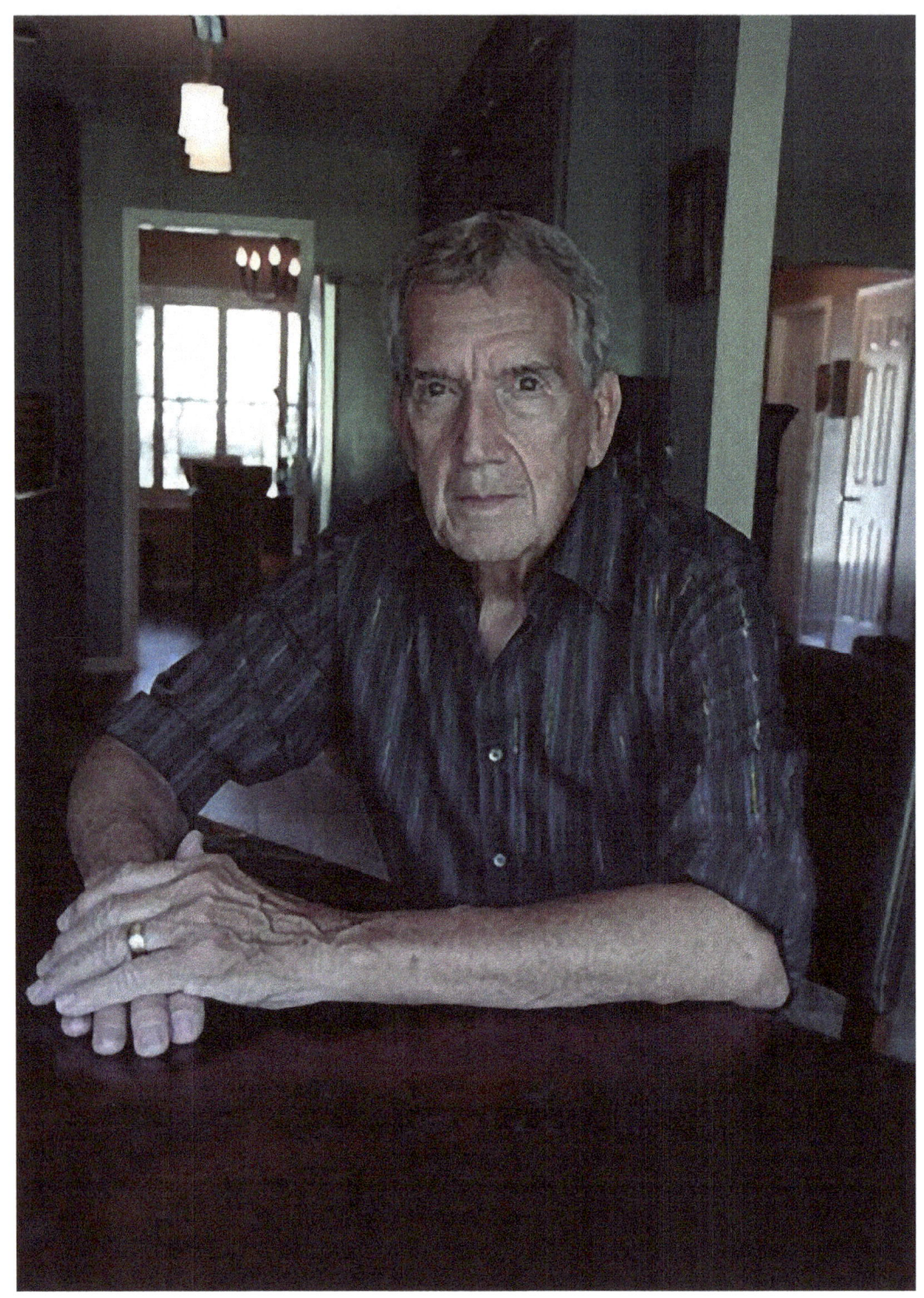

Danny Jones

Danny Jones

I don't have a studio. I sit right here on the couch and paint. I need a quiet place. I have to have something that I can glance up at from time to time, so I'll turn on a crime show or something like that - something you don't have to watch intently. Watercolor is real easy. I can just lay it flat right on that coffee table. Oil paint, I have to have up on an easel. Lynn (my wife) puts all kinds of stuff under it so I won't get paint everywhere. It'll take me a few days to complete something. I've painted more since we've moved to Wimberley than I did for years and years. Wimberley, Texas inspires me. The Wimberley Valley Art League definitely inspires me to get things ready for the next show. I also do a lot of teaching. I've done workshops in watercolor and sculpture. I love doing that sculpture portrait workshop. The students in my workshops are mostly retired people, but not all.

I did a series of paintings in San Miguel de Allende that have hidden faces. The backgrounds are abstract and there's a realistic piece in the middle. The last thing I do is I hide all these faces in the background. I did this "Day of the Dead" series. This is where people visit the graves and remember their loved ones. So these little hidden faces all represent people that were in that person's life. This textured part on the canvas is plaster. That's the first thing I do, put plaster in places on the canvas and then cover it in house paint to hold it on. From there I do the realistic part and then the last thing I do is the faces.

I first went to San Miguel in the 1960s. It was a different place altogether than it is today. That was before most Americans had discovered it. I attended the art school there. It was the first time Lynn had ever been out of the U.S. and nearly the first time she had ever been out of Arkansas or Texas. I talked her into going to San Miguel. We took our two young kids and had hotel reservations for two nights. I said let's go down there and if you don't like it we'll come right back. We drove down and ended staying two months. Our daughter was five and our son ten. It was great; both our kids learned to speak Spanish there.

We took a side trip to Guanajuato, Mexico. We went there to see the mummies. There's something in the soil that mummifies people. And in Mexico when you're buried, you have to rent the space where you're buried. And if the family stops paying the rent, they dig you up and scatter your bones around the back of the cemetery. So you see all these human bones in the back of the cemeteries all the time. So when they were digging up these people in Guanajuato, they discovered this about the soil: that it mummifies you. And they're exactly like they were, other than body fluids. So they're really creepy. You go down this spiral staircase into this tunnel in the ground with real dim lighting. And all the mummies are just propped up against the walls. People were picking off skin for souvenirs. So they have put them behind glass now.

The first summer we were retired we worked in Yellowstone National Park. I was a tour guide, driving one of those big Yellowstone buses. I had to study very hard to learn all about it. But when the historian rode my bus to see how well I did, he said, oh, everybody loved your trip, but he graded me down for *embellishing*. We stayed nearly four months in Yellowstone and lived in a dorm. Lynn loved it because she didn't have to cook for four months. We'd have three-day weekends and we'd go all over the place up in that area. Devil's Tower was one place. I didn't realize until we went there that it's actually the center of a volcano that had erupted. The lava came up and then cooled down and all the land around it eroded away and left the core of the volcano standing like a tower.

I was born in Graham Chapel, Texas. Well, I was born in Slaton, but my parents lived in Graham Chapel which is a few miles out of Post, Texas. The closest school was in Post, and they didn't even have an art dept at all, not in the elementary, middle school or high school. I knew I could draw, but I thought if I majored in art in college, I'd be too far behind. I knew I wanted to teach. I was real good in math so I started off as a math major. I was going to be a math teacher. I went to West Texas State University in Canyon, Texas. In my sophomore year I took an art class just for the heck of it. The teacher said, what the hell you are you doing as a math major. Ms. McNeely was the art teacher who said that. So she convinced me to switch majors. I really was glad I did because I loved teaching art. I actually taught math one year at La Vega High School in Waco, Texas. I was Teacher of the Year there that one year I taught math. I had gotten involved with the senior play helping them get ready, because they didn't have a drama teacher. I didn't know much about it, but I kind of knew what would look good on the stage. The students actually made up the play and it was real good. I'm sure all the seniors talked everybody into voting for me for Teacher of the Year.

I think I really decided I was an artist in first grade. That was the first year you could go to school back then; they didn't have kindergarten. The teacher asked me if I would do a Christmas scene on the blackboard. She must have seen that I was good at drawing. I did some kind of Christmas scene on the blackboard with colored chalk. From then on, I did all kinds of art things in the Post schools. People knew I could do art, so they'd call me to create something. I should have trusted my abilities and started off as an art major in college.

I taught art for thirty-five years. The first few years I taught, I'd go back-and-forth between the junior high and high school. Then I started teaching just high school. Many of my years of teaching were at Mansfield High School. When I started, I was the only art teacher and Mansfield was growing like crazy. After a few years they were in need of a second high school but voters didn't approve a bond to build one. The year I retired we had nearly six thousand kids in that one high school. We had ten art teachers and I was head of the art department. They were really very supportive of me and my art program. In fact, I have a school named after me: Danny Jones Middle School in Mansfield. Now there are six high schools in Mansfield.

I loved teaching. It was so much fun. I still keep in contact with lots of my former students and I go back for reunions. I've got quite a few former students who are art teachers and college professors. One is an artist in New York City and is doing really well there. Who knows, he may be the next famous breakout artist. I also have a lot of architects that are former students. I hope all the students I've had appreciate art. Whether they do it as a profession or not, I hope they're glad they took art and enjoyed it. I've always said I can teach anybody to draw and I can. When people say "I can't do art," I say it's teachable or there wouldn't be art schools. It's really important for people to realize that. I've had lot of students that were amazing in photography that couldn't draw a lick until I taught them. They might be incredible on a pottery wheel, so who cares if they can't draw very well.

In 1988 I was introduced to Wimberley because the Superintendent of schools in Mansfield became the Superintendent in Wimberley. He asked if I would be interested in coming down to Wimberley and being an art teacher. My son was going into his freshman year in high school and my daughter was in elementary, so it was a perfect time if we wanted to move. We came down and really fell in love with the place and were ready to move. I said my wife needs an elementary teaching job. He said we have this one elementary teacher we're pretty positive she's leaving. Her husband got a job somewhere else and your wife can have that job. We were ready to pack and move to Wimberley. My Principal, Vernon Newsom, then got a call asking him to come to be the Assistant Superintendent in Wimberley, and his wife was an elementary teacher, so she got Lynn's job. So we couldn't move. In 2014 both our kids were living in Austin and they kept pushing us to move down. Mansfield had grown so much, our friends had gone off different places, so we decided to move to Austin. We found we couldn't afford to live in Austin and we started looking at Wimberley again and found this house. We are now so very glad we moved to wonderful Wimberley!

Some part of art is for anybody. Sometimes creativity gets stifled. For instance, give a very young child some paints or crayons and ask them to create a tree. Most of time kids can create these amazing trees that are fascinating to look at. Later when they get into school they may get a handout with a tree to color. They may think: this is what a tree is supposed to look like, which may affect their creativity. So they may change their whole idea away from something that had been much more creative to begin with.

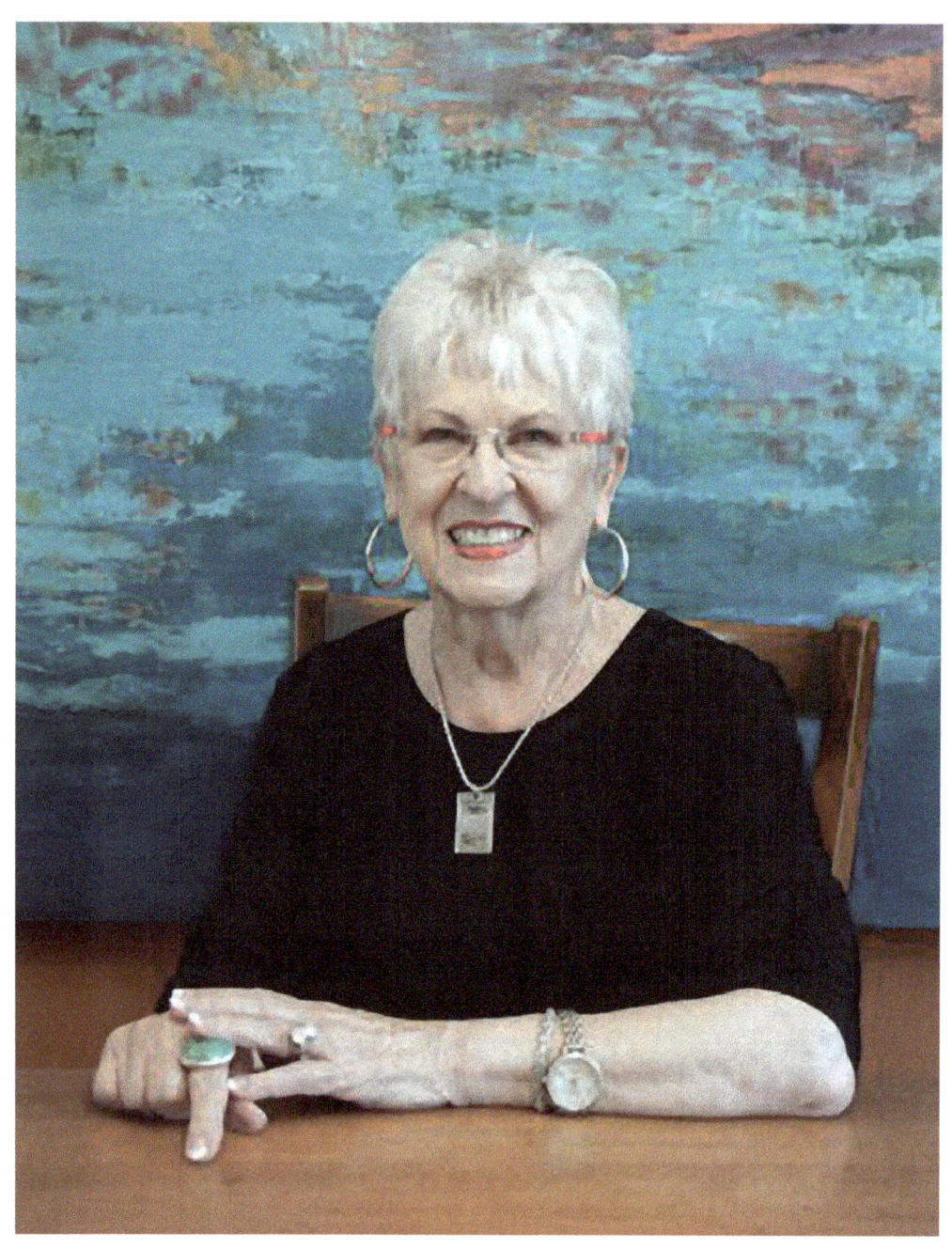

Maxine Price

Maxine Price

My first memory of art was from kindergarten, when I drew a face and the teacher put it up on the bulletin board. I liked that, because I was always really shy. I've drawn all my life since then. All I really ever wanted to do was be an artist.

My Dad was in the military, so I went to four different high schools in four different states. The last one was in Fairfax, Virginia. At the time, my Dad was stationed at the Pentagon. I had a boyfriend, so I wanted to stay in Virginia, but my Dad said I could go to college anywhere I wanted to, as long as it was in Texas. That did not make me happy. I had never seen the University of Texas campus, but we came in August and found a room and it didn't take me long to fall in love with it.

I first became a successful portrait artist. A lot of my portraits hang on the campus of the University of Texas. I did well at it, but eventually I got tired of it. I got tired of dealing with some people's ideas of what they looked like. I could tell you some stories about that! So at some point I started thinking about changing what I was doing. I wanted to paint from my imagination, and that's what I've done. I think I've been successful at that, too. I think everything I've done as an artist has led to the next thing. It was very difficult to change from being a realistic, detailed portrait artist to become an abstract painter. It took a while.

I have a degree in art, but I also took a lot of workshops from well-known artists. The one who really got me started was Maxine Masterfield, out of Florida. She just got bottles and squirted inks all over everything and laid papers over them. It was just the wildest thing I ever saw. I played with that for a long time. It was very freeing in so many ways. I've gotten feedback and ideas from a number of different artists. I've learned a lot from a lot of different teachers. Artists are just the most sharing people, which I think is wonderful. I've had so many mentors and muses throughout my years as an artist.

I recently found a book where I had written down my goals when we first moved here to Wimberley in 1998. I found one goal that was to do juried outdoor booth shows to get people's reactions to my work, because I was all over the place. I did landscapes, I did poured inks, I did acrylics and finally got down to oils and a palate knife. I found another one of my goals from that book was to get into galleries. It's fun to go back and see goals you've written and see that you accomplished them. I've been very lucky getting in some of the galleries. Some of it was just pure luck. One in Houston was a little bitty gallery. A friend from Austin was doing a show there and asked if I would come do the show with him. I did and I'm still there. It has doubled and tripled in size and I'm still with them. It's one of the top galleries in Houston now. The same kind of thing happened in Austin. I was in a tiny gallery right off

South Congress street with a couple of other artists. We sold to people from all over the world. When that gallery closed, a guy down the street at another gallery said he knew my work and wanted me to show there. Now that gallery has grown and doubled. Some galleries have even found me on my website. So it's been really nice. I've not had to go out knocking on doors.

I like a challenge. In all of my abstract work, I've worked in series. I'll work with a series until I feel like I've exhausted all my ideas in that particular series. I did one series where I started with a few little pieces, while listening to Eric Clapton jazz music from his *Unplugged* album. I painted to the rhythm of the music with a palette knife. I just got intrigued with that, and then I did a bigger one and then a bigger one. Frank, my husband, came out to the studio one day and I was doing a 4'x4' piece. He said, Max, what are you doing? You don't even know if these will sell. I said, I don't care. I'm having so much fun! I didn't stop until I felt I had done all I wanted to do with that series. Later I got a commission from a man who called me from Colorado. He was very specific about what he wanted his painting to look like, down to the colors and almost down to the number of leaves he wanted on the trees. He found out about my Eric Clapton series, and asked me what kind of music I would listen to when I painted his piece. I asked what he wanted me to listen to, and he said, George Winston. I had never heard of George Winston, but I bought the album, and that's what I painted to!

I've just started a whole new series about dreams and poems. There's a drawing I did around twenty-five years ago about my alligator dream. I did some research recently on what it means to dream about an alligator. I found out if an alligator is attacking you, you need to watch your back. If you're taming the alligator (which I was) it means that you're on the road to something good, and positive things will come pouring your way and you won't be able to embrace all of them. Many opportunities and chances will be shown to you and your only assignment is to choose the right ones for you, and make sure you use this time in your life to get back in control of things and improve the overall quality of your life. The strange thing to me is, I had this dream at the time I was changing from being a portrait artist to working from my imagination. So that's part of why I started this series of dreams and poems. I'm not a poet, but I'm really enjoying it.

I actually have more ideas than I can possibly do. I'm always putting more ideas in the back of my head. They just stay back there and kind of percolate. Then, one will come forward and I'll think I need to do that now. I get ideas everywhere I go. I sometimes stop and photograph the pavement and think that would make a great abstract. I'm always looking at design. I'm inspired by so many things. I'm inspired by weathered and rusted poles. Even the foil liner of a to-go box can inspire me. A few days ago, I had Frank hold up a pan that he had used while he was grilling. There was grease running in it. It was a perfect design, so I took a picture with my cell phone. I'll use that someday. All of these ideas will become paintings someday.

Jan Fitzhugh

I never thought of myself as an artist until I moved to Wimberley and found myself surrounded by other artists. Before that, I was working in a very demanding, high-stress career and occasionally dabbling in art in a tiny corner of my kitchen. I never considered calling myself an artist until it was my real job.

While I was working in senior healthcare, I'd sneak away every now and then for a day or two to take an art workshop. I found myself dreaming that someday I'd quit my job and teach those workshops. Selling my work was never in the plan. I took the leap, quit my job and jumped into art full time. I have no regrets. I'm grateful now to wake up every morning and immerse myself in the world of art.

I have a beautiful studio behind my home where I work and teach others the same techniques I use. The studio is a peaceful place where worries and problems are checked at the door. Well, there is the occasional soldering disaster that takes place within those walls, but I can always start over on that piece tomorrow and fix it.

I was recently asked: If you could have dinner with any three artists in the world or even beyond in the celestial world who would they be? I knew that I wanted to sit down with Beverly Mangham and Gil Bruvel, because the conversation would be real and rich. It seemed impossible to come up with a third on such short notice. There were too many great artists to choose from. Finally, I knew it would have to be Keith Lo Bue, an artist living in Australia who calls himself a *stuffsmith*. What a great conversation this would be!

I've learned from and am inspired by several well-known jewelry artists. Susan Lenart Kazmer inspires me to remember that the sky has no limit. Richard Salley inspires me to forge-on and keep perfecting my skills. Keith Lo Bue inspires me to think outside the box, make sure whatever I design and build will never fall apart and that glue is NEVER an option! My real inspiration and drive to create, however, came from my wonderful mother. She was an artist and a dreamer. She raised me in a world of art and design and especially one of dreams. For my entire life we spent most of our time together immersed in one creative endeavor or another. Whether it was painting a chair, building a bird cage or designing the interior of a home, hotel or country club, we were creating. We spent our days and nights working on projects together and talking and dreaming about the ones on the horizon. The first piece of jewelry I ever made, I made for her. It's hanging in my closet.

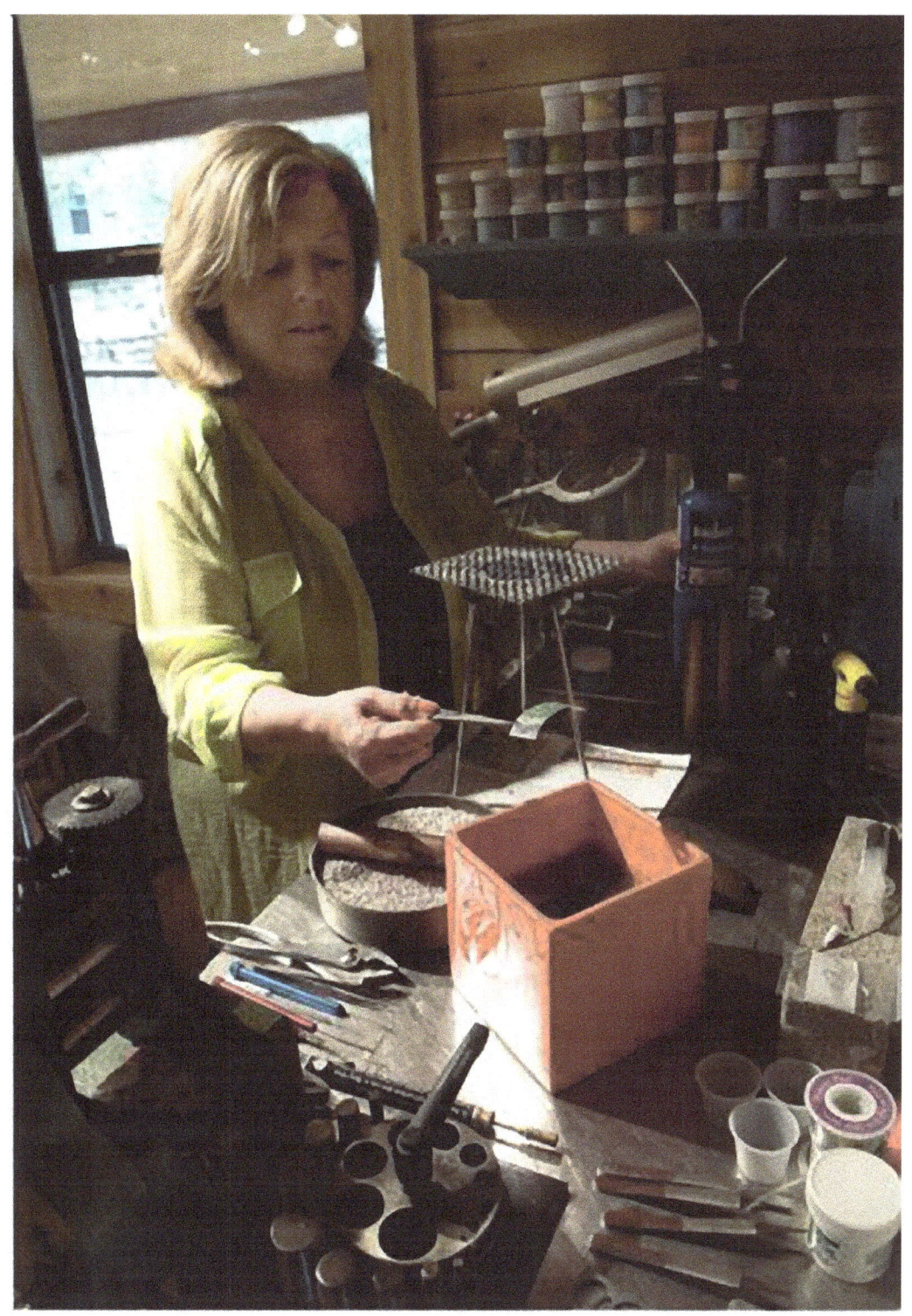

Jan Fitzhugh

Bob Cook

I lusted for a Brownie Hawkeye camera when I was just six years old. I went out and bought my first roll of film and took twelve Pulitzer Prize winning shots with that first single roll of film. But wait there was some technical problem when I opened the camera and exposed every single masterpiece. That was my start in photography.

All my life I was to some degree an art collector and a pretty good photographer. In college I worked summers in a big studio in New York. I met Dan Rubin who was the team photographer for the New York Giants. He hired me to be the assistant photographer for the team. My job was to go to every game and bang away, get every shot I could. Dan would shoot the players for promotional shots, but he couldn't be everywhere. That was my job.

My wife, Zeina and I took our first cruise when we lived in Roanoke, Virginia. We were solar eclipse chasing and this cruise offered the opportunity to see the eclipse. We sailed for days and days. Do you know how big the Pacific Ocean is? It was like being in jail and being forced to eat five meals a day. I was so bored at watching the waves, I went to the ship's library and picked up a book called *Drawing on the Right Side of the Brain* by Dr. Betty Edwards. I studied and did pencil drawings for the rest of the cruise. I just did what she said and finished some pretty good drawings.

When I got home, I took a workshop with Brian Bomeisler, Dr. Edwards' son and began to work some color into my drawings. Now I work in pretty much every medium. I've had limited college training in art at Texas State University, but I've benefited more by being in a community of artists in the Texas Hill Country and by having studied with numerous instructors in workshops. That's where you pick up all the tips and you benefit from critique. In photography workshops you pick up the nerd tricks.

There is an age-old art war between painters and photographers. The photographers complain that they don't win the awards and they aren't typically rolling in the money of the lucrative field of fine art. The painters complain that photographers push a button and make as many prints of a photograph as they want. I do both and I can tell you the only painters who suffer are those who paint plein air. Photographers buy gasoline, drive for nine hours to Big Bend in west Texas, sleep in a lumpy bed in a junk motel, get up before daylight to go out in the freezing cold and hope for a sunrise. Painters relax in their studio, make languid brush strokes and are fed grapes by their spouse.

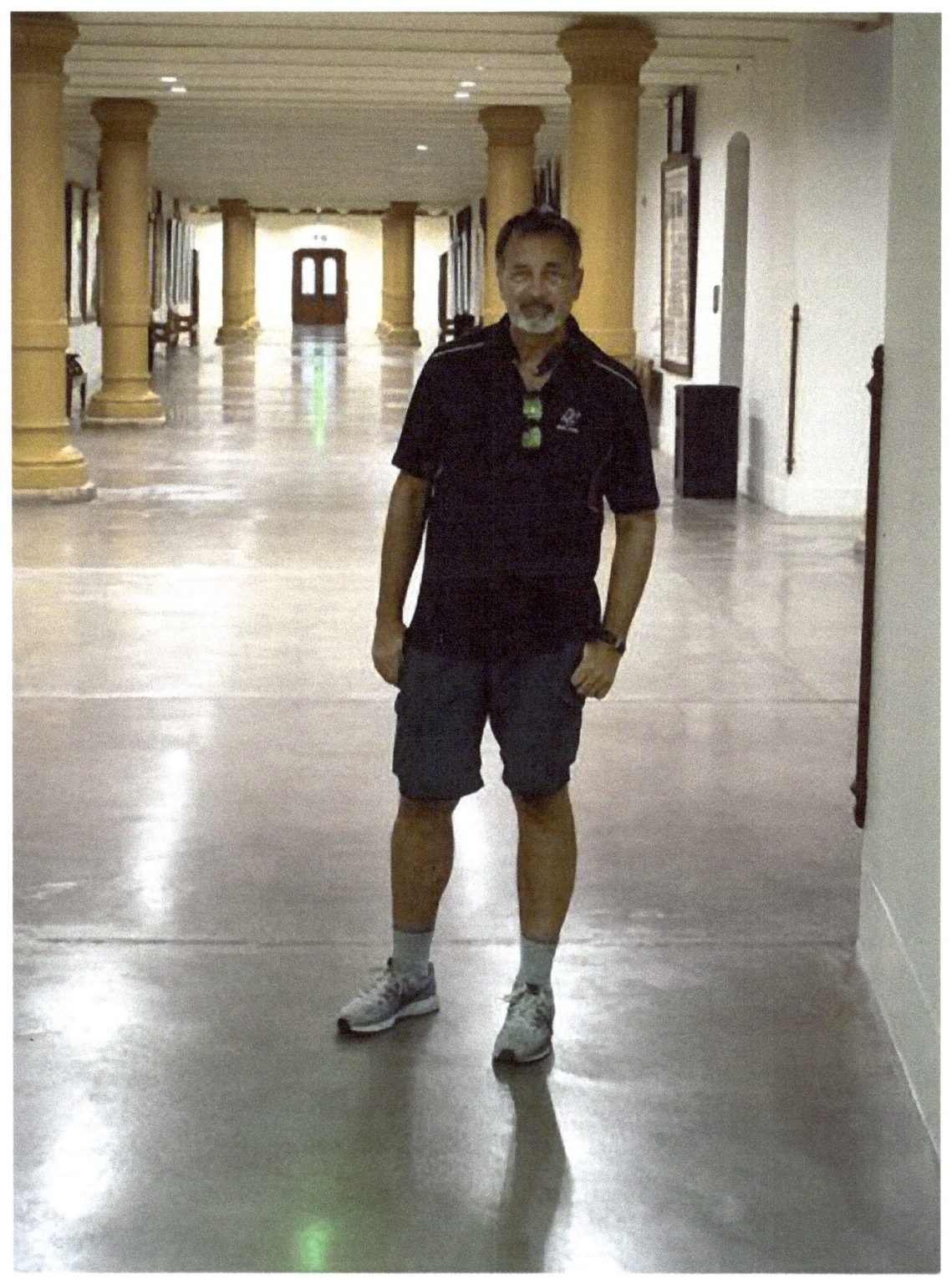

Bob Cook

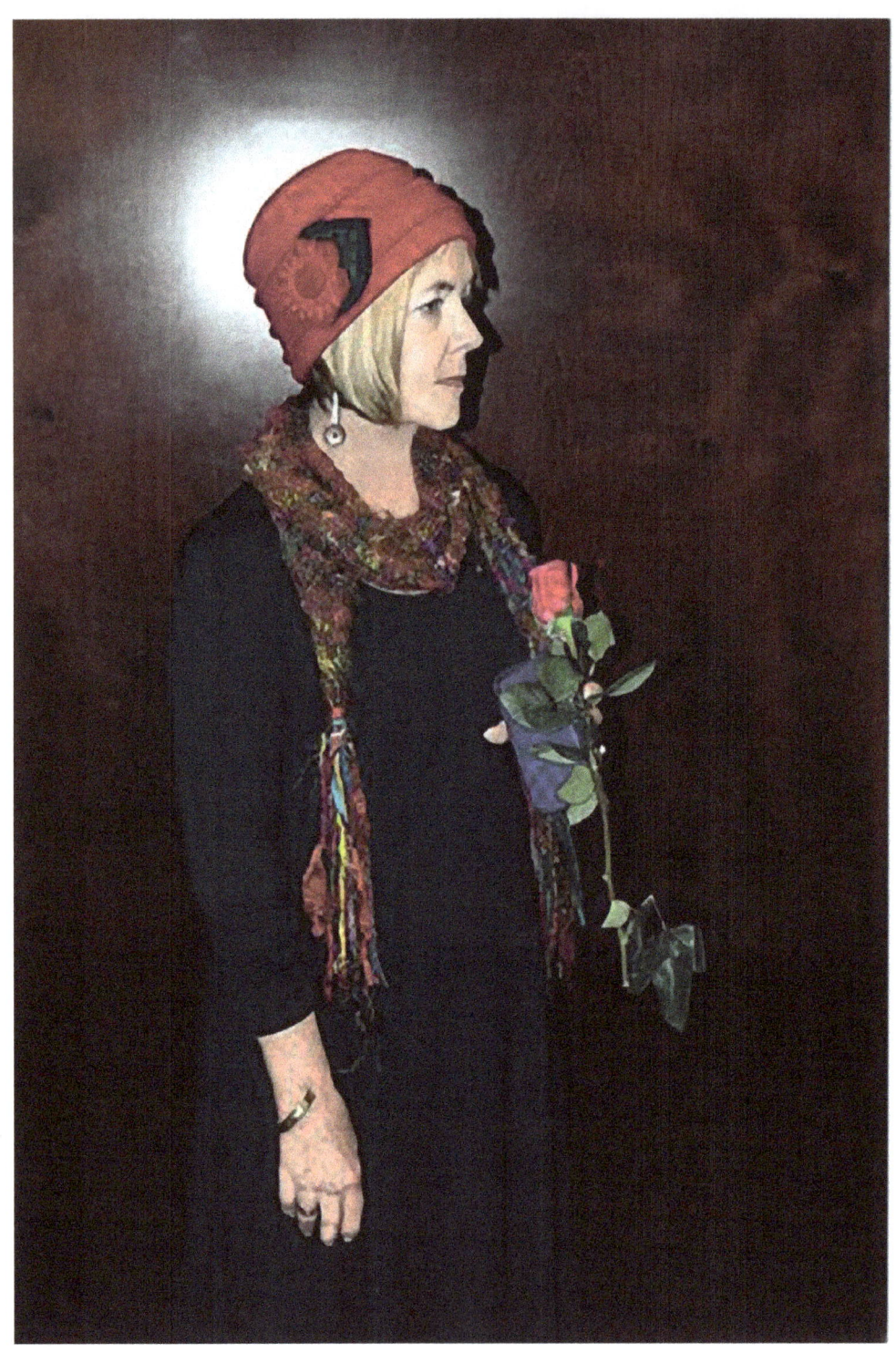

Martha Gibson

Martha Gibson

I have a very clear memory of the moment I first knew I wanted to be an artist. My aunt, Burmah Burris, my father's sister, was an illustrator who lived in New York. On holidays she would come home to Mississippi to stay with her parents. We would be there also. One time, when I was probably eight or nine years old, she was in the bedroom and she had her drawing board in front of her and she was drawing. She was working on her illustration work from New York and I thought that's what I want to do. I want to be an artist. From that moment on I just knew it.

I guess I was probably in high school when I really began to consider myself an artist. I had a really good high school art teacher. She was good, not only with studio art, but also art history which I think was really important. I can't remember if we ever had a discussion about my future in art, but I majored in art in college, so we probably did. That was a long time ago, but I know she changed my whole perspective of art.

When I was working as a high school art teacher, I didn't really have time to be serious about my artwork. I'd say that when I retired from teaching, my artwork became more serious. When I first came to Wimberley, Texas I got introduced to a lot of other artists that inspired me. I was painting landscapes just like everybody else and I realized that wasn't for me. So that's when I got into mixed media and rediscovered image transfer, which is a process I use for a lot of my work.

Choosing the subject matter for my art is usually pretty random. Sometimes I have an idea and I go looking for it, but most of the time I see an object or a scene that I photograph and that kind of sparks the beginning of a piece of artwork. I collect images and assemblage materials and eventually they come together. That sometimes takes a while. It may be years later that I can pull those things together to make a piece of art. I think that artwork needs to tell a story, otherwise it's just decorative. So I try to tell a story with my paintings and my mixed media work. I want the person looking at it to want to know more about what's going on. Sometimes I finish a piece and I don't want to let it go. If I fall in love with it, it just grabs me and I know I can't let it go, so it stays in my house. I still like to show it, but if it's a favorite I don't sell it.

My art mentors would include my aunt Burmah who was always very supportive of me. She came to live with us at the end of her life, so we got to spend a lot of time together talking about art. Before that, I used to drive to Mississippi just to spend time with her. Other mentors include my friend George Krause and just so many of my other art friends in Wimberley. I'm also inspired looking at artwork in museums and galleries. I always get really excited and optimistic about what I could do when I go to galleries and museums. Seeing new things and other artwork sparks my creativity.

Trisha McWaters

In my twenties, a friend said to me that my photography was different, or that I had an eye for it and so that's when I started to think differently about my work. I've always credited her for where I've come. I also had a friend named Heather in the 1980s who was a graphic designer and a working artist. Hanging around with her and making art with her, even just learning new words and new techniques from her also really impacted my art. Other artists who have probably influenced my work are Diane Arbus and Jean-Michel Basquiat.

In 1985 I went to the Art Institute of Houston to study photography. That's when I probably started to consider my art real. I realized my work was so different, in that it was abstract. I had some really good instructors that happened to be fine art photographers, not commercial photographers. They really helped me see the fine art component in my work. During school I did portraits and commercial work and other things, but what I was called to do for myself and my own satisfaction were shapes and forms, colors and shadows—rusty things.

I'm not really trying to tell a story with my art. More times than not, it's an intuitive process or a spiritual process. My eye is good enough that I recognize a good solid scene, as far as composition goes, and that draws me to it. But sometimes I might click the shutter and have no idea what the image will later become or what it will mean. Sometimes it becomes clear when I review it on the computer screen, but it might be a year or two later when the image or the meaning is revealed to me. Over the years the subject matter in my work might still be the same, but what I see in the images or the objects or what I bring forth to the viewer has more depth. Oftentimes, it makes a statement about the world or spirit or goodness, or what's not so good, rather than just being an image.

I don't really need anything to spark my creativity today. I don't say that lightly or in a boastful way, but for so many years I was blocked. When photography switched from film to digital, I didn't stay with it. I allowed myself to be intimidated by it, so it took some work for me to break free of that block. I'm not saying I create a piece every day that's solid, that I can hold in my hands or hang on the wall, but almost every day I'll create an image with some words or something like that. My assemblage work almost always starts with a photograph, oftentimes printed on watercolor paper or canvas, so that I can draw, or paint or write on it. I love to have a foundational piece that's a pattern and then build on it from there. The assemblage work requires more thought and more effort and oftentimes more emotion. It usually stems from something that I need to say that might not be something joyful or happy and so that causes a little creative anxiety in me. It might be on my table in progress for several weeks before I finish it.

The series I did about my mom is probably the most important work I've done. It was therapeutic process about some things I was trying to heal between us and our relationship. The process allowed me to work through it completely and heal it for both myself and for her. By that time, she, of course, had already left the planet.

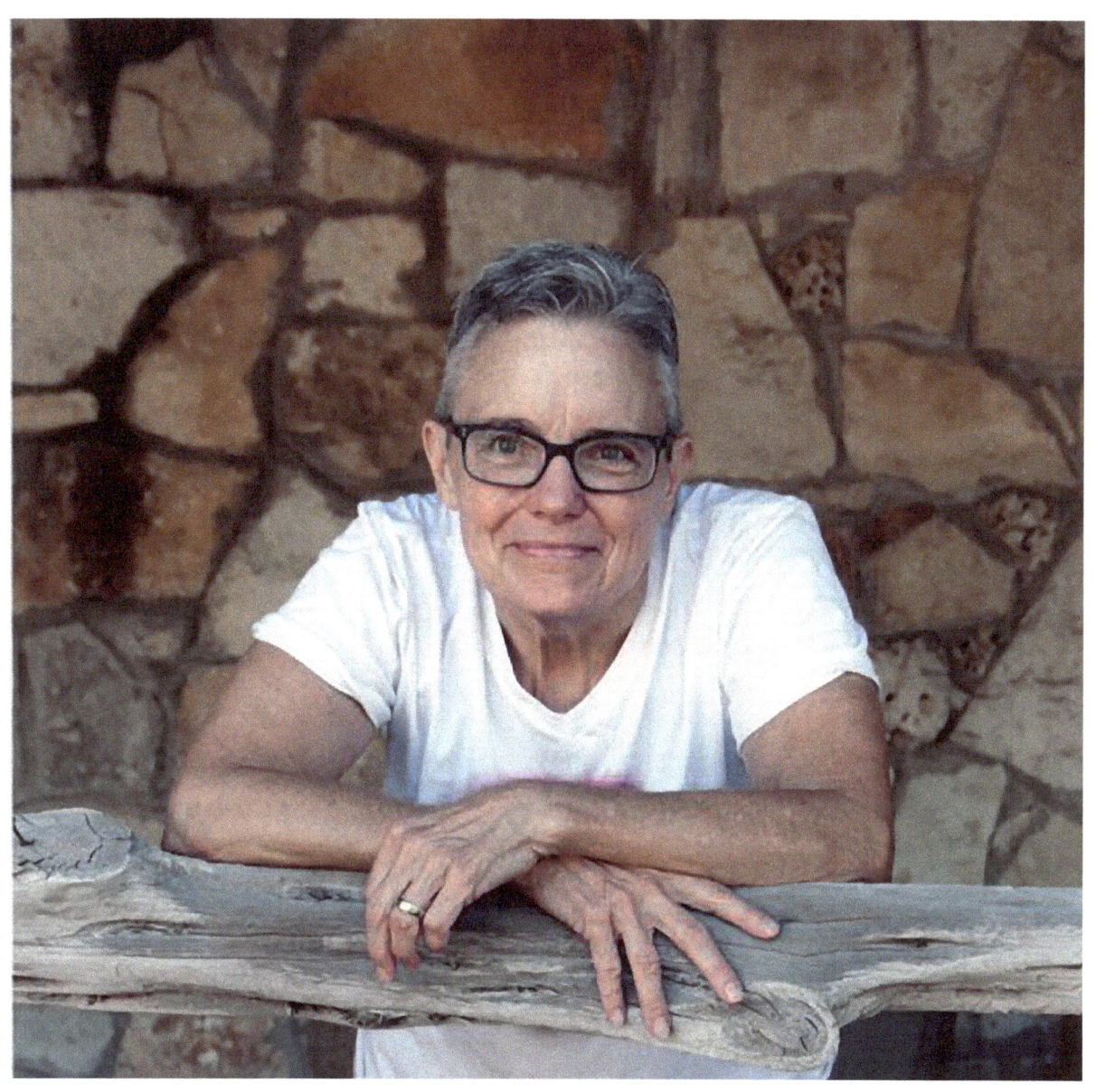

Trisha McWaters

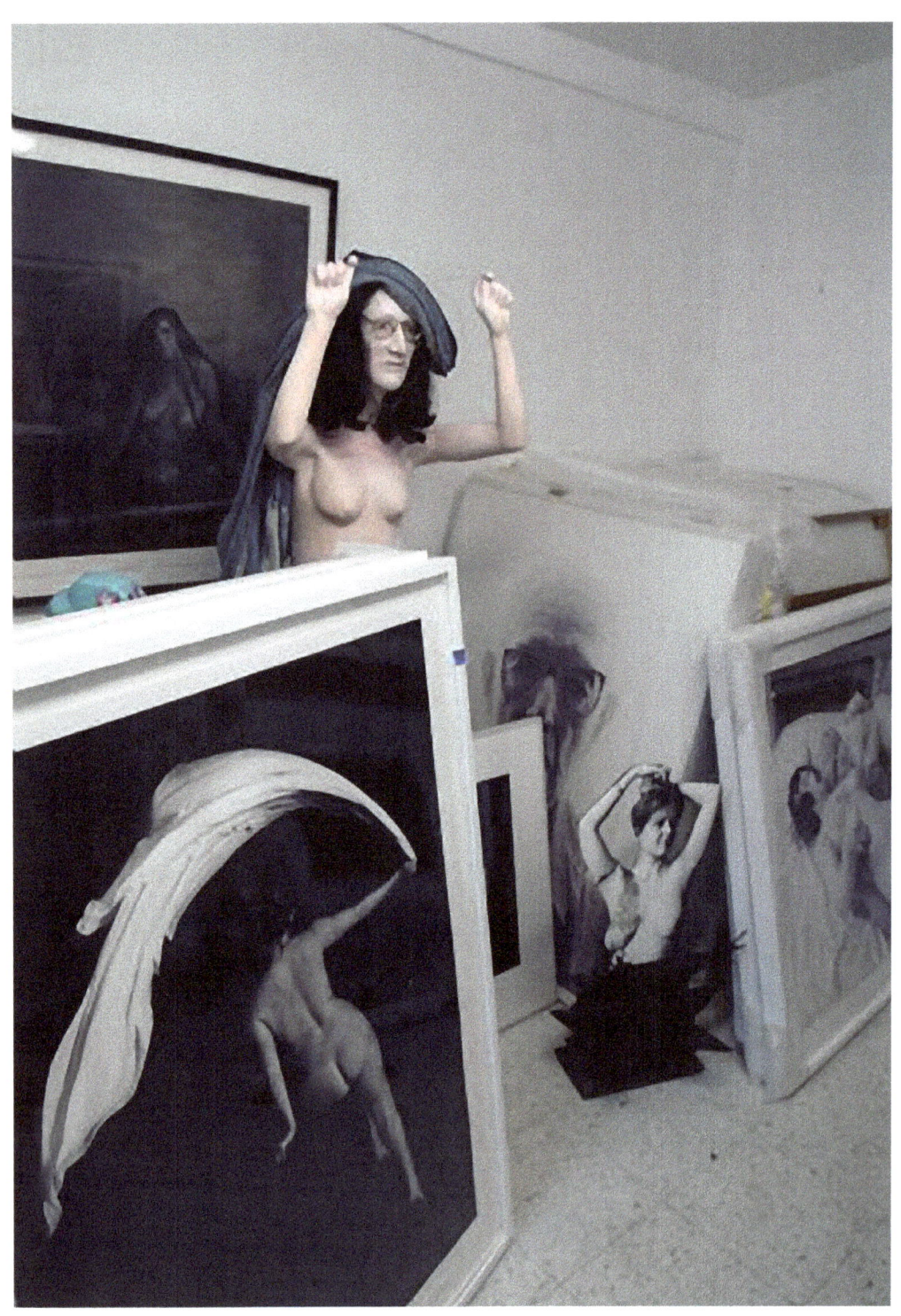

Art by George Krause

The Atelier

A closer look at the artistic environment includes studios and workspaces where art is made. For the most part, these are private places, sanctums that contain physical evidence of inventive activity. Some are tidy enough to concentrate on the project at hand. Others are as jumbled and messy as the unfinished ideas that clutter a creative mind. They contain old brushes and dried paint palettes. There are wood shavings and plaster casts, splatters of wax and hoists and pulleys. In every studio there is evidence of someone's passion. Some workplaces are high-tech marvels and others are just good enough to get the job done. They are more than a collection of tools and ideas. They are the places where art happens.

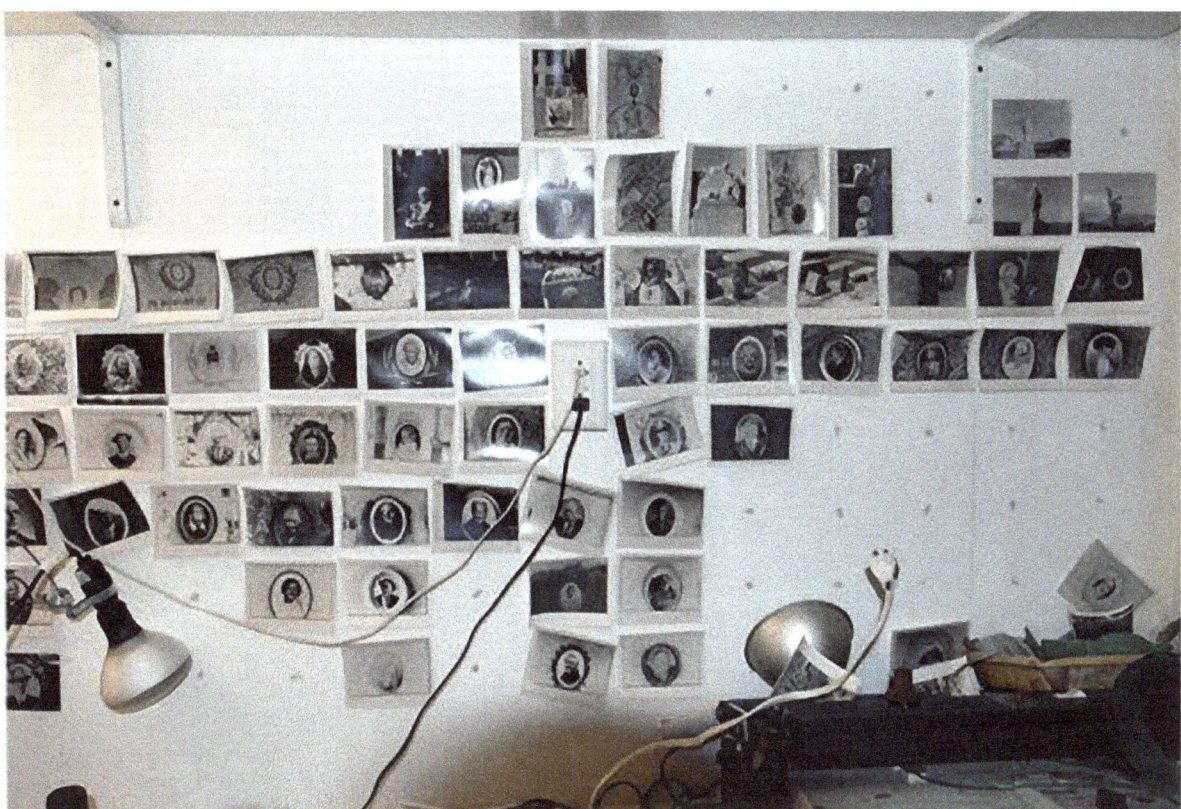

In George Krause's studio

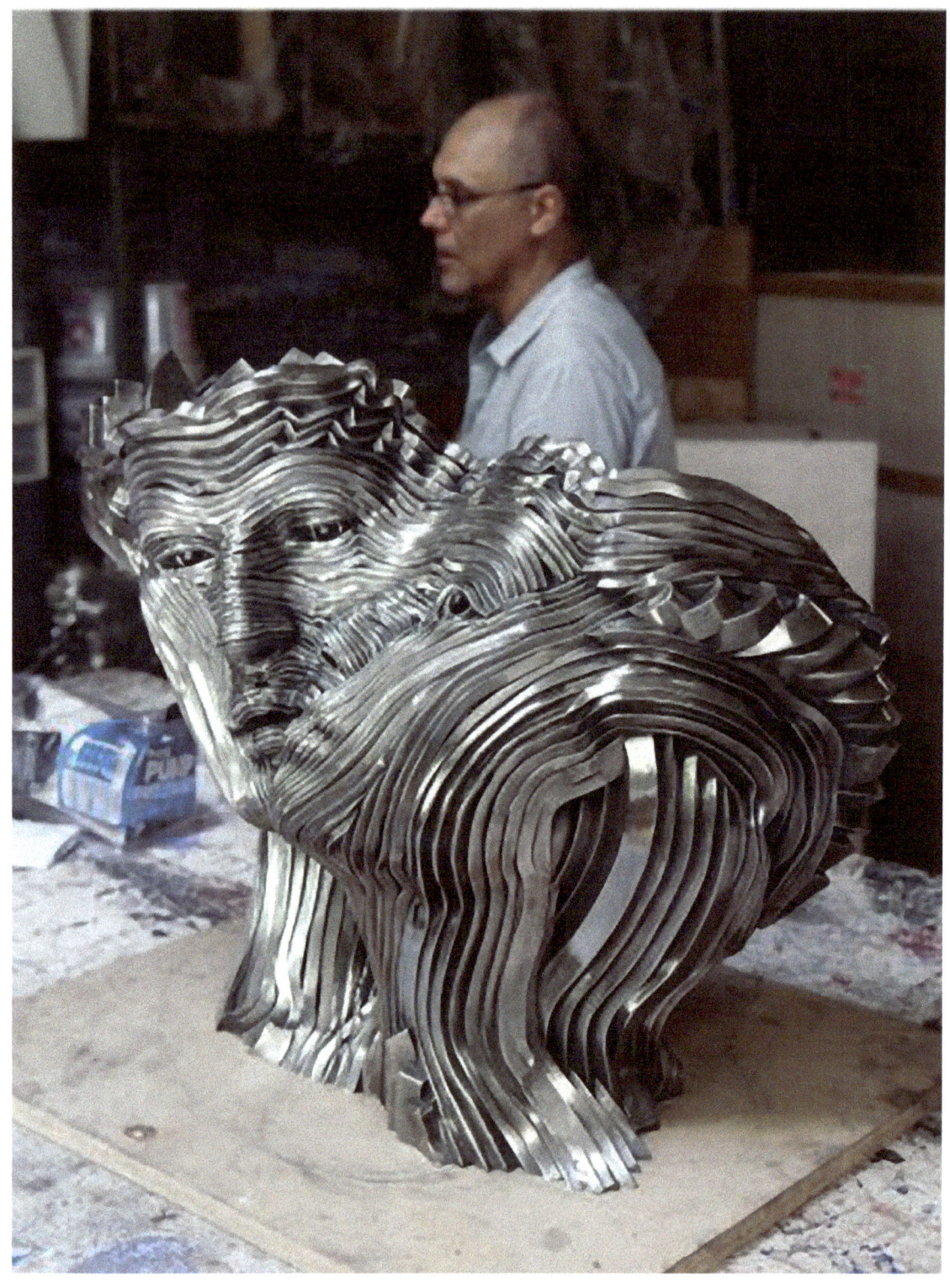

Gil Bruvel's studio

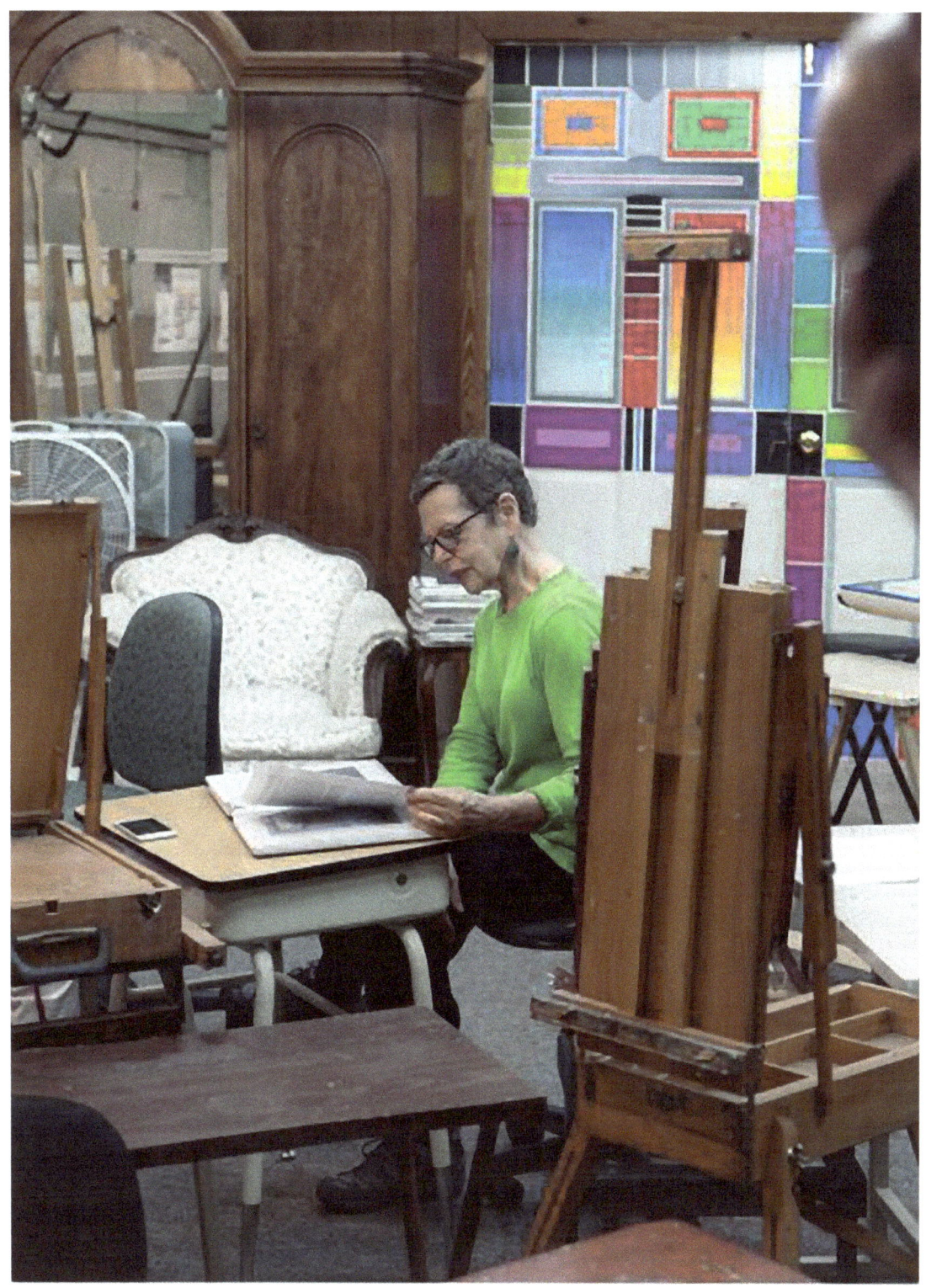

Lilli Pell in her studio

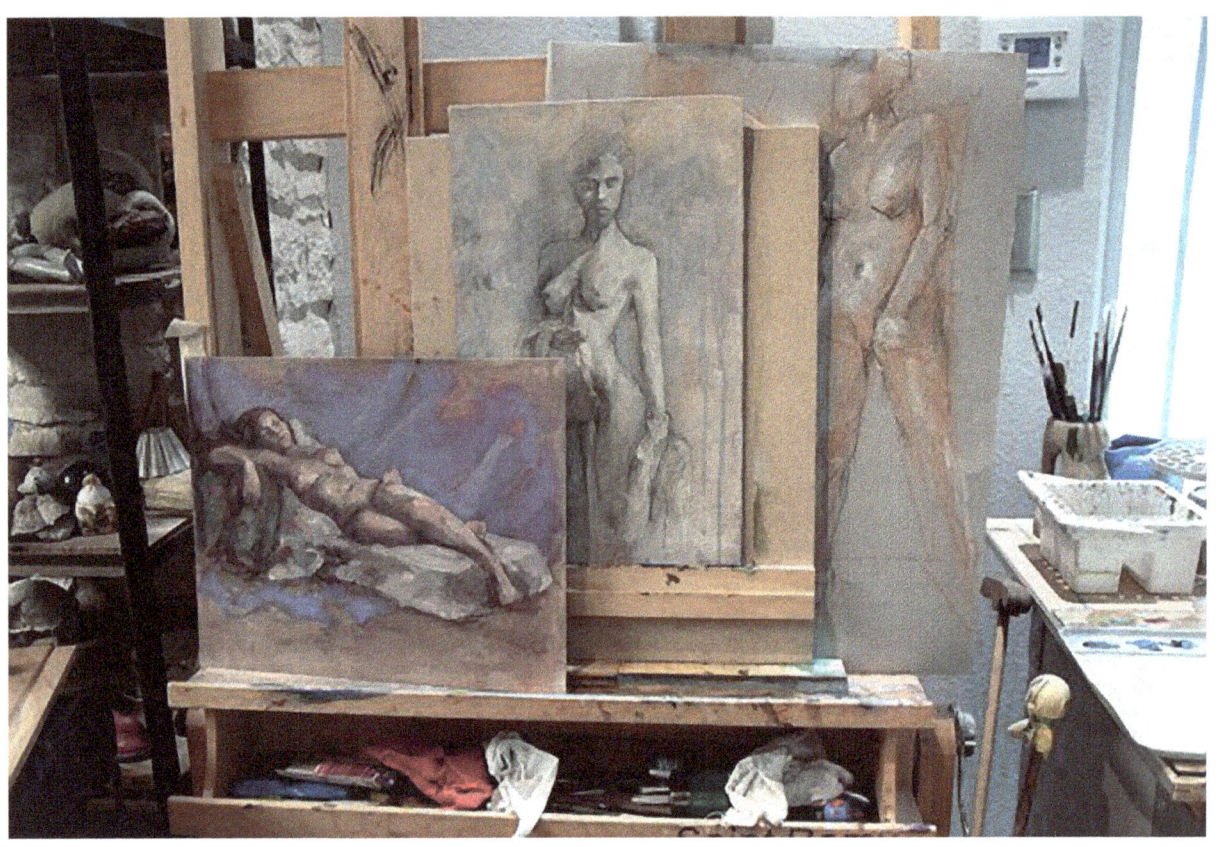

Nudes in Cleve Ragan's studio

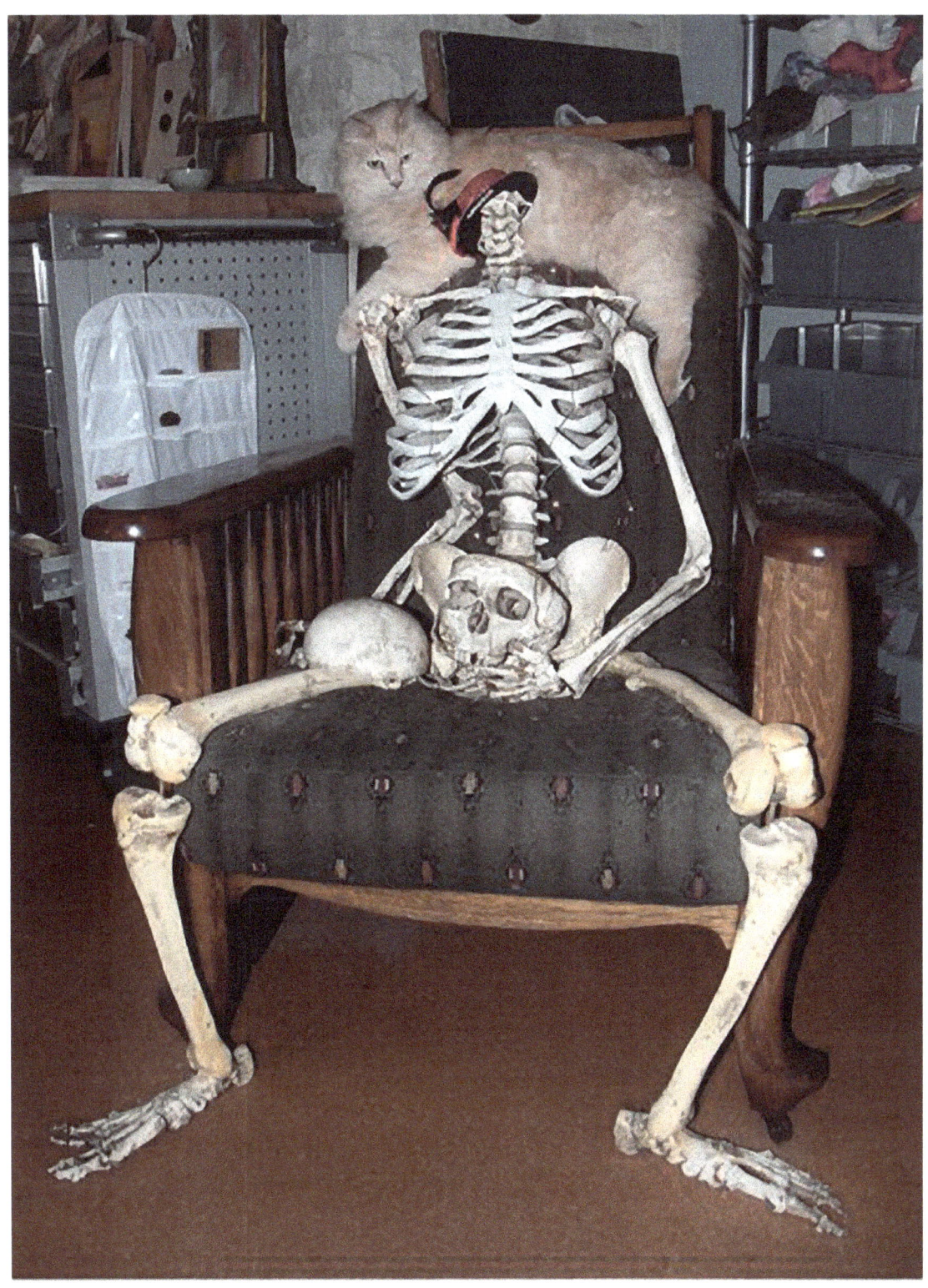

Otis and friend in Cleve Ragan's studio

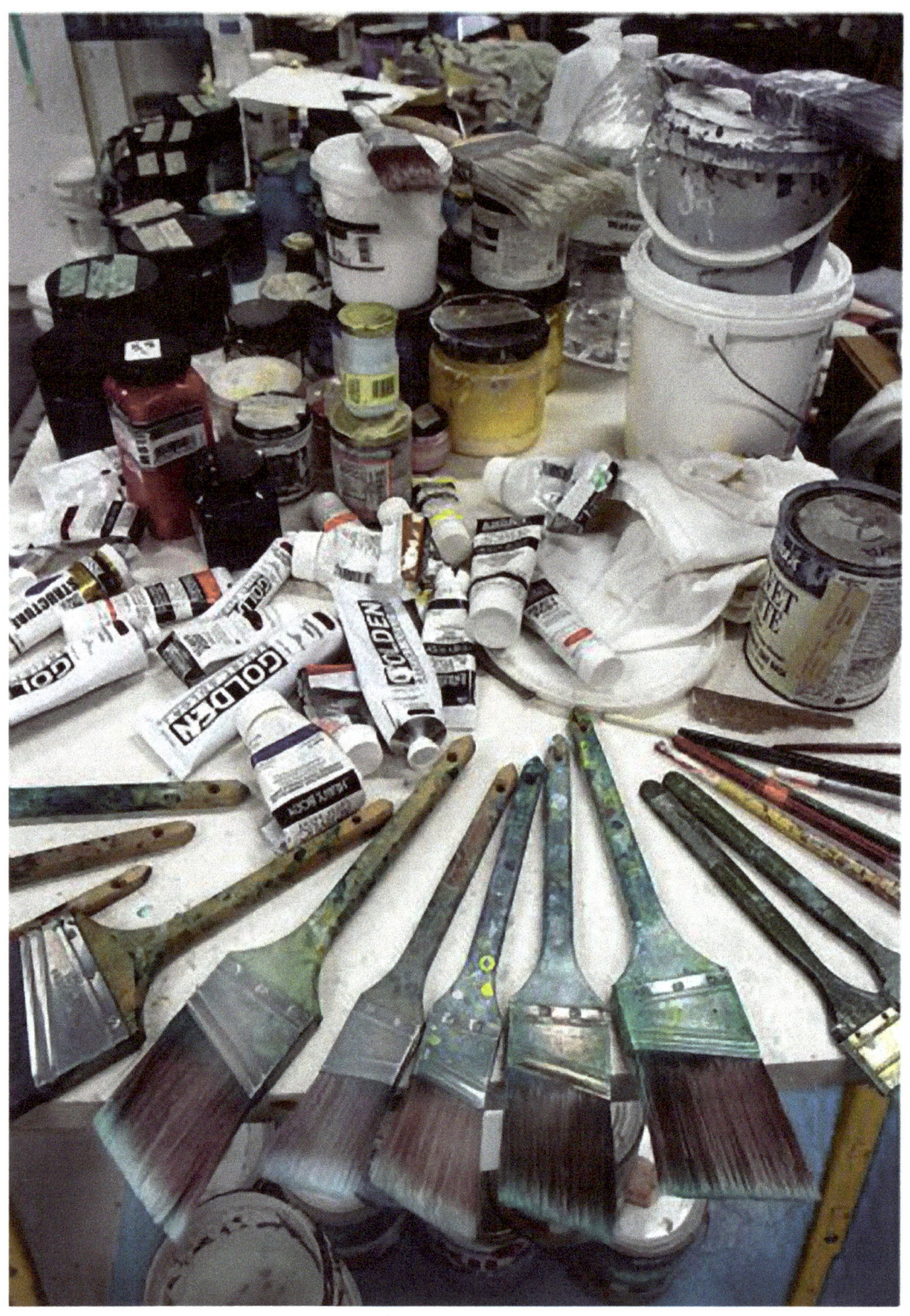

Denny McCoy's tools

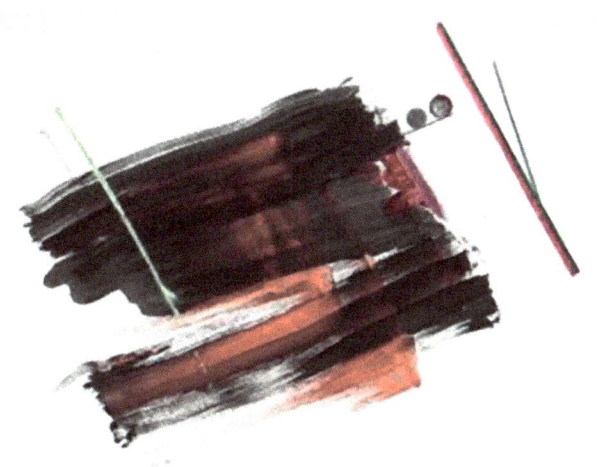

a page from Denny McCoy's sketchpad

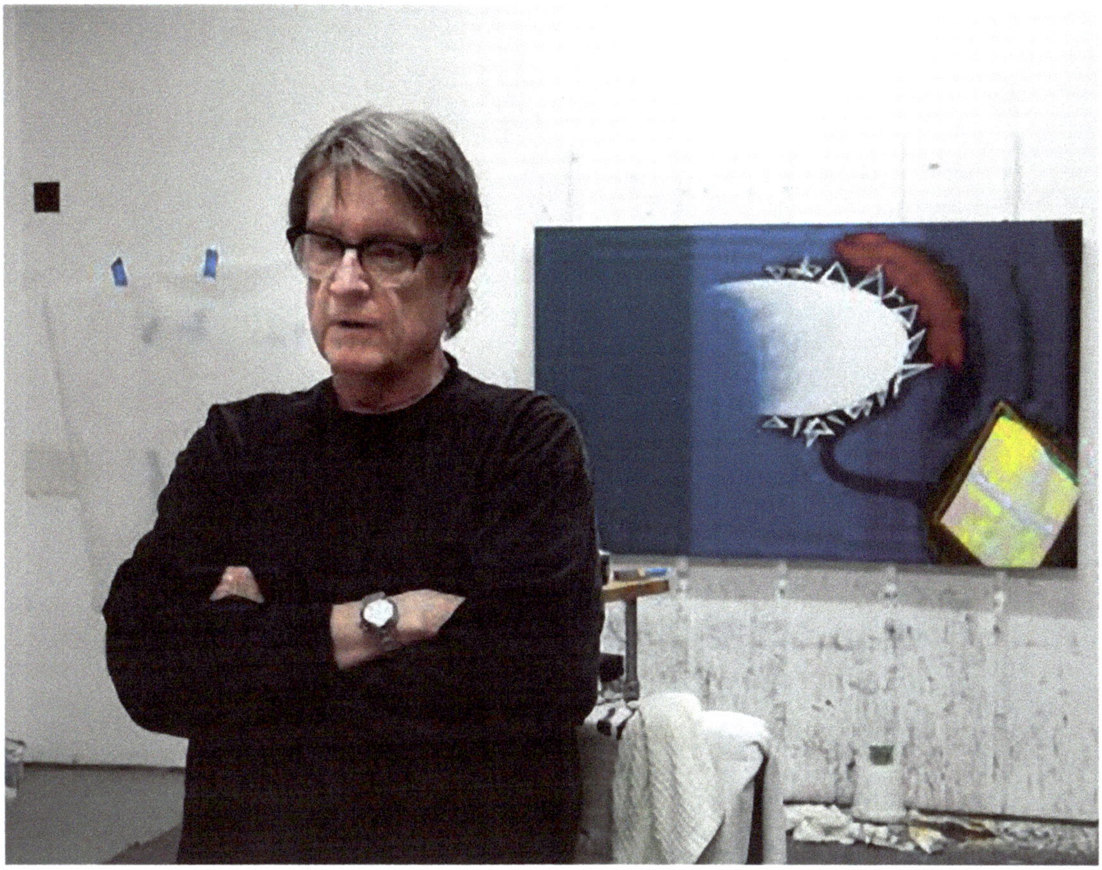

Denny McCoy with a painting in progress

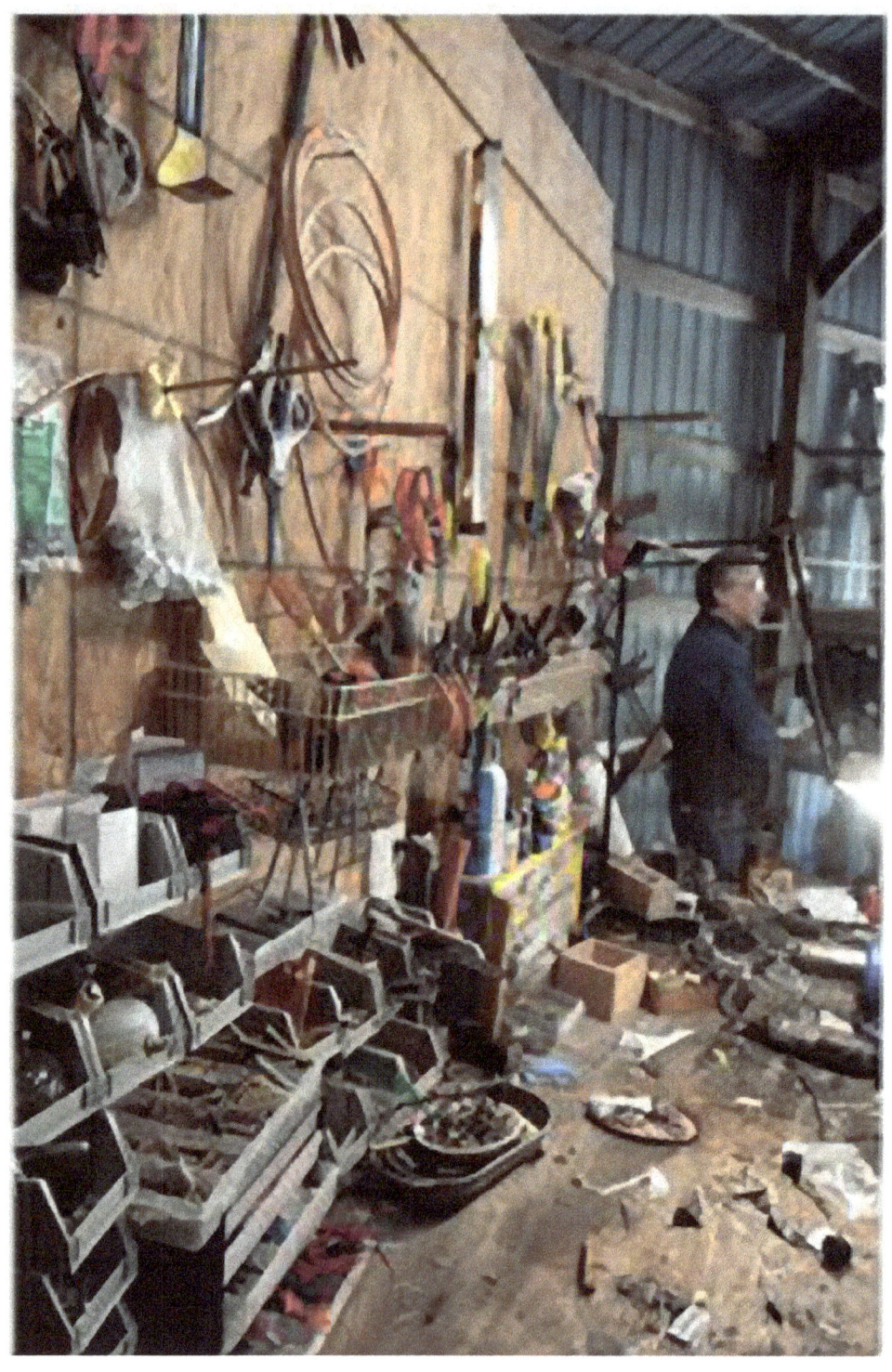

Kent White's Studio

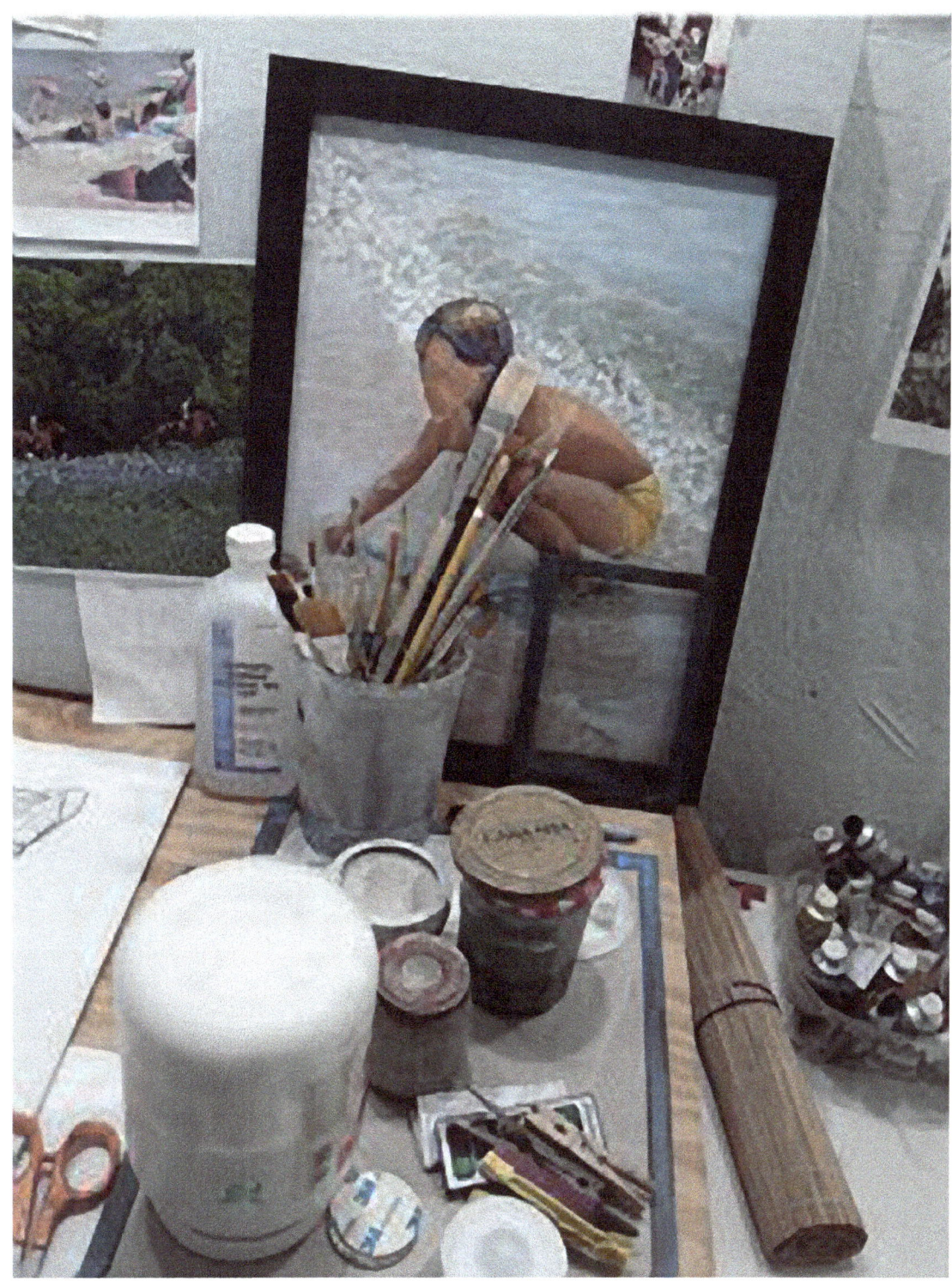

Judy Guimont's Studio

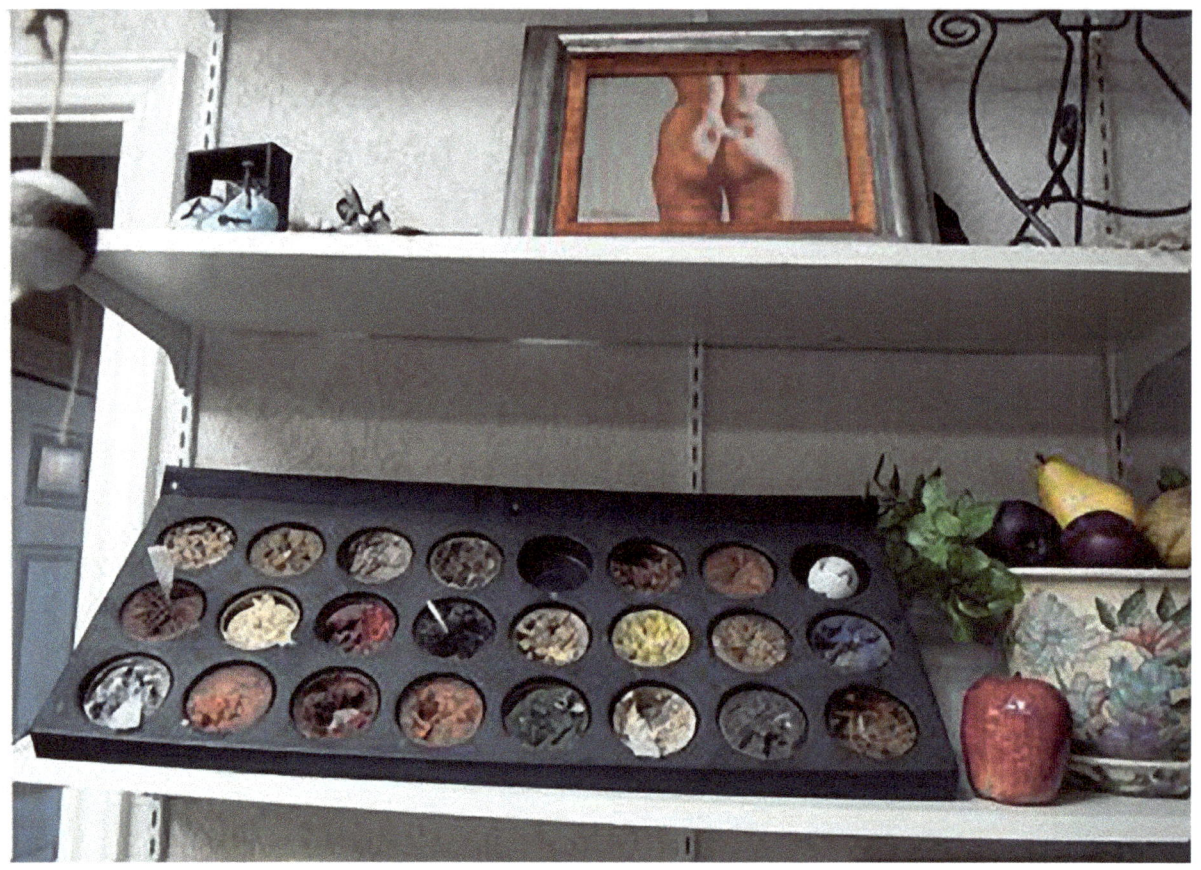

Betty Rhodes' studio

Community: the Creative Enclave

Each art community has its own sensibility and its own identity, a rich and vibrant brew of all who inhabit it. In our community, in Wimberley, Texas, the creative spirit is well represented by visual artists, sculptors, musicians, performance artists and aging hippies. This place is buzzing with imagination.

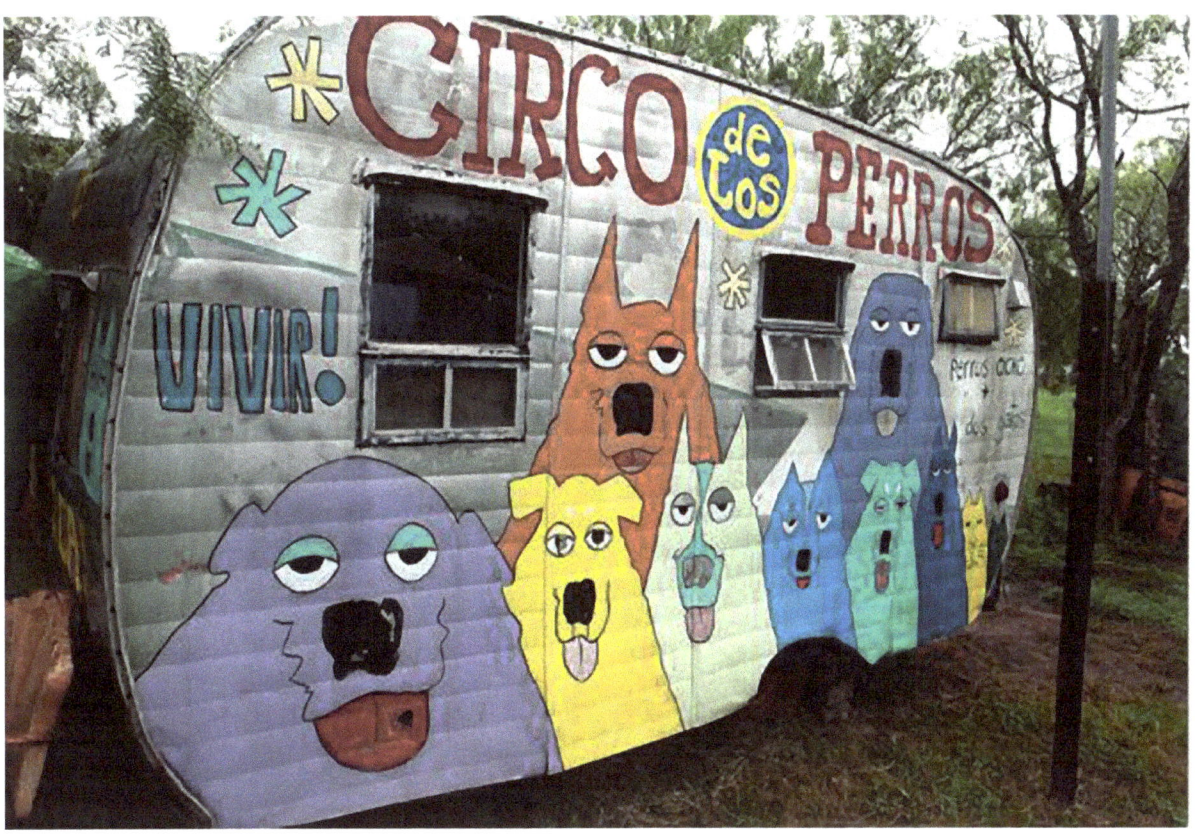

"Perros" mural at Eye of the Dog Art Center

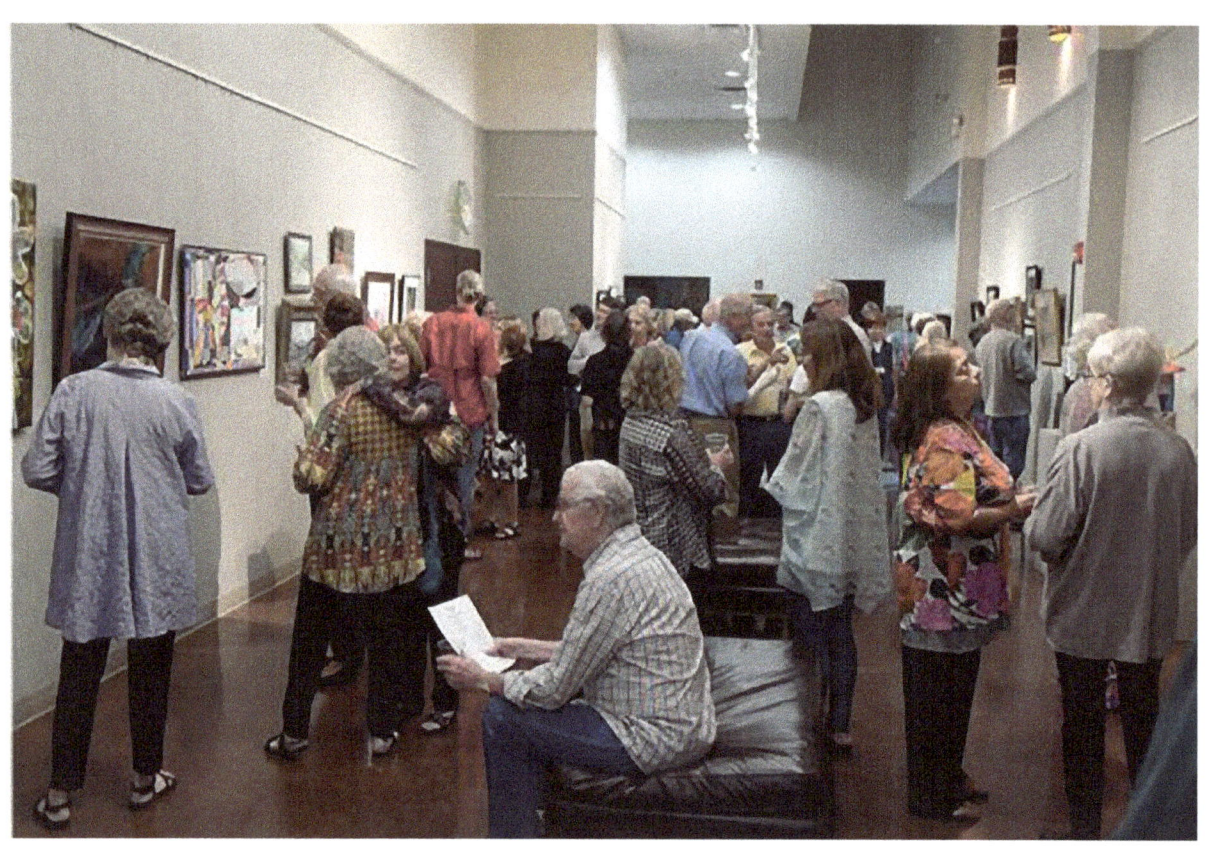

Wimberley Valley Art League reception

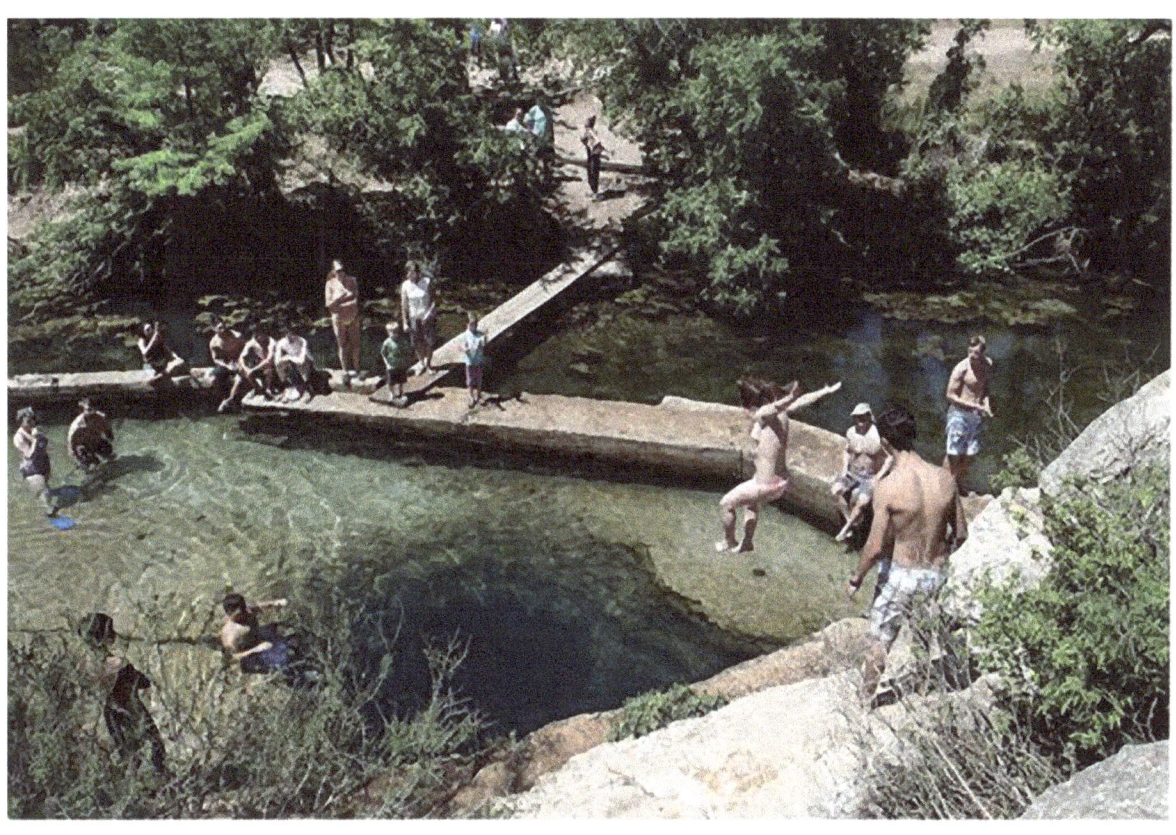

Jacob's Well

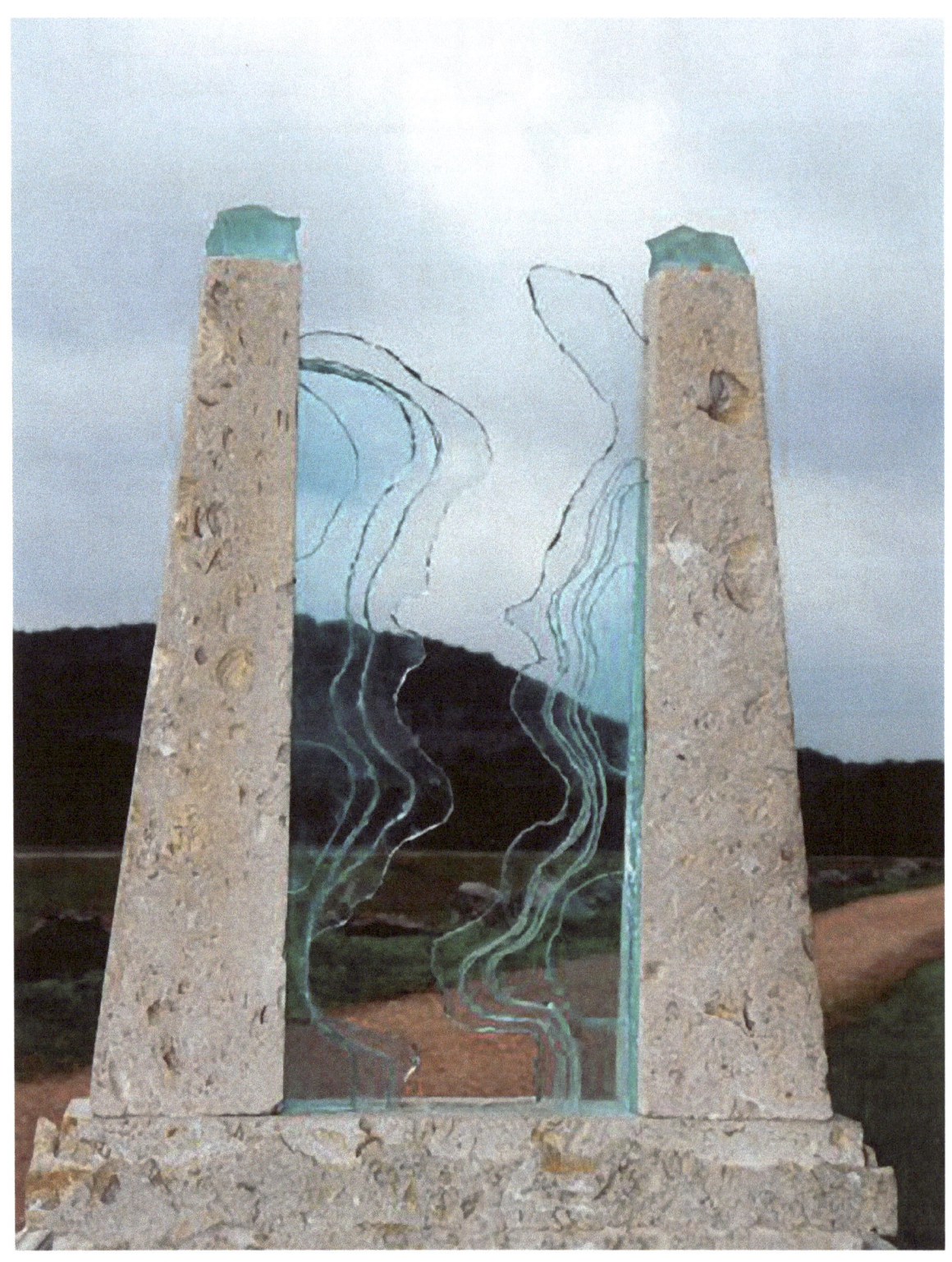

Flood Memorial prototype by J.J. Priour

Yet community becomes most important when the unexpected occurs or when tragedy comes to call.

The Flood: Wimberley is bisected by the Blanco River just to its north. Cypress Creek joins the Blanco at the town square. These two waterways afford a beautiful and tranquil backdrop for our town. But as is the nature of all bodies of water, they can become raging and uncontrolled when nature takes a dark turn. On Memorial Day weekend, 2015, with an unusually heavy rainfall near the headwaters of the Blanco in Kendall county, some 70 miles to the northwest of Wimberley, the river unleashed its fury. A forty-five foot wall of water roared down the narrow Blanco River bed. Four-hundred year-old Cypress trees snapped apart like toothpicks. Their huge trunks, roiling with the river, created a destructive force that nothing in its path could withstand. Three hundred and fifty homes were washed away, claiming thirteen lives in the process. Eight of those, close friends from three separate families, perished together in a vacation home on the river's bank. Thousands of other homes were destroyed or damaged beyond repair. Just five months later, on Halloween, another flood, this time Cypress Creek, devastated many downtown businesses.

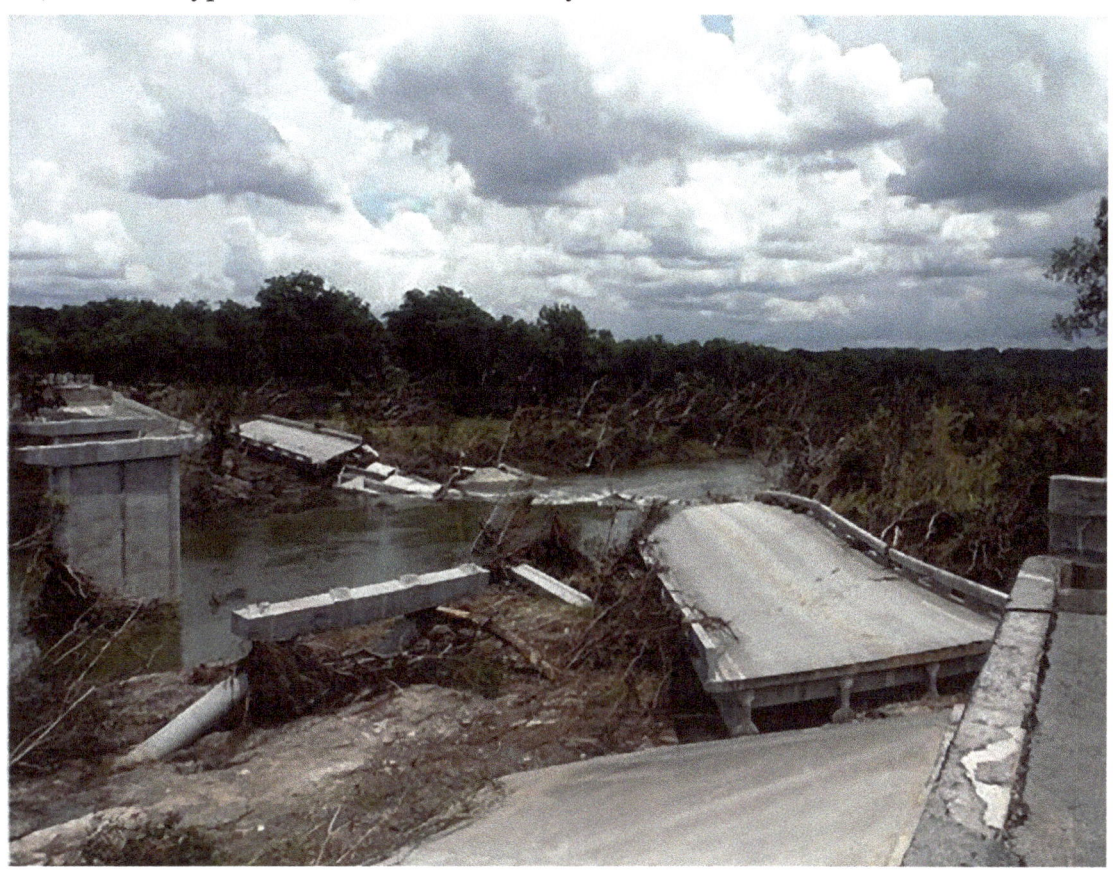

Fischer Bridge after the 2015 Memorial Day Flood

Nevertheless, the spirit of the citizens of Wimberley was strong. Neighbors rallied to help neighbors cleanup and rebuild their lives.

Those in the art community took on a special role. Drawing on the power of art to heal, artists helped townspeople endure with projects like the making of cyanotype nature-prayer flags to hang in homes and businesses. One month after the Memorial Day flood, the Wimberley Valley Art League (WVAL) put together an art show and sale: 100 for 100, with a goal to get one hundred donated works of art, each to sell for $100 as a way to raise money for those individuals whose lives had been shattered by the flood. In fact, more than four hundred pieces of art poured in from area artists. WVAL raised over $45,000 in just three hours to assist in this cause.

There was an initiative launched to create an artistic statement—a monument—with the thought of a future park: a place to remember those who lost their lives or suffered devastating property damage, and a place for contemplation. A region-wide design competition, encouraged area artists to create a work that reflected Wimberley's spirit of community, resolve and resilience in the face of tragedy. Twelve remarkable monument designs were submitted. Following a series of events that included community input, public vote and comment, a design was chosen for the centerpiece monument for the park. The winning design was offered by local area sculptor J.J. Priour. Fashioned entirely from native materials the monument is constructed with central Texas fossiliferous limestone and glass, used as a metaphor for water. Here our remembrance of our friends, our relationship with our beautiful slice of Texas, and our commitment to honor the surrounding environment was made permanent.

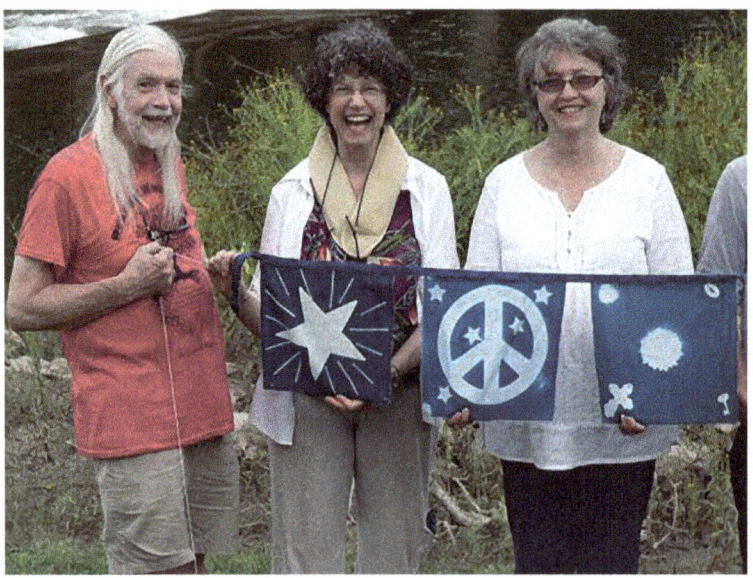

Herb Smith, Susan Zimmerman,and Myra Allen at Wimberly
Strong flag ceremony

A community creates a shared soul by virtue of what people see, hear, smell, taste and touch every day. Our artists bond over their work, of course. But artists bond over many other things besides their work. They bond over their pets, their gardens, the food they prepare for their friends and family for regular family dinners and for special occasions, and they bond over the views of our beautiful valley. Not everybody embraces community. Some prefer to watch from the sidelines. Some artists are too involved with their own work, or too shy, or do not want their ideas contaminated by outside influences. There may be more benefits to exchanging ideas than working in a vacuum, but inspiration is ephemeral, and it is best to go with what is working at the moment. Still, when creativity goes stagnant, it doesn't hurt to look at what others are doing. There is a creative communal vibe wherever artists congregate and show their work, and it is vast enough to feed off of in times of drought.

Many of the artists in this book teach, and even more attend classes to learn a new technique in a medium in which they may already be highly accomplished. Stellar brush artists can explore new avenues of creativity by learning to wield a palette knife. Photographers can learn about technological advances in their craft. Potters can become sculptors.

Artists probably do not attract one another any more than gun enthusiasts, Master Naturalists or tattoo aficionados. And like those other groups they learn from one another and their assemblies are of like-minded people. A community can be a powerful artistic muse. What makes a community? Certainly, shared values, shared experiences and shared appreciations. Here, in the Wimberley valley, there are individuals and organizations that offer generous stimulation and artistic knowledge enough to make this small area of the hill country a creative enclave.

A search of Texas hill country art organizations reveals a variety of similar manifestos and mission statements. Basically, they all want to promote the work of local artists and instill a community-wide interest in art.

The Wimberley Valley Art League (WVAL) began over thirty years ago with about that many artists and has grown to over two-hundred members. Many of those people volunteer to frame and hang the yearly student art show that exhibits the work of elementary and high school art students. Some of the valley's next generations of artists are the beneficiaries of that show. The WVAL has more than achieved its goals through juried art shows at the community center, art workshops, and studio tours. Wimberley Arts Fest is a spring event that draws artists from across the country, Canada and Mexico. Some of those artists go back home with mental images of the hill country that are later translated onto canvas or some other artistic medium.

The Wimberley Valley Arts and Cultural Alliance is an umbrella organization that promotes visual and performing arts. Among their goals is to connect art and cultural activities with geography and the natural environment of the Wimberley valley. One of their projects was the creation of fifty artist-painted giant boots, that were commissioned by local businesses and sit in front of their establishments. Some of those boots appear in this book and have become popular photo opportunities for Wimberley visitors.

Eye of the Dog is an artistic commune between Wimberley and San Marcos, Texas that exudes creativity and is so saturated with artistic creations that the acreage it sits on is running out of space. It is an indoor/outdoor gallery and teaching facility.

The Texas Bold Beauty Project is a photography exhibit initiated by Bob Cook, one of the artists in this book. It depicts women with disabilities and tells their stories. The project seeks to raise awareness of the women's strength, sensuality and spirit, and in the process, change the perceptions of beauty. The exhibit has been shown in venues around Wimberley, San Marcos, and Austin, Texas. It came about when Bob energized an army of volunteers to choreograph multiple exhibitions that we all knew we would feel good about. And we did.

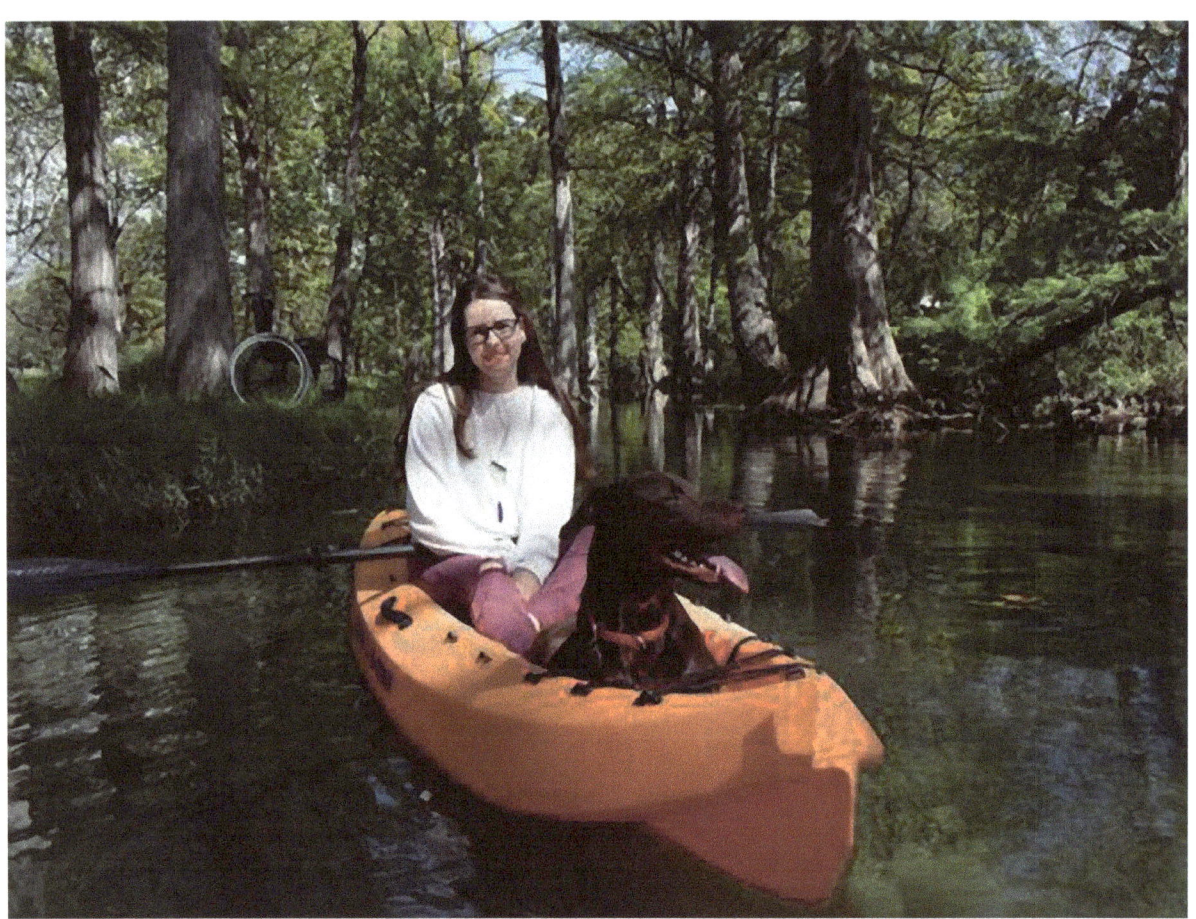

Erin Hoyt and her service dog Hank participating in The Texas Bold Beauty Project

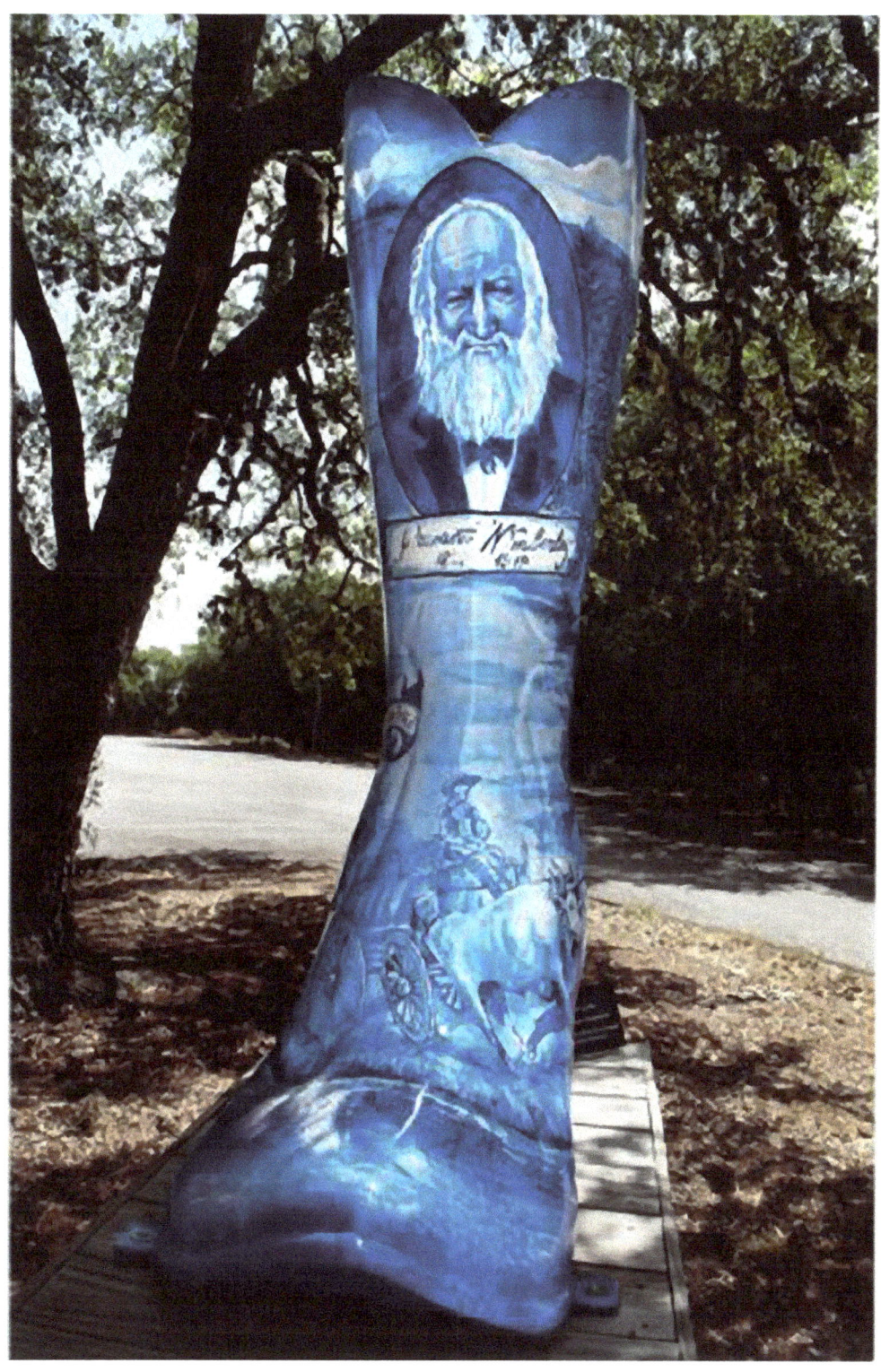

BOOTIFUL WIMBERLEY "Pleasant Wimberley" by Jic Clubb

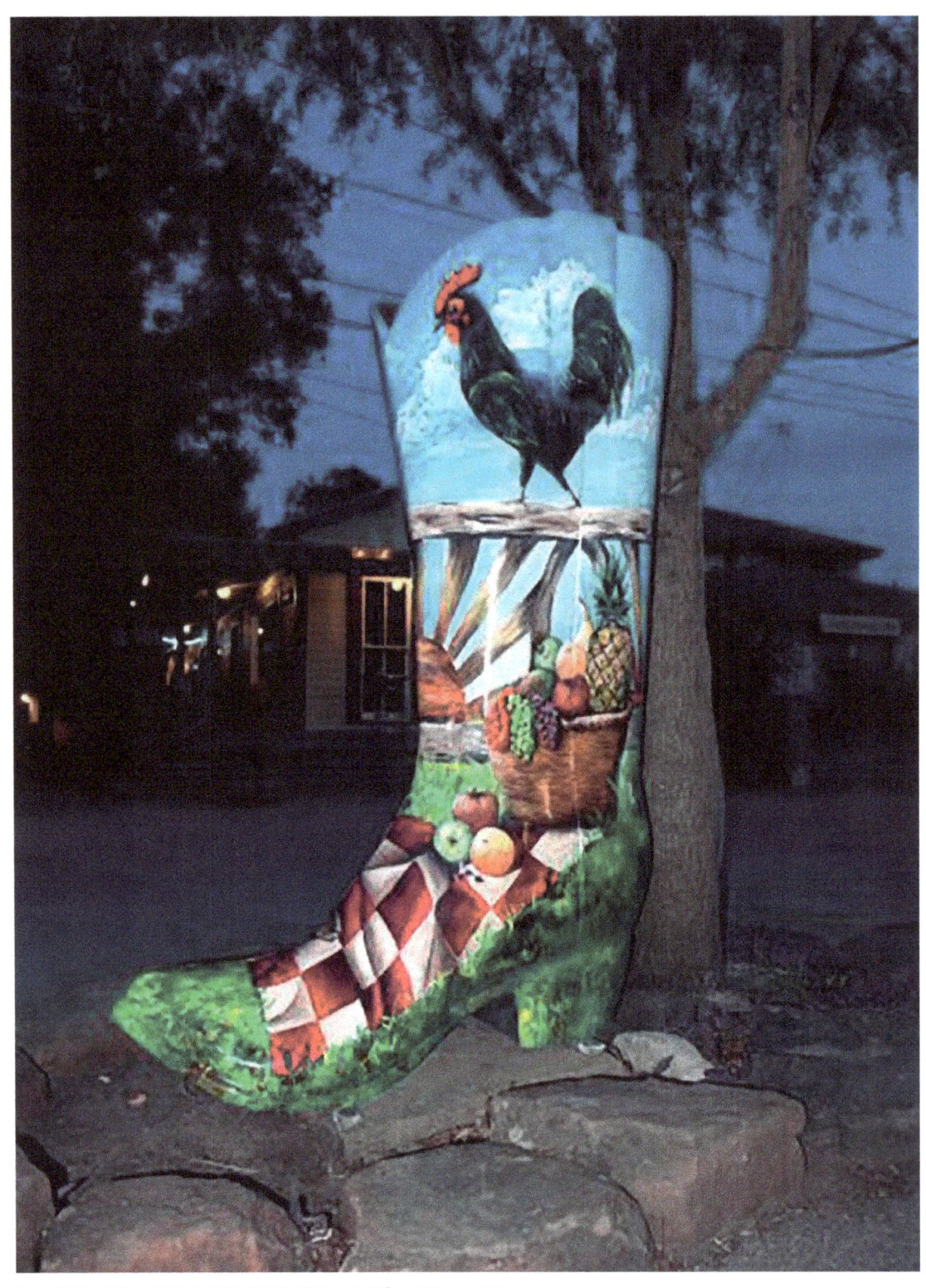

BOOTIFUL WIMBERLEY "Picnic" by Diana Weems

146

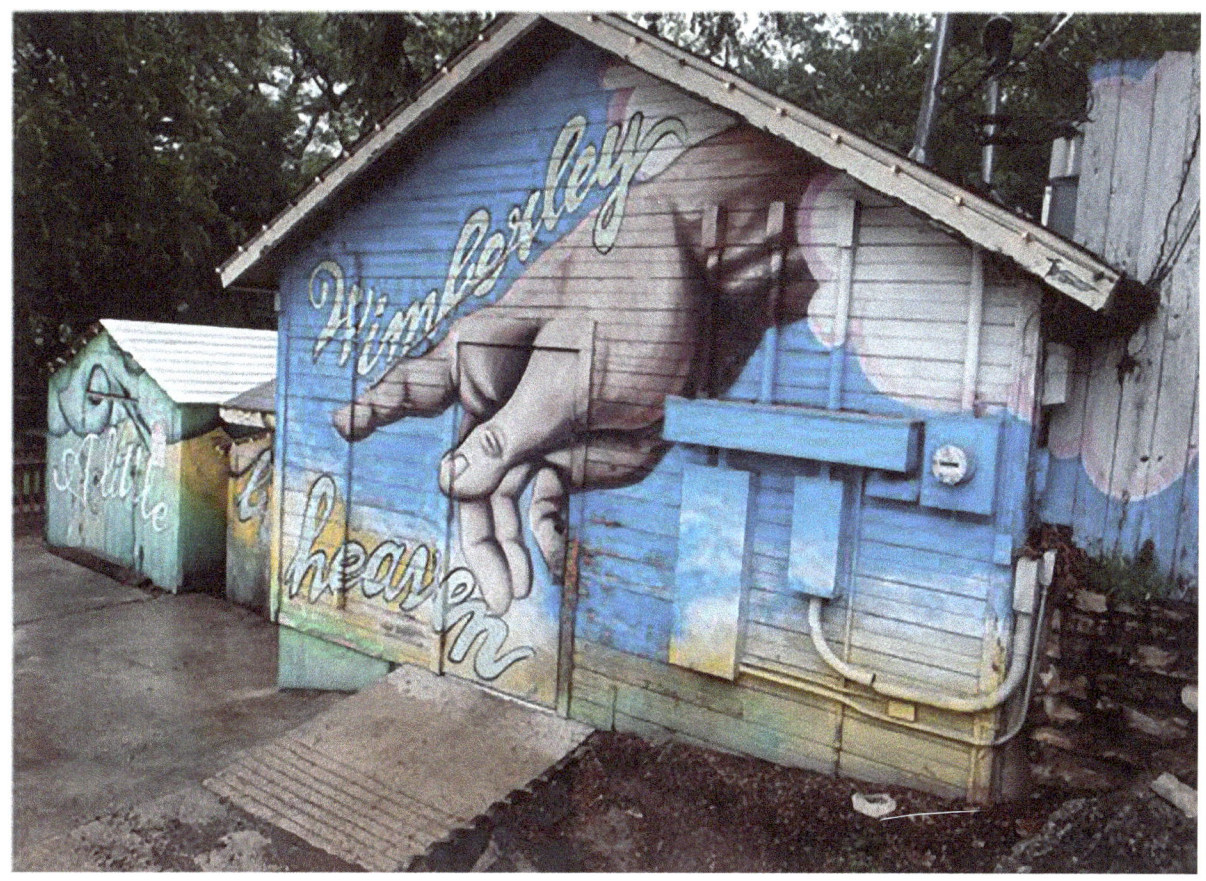

Wimberley mural

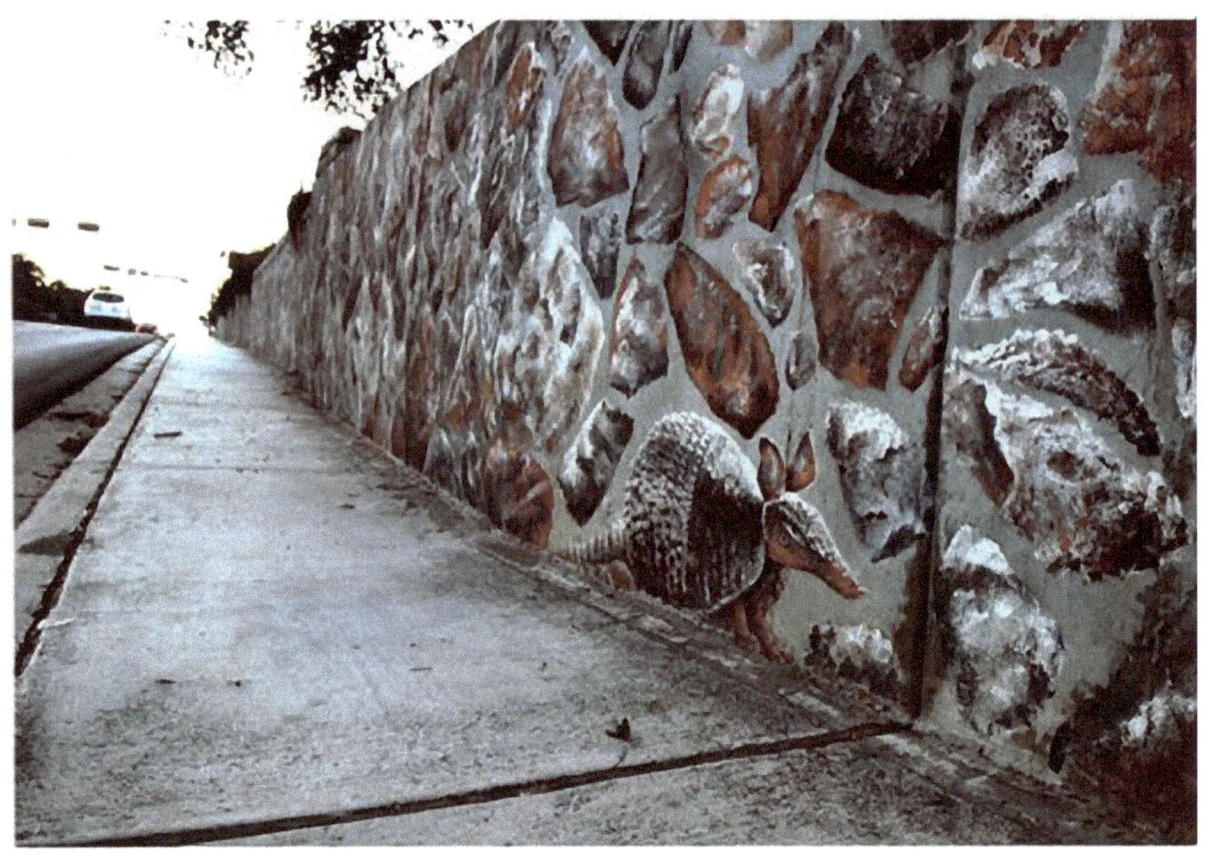

RR12 wall mural by Sharon Carter

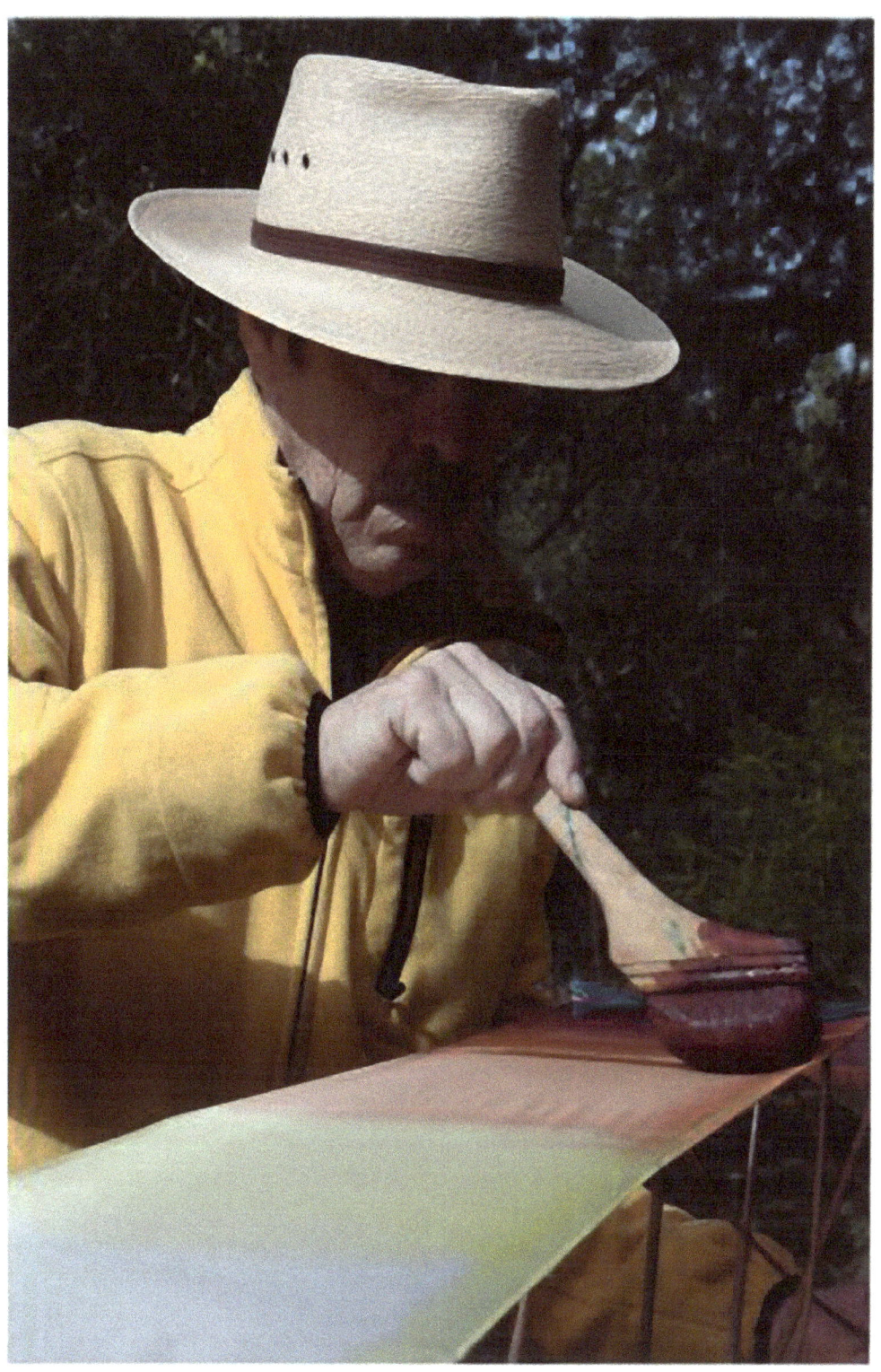

Dye Lessons by Tim Leibrock

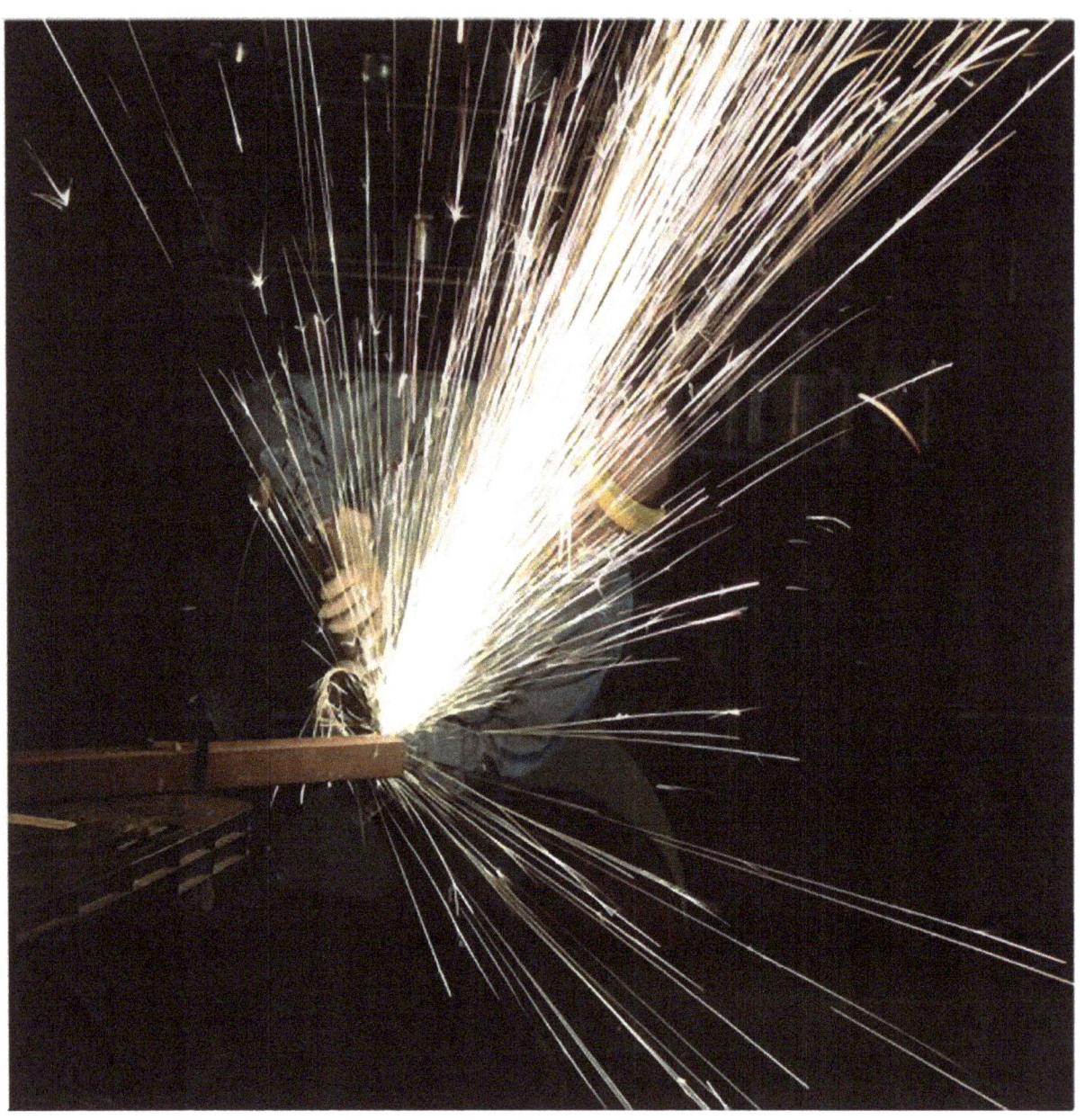

Solon Williams makes more than sparks

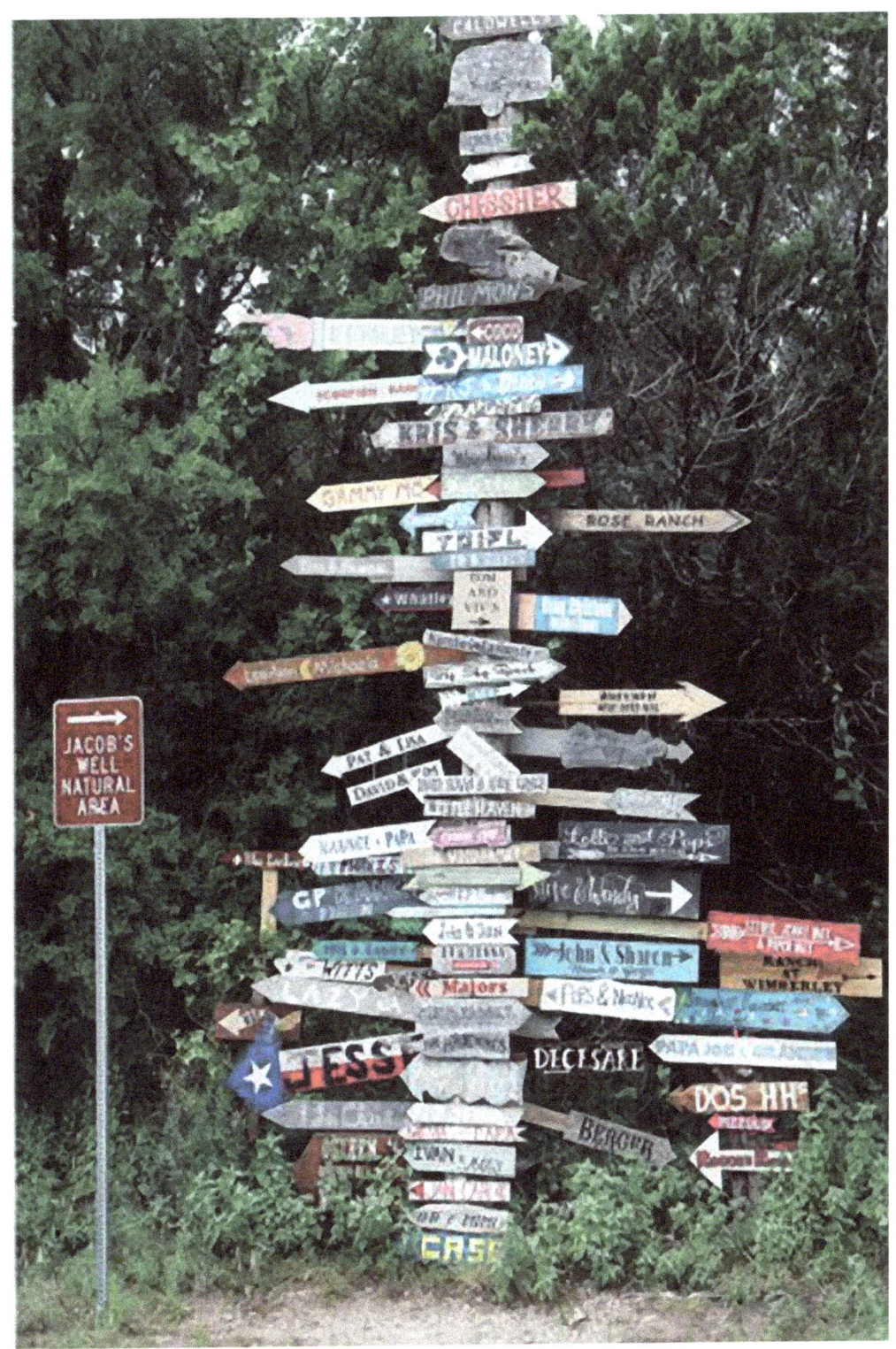

Jacob's Well road sign

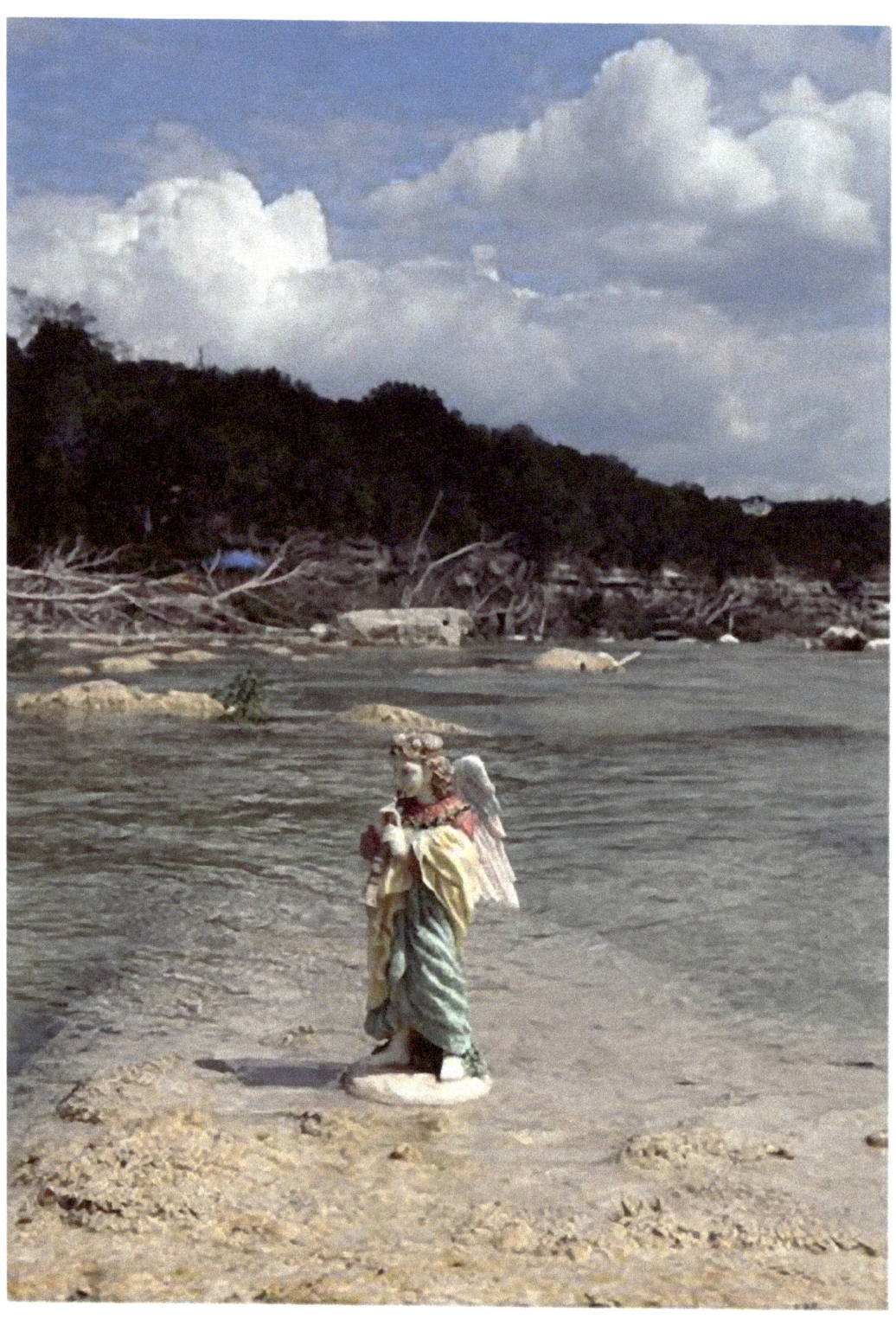

Blanco River Angel found after the 2015 flood

www.ingramcontent.com/pod-product-compliance
Lightning Source LLC
Chambersburg PA
CBHW052137170526
45162CB00004B/43